Charles Schneider would like to thank the following people:

Erika Clowes, John Goldsmith, Glenn Bray, Bill Smith, John Carney, Heather Allen, Mike Caveney, Donald R. Adamski (Executive VP and General Manager of DeMoulin Brothers), and all the people who ever worked in the DeMoulin factory.

Editor: Gary Groth
Designer: Jacob Covey
Production: Paul Baresh
Associate Publisher: Eric Reynolds
Publishers: Gary Groth & Kim Thompson

Catalogue 439 is copyright © 2010 Fantagraphics Books. Appreciation is copyright © 2010 David Copperfield. "Inside the Goat Factory" is copyright 2010 Charles Schneider. "Canned Snakes, Mechanical Goats, and Spitting Skeletons: Making Sense of the 1930 DeMoulin Bros & Co. Catalog" is copyright © 2010 William D. Moore. Photographs of DeMoulin burlesque paraphernalia by Heather Allen. All historical photographs provided courtesy of John Goldsmith/DeMoulin Museum and DeMoulin Brothers and Company. All rights reserved. Permission to quote or reproduce material for reviews must be obtained from the publisher. Fantagraphics Books, Inc. 7563 Lake City Way, Seattle, WA 98115.

To receive a free catalogue of fine comics and books, including graphic novels, prose novels, essays, and strange compilations of esoteric and marginal pop cultural aberrations, call 1-800-657-1100 or visit our website at Fantagraphics.com.

Distributed in the U.S. by W.W. Norton and Company, Inc. (212-354-5500)
Distributed in Canada by the Canadian Manda Group (416-516-0911)
Distributed in the U.K. by Turnaround Distribution (208-829-3009)
Distributed to comics stores by Diamond Comics Distributors (800-452-6642)

ISBN 978-1-60699-367-5

Printed in China.

Opposite: The DeMoulin Bros. & Co. woodworking shop, circa 1915. Note man working on trick chair.

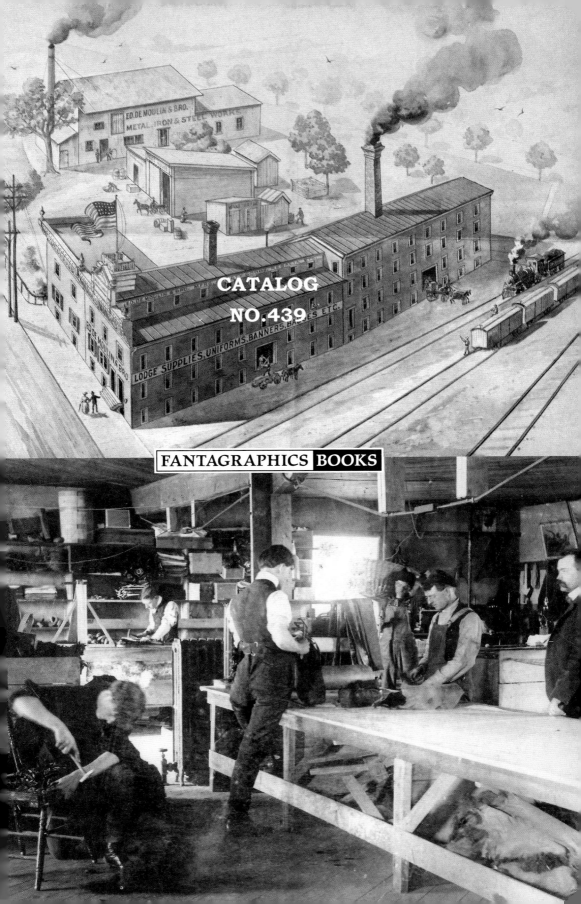

AN APPRECIATION
by
DAVID COPPERFIELD

THIS CATALOG IS A TIME MACHINE. Can you imagine, in today's world of lawyers and lawsuits, inviting someone to sit in an exploding-collapsing chair? Well, truth be told, I do it all the time, but I've been studying, preserving, and sharing DeMoulin Brothers' "Burlesque and Side Degree Paraphernalia" for at least twelve happy years (and I make sure that my insurance premiums are paid). In fact, I'm a pretty avid archivist of DeMoulin Brothers items. Proudly displayed in my museum I have everything from the Traitor's Judgment Stand to the Throne of Honor, from the Invisible Paddle Machine to the original art and printing cuts used to make this very catalog. This catalog makes me feel like a kid in a toy store. I flip through the pages thinking, "Need it, got it, got it, need it." These items take me back; they're the magic shop gags of my childhood—the squirting nickels, the whoopee cushions, the joy buzzers—writ large.

They were designed as initiation devices to be used as part of secret society rituals. Back in the day, fraternal organizations were all the rage, and the world was the DeMoulin Brothers' exploding cigar. But these are practical jokes of a high order. The skill and craft that went into each piece is astonishing. And the plots of these devices seem to have been devised by the comically sadistic, politically incorrect sensibility of a Bugs Bunny. Because of the cleverness and detail, they remind me a lot of vintage magic equipment. In fact I view the DeMoulin Brothers items as cousins of antique magic equipment and illusions. Same kind of look, same kind of care, and craftsmanship of a sort that has all but vanished from today's world. And many of the items still collapse, explode, spray, and shock as if they were just finished yesterday. Not only don't they make them like that any more, they don't make them. Period. It's up to the collectors and historians to rescue these wonderfully strange things and preserve them, and the sensibility they arose from, for future generations. Although doing so can be hazardous to your health, as I found out when I demonstrated a DeMoulin Brothers Spanker (item no. D451 in this catalog) on the Conan O'Brien show.

Once upon a time, corporal punishment was considered part of every grammar school curriculum, and I guess spanking paddles, which look like miniature oars, were commonplace items. The DeMoulin Brothers' paddle comes with a surprise: a .38 caliber blank that goes off with a hell of a bang when the paddle makes contact with the victim's butt.

On the Conan show, I was the victim. Now, Conan's a smart guy—a Harvard guy, in fact—but a novice with DeMoulin Brothers props. And so, with the cameras rolling, Conan wound up like Babe Ruth and smacked me square on the ass. Only he had the wrong side of the paddle ass-ward; he had the side that contained the loaded blank facing toward me. So when the blank went off it burned a hole through my pants, and through the top couple layers of skin, leaving a permanent memento on my otherwise baby-soft cheek, which I've come to regard as a souvenir from NBC.

It's great to see the incredible DeMoulin Brothers catalog #439 back in print. Enjoy the bizarre, amusing, and illuminating journey you are about to take.

—David Copperfield
Musha Cay Island, Bahamas
March 2010

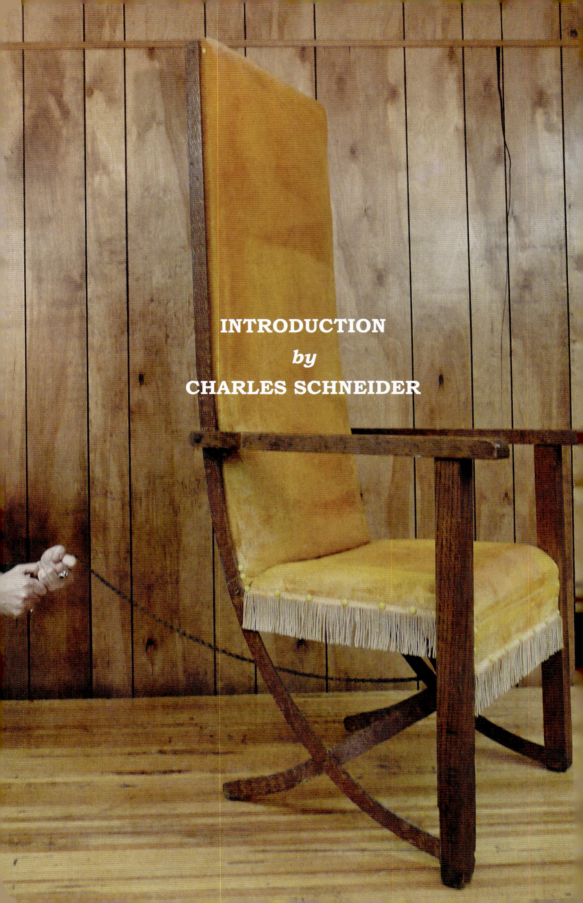

INTRODUCTION
by
CHARLES SCHNEIDER

INSIDE THE GOAT FACTORY

YOU HOLD IN YOUR HANDS ONE OF THE MOST BIZARRE AND WONDERFUL CATALOGS TO HAVE EVER SPILLED FORTH FROM THE MIND OF MAN. It is the sort of thing that could have only been produced during a specific time and at a certain place in American history, and this takes some explaining to appreciate.

In the late 1890s as much as 40% of the male population of the U.S. belonged to some sort of fraternal order. The same spirit which drove men West searching for gold created the need for brotherhood and camaraderie. This took the form of innumerable fraternal organizations. There were The Modern Woodmen of America, the Knights of the Maccabees, The Woodmen of the World, the Knights of Pythias, The Improved Order of Redmen, the Benevolent and Protective Order of Elks, the Odd Fellows, the Freemasons, and many others.

There were even organizations, such as E. Clampus Vitus, which sprang up as a response to and a parody of more serious groups. Still, these allowed men to get together and commiserate, fraternize, and take part in pseudo-esoteric rituals. Some men often belonged to multiple secret groups. The names tend to sound exotic and mysterious, and it appears that many of these groups appropriated their ritual symbolism and charity work from that of older and very serious organizations.

As the twentieth century dawned, the need to expand one's consciousness through the initiatory process became increasingly important, almost as if the male psyche was mirroring the creativity and wild abandon of the new century. Charity was the public function of many groups, but initiating new members was their primary function. This usually happened amidst ritual couched in classical symbolism, teaching the initiate key life lessons whilst taking part in a highly secretive, possibly ancient and greatly empowering ritual drama.

Although fraternal organizations had existed in America before the days of the Founding Fathers, their membership reached an all-time high after 1890, achieving its zenith just prior to the first world war. Many fraternal groups offered health insurance and death benefits, free of charge, to members who could not afford them from a commercial company, thus drawing many men in during troubled times.

The origin of the DeMoulin Brothers' line of burlesque and side degree contraptions bears telling. The Modern Woodmen of America (MWA) was founded in Iowa in 1883 by Joseph Cullen Root, primarily as a fraternal benefit organization. Men could socialize in the nationwide chain of camps, and also enjoyed the benefits of life insurance. No one tells the amazing tale better than John Goldsmith, who wrote in his article "Bucking Goats and Lung Testers":

> The Modern Woodmen of America grew slowly, but their fate changed drastically when a little-known attorney from Greenville, Illinois named William A. Northcott was elected the organization's Head Consul in 1890. One of the first challenges that Northcott tried to tackle was the organization's lackluster membership. He felt that the MWA needed something to entice new members beyond the insurance benefits.
>
> Northcott consulted another Greenville man, Ed DeMoulin, who was a photographer by trade but also a crafty inventor who already had received a patent on a trick photography camera attachment. DeMoulin conferred with his brothers Erastus and U.S., and the trio concluded that the Woodmen needed more humorous rites of initiation for its prospective members. Ed, blessed with a quirky sense of humor to complement his inventiveness, devised the "molten lead test" that a new member was told he must pass in order to gain acceptance by his fellow Woodmen. A pot resting on a tripod above an alcohol stove gave the impression that the poor fellow would be placing his hands into a boiling brew. In reality, dry mercury powder was sprinkled into cold water to give the illusion of bubbling, hot lead.
>
> Sensing he had stumbled upon a potential commercial venture, Ed opened a lodge and fraternal paraphernalia business. With Northcott as a silent partner and backed with the business savvy of U.S. and the blacksmithing skills of Erastus, Ed DeMoulin's business soon cornered the market of the Modern Woodmen of America. The "molten lead test" was followed by bucking goats, lung testers, surprise chairs, and paddle machines. The DeMoulins accumulated patents on dozens of initiation devices and their growth coincided with that of the MWA. Under Northcott's tenure as the Woodmen's Head Consul, the group saw its membership explode from 40,000 to 600,000. Noting the success of the Modern Woodmen of America, other lodges began incorporating these crazy initiation practices, and DeMoulin Bros. catered to their needs. There is no evidence that Masonic lodges used such informal and unapproved initiation pranks.

Indeed, many of the pranks and devices seem rooted in the public's (or the DeMoulin Brothers') heightened, cartoon conception of what a secret society initiation might be like; a far cry from the reality of such an event.

The trappings of the torture chamber, the pointed hoods of the Spanish Inquisition, and some of the earlier displays of "gore and splatter" special effects all contributed to the catalog's abundant terror tactics. The advent and novelty of

The DeMoulin Brothers and their wives, circa 1895. From left to right: Ed, Ulysses, and Erastus.

electricity served to inspire the factory's inventors to newer, more shocking heights, inspirations of a prankster's most outlandish nightmares. A dash of the macabre was blended with a genius's love of oddball gadgetry. In fact, Ed DeMoulin was fascinated by inventions and gimcracks of all sorts. He was the first man in town to drive a fancy new car, and adored the creation and celebration of mechanical wonders. He started the business. His brother, Ulysses, whom everyone called U.S., ran the factory. A self-made "expert," he was a prim and proper fellow, businesslike and brilliantly efficient. The third brother was Erastus, or "Ras," the most hands-on member of the family. He was a vastly experienced blacksmith, a true family man who liked to hang out with the workers in the factory. Together, the three diverse personalities merged into the perfect combination of impish invention, practical scientific mechanics, and marketing brilliance.

Carpets and chairs could now have nearly invisible copper wires run across them, charged with enough power from a hand-cranked "Magneto Battery" to drop a man to his knees. If this didn't scare him, the deafening report from a blank cartridge firing simultaneously would do the trick. A jet of water or talcum powder right in the eyes wouldn't hurt either. The combination must have been quite disorienting. It is interesting to note that the French theatre of panic and terror, The Grand Guignol, experienced a similar rise in popularity following the great world wars—and suffered as the war machines were oiled up again.

Still, the metaphor of taking a walk on a perilous path comes through in the form of literally electrified pathways or "rough roads."

ROUGH ROADS

BRIDGE

This bridge is 26 inches wide between the rails. It is a substantial and handsome piece of paraphernalia. The posts and rails are of gas pipe finished in aluminum. The floor is of wood and metal, nicely finished and ornamented, and is suspended from the rail posts so it will readily swing with each step which the pilgrim takes. This motion creates a peculiar sensation and causes him to repeatedly grasp one or both of the rails, each time receiving an electric shock. The bridge may be quickly taken apart, occupying but little space for storing, and may be as quickly set up for use. Weight of 1895R, packed, 235 pounds; 1896 R, 170 pounds.

IMPORTANT NOTE—If desired, we can arrange one or more independent sections of our Electric Hot Road and our Electric Bridge so all can be operated with but one battery without additional cost for arrangement. A very fine rough road is made as follows: A few yards of Rocky Road, a few yards of Electric Hot Road, The Electric Bridge, another few yards of Electric Hot Road, and finally another section of Rocky Road.

1895R—Electric Swinging Bridge, 14 feet long, three posts on each side..$72.15
1896R—Electric Swinging Bridge, 8 feet long, two posts on each side ... 52.50
1897R—Magneto Battery and Cord; necessary if desire pilgrim to receive electric shock 12.50

ROUGH OR ROCKY ROAD

The road is a mat of double canvas with irregular articles sewed between same. Can be rolled up in a small space when not in use. Carpet is made 22 or 44 inches wide, and can be furnished in any length; (usually ordered in lengths of three to five yards).

1886R—Rocky Road, 44 inches wide, per running yard ....$ 4.50
1887R—Rocky Road, 22 inches wide, per running yard 2.65

ELECTRIC HOT ROAD

This improved Electric Carpet is made very substantial. Our manner of construction does away with all wires, buttons, etc., hence short circuiting is impossible; nothing to get out of order by broken connections or by buttons coming off. Candidate will receive the full "benefit" whether he stands on one foot or both. Occupies but little space; a three-yard length can be rolled up in a roll four inches in diameter. Carpet is made 25 or 50 inches wide, and can be furnished by the yard in any length desired. (Usually ordered in lengths of three to five yards.)

1888R—Electric Carpet, 50 inches wide; per running yard ....$ 6.90
1889R—Electric Carpet, 25 inches wide; per running yard 3.60
1890R—Battery and cord 12.50

No. 1888R Electric Carpet is preferable on account of the width, which prevents the candidate from striding the carpet in order to get away from the current.

ELECTRIC SPIKED PATHWAY

1891R—Electric Spiked Pathway, substantially made; rubber spikes (an exact imitation of steel) securely fastened; short circuiting absolutely impossible; 22 inches wide; per running yard $11.15
1892R—Battery and cord 12.50

TRIPPING RUG

1893R—Tripping Rug, size 20x36 inches, of heavy canvas, with handles; used to trip candidates $ 1.40

HOBBLES OR SHACKLES

1894R—Hobbles or Shackles, consisting of two strong leather straps with buckles, fastened together with a stout 12-inch chain. These are to be strapped to candidates' ankles like handcuffs $ 1.00

ROLLER PATHWAY

For Rough Road or Bridge

1898R—Roller Pathway, 6 feet long, with plank back and stand on which to rest upper end......$21.00
1899R—Roller Pathway, 6 feet long, without plank back 19.20

Either of the above made to hinge in center, occupies but little space for storage; extra. 2.00 Weight, packed, 95 pounds.

UNEVEN ROAD

1900R—The Uneven and Moving Road is built in uneven connected sections arranged in such a manner that they drop suddenly and rise again as candidates walk over them. The Road is 20 feet long, built in a very substantial manner and folds into a small space; (weight, packed, 70 pounds) $18.30

ZIG ZAG ROAD

1901R—Zig Zag Road, substantially made of very strong material, 27 inches wide, three yards long; hummocks securely fastened; strong rope at each of the four corners so it may be moved while candidates are on it......$11.15
1902R—Zig Zag Road, same as 1901R, but 5 yards long 18.00

This is the only page of odd paraphernalia from another DeMoulin catalog dedicated to the Royal Arch Masons. Most atypical.

—10—

The side degree business really started with a series of mechanical goats. These were originally wool-bodied, replica goats with actual horns attached to three, or more, asymmetrical wheels. The initiate would be blind-folded with one of the DeMoulin Brothers' best-selling "hoodwinks," and placed on the faux animal. He would be given a "goat ride," the wobbly wheels and erratic motions ensuring that he would eventually get bucked off, onto the floor. Sometimes the carpet he landed on was electrified, ensuring a most memorable evening for all. The DeMoulin factory created diverse goats of various function, design, and price, such as "The Fuzzy Wonder," "The Royal Bumper," "Ferris Wheel Goat," "A Low Down Buck," and "The Rollicking Mustang Goat." A camel, donkey or tiger body could be had for an extra ten dollars.

One such camel, dubbed "Humpy Dump," had a lot of character. Oddly, he does not appear in this ultimate catalogue. Perhaps a $31.00 rubber-tired camel was not a priority in 1930 when you could purchase the Rollicking Mustang Goat for a mere 21 bucks. An intact "Humpy Dump" is now one of the rarest of all DeMoulin collectibles. The catalog copy almost creates a mythos, suggesting a veritable zoo of commingling, fraternal beasties. The descriptive text suggests that "He has been associated with the goat family so much that he has acquired many of their characteristics. The ups and downs in this world will be thoroughly instilled and vividly shown to the candidate." For additional sums, any of the creatures could come with electrified stirrups and the ability to blast water in the rider's face.

The original DeMoulin goats had actual goat horns which were shipped in from New Mexico. One hot day in 1900 a trainload of 3,800 pairs of horns arrived, after traveling in a humid freight car. The horns sat out in the sun and cooked further in the boiling Greenville, Illinois summer sun. And they started to stink. And STINK. So much so that when the wind shifted and blew the stench across town, the local merchants became distraught. The story goes that they wanted to run the DeMoulin brothers out of town for being such irresponsible goat-makers. A few years later the company switched to simulated horns made out of molten metal in the factory's blacksmithing shop.

The Low-Down Buck, the last model of mechanical goat produced by the factory in 1923. Note the Buck's metal horns.

Clockwise from top left: 1955 factory fire; DeMoulin Bros. & Co. today; a vintage magneto battery used for shocking unsuspecting initiates; the contemporary uniform showroom.

Today, the vast, nondescript building in Greenville produces a substantial percentage of the nation's marching band uniforms, serving colleges and high schools around the world. The old pond remains, out of which the brothers are said to have fished from their office windows. Yet, it will always be "The Goat Factory." A few old-timers may still be found in Greenville who call it by this affectionate name. Although DeMoulin Bros. shifted its focus to church furniture, graduation caps and gowns, and band uniforms, the company proudly acknowledges its unique and whimsical history.

From the early 1890s until the 1930s, Greenville was the center of the most remarkable and different sort of productivity. All of the proper pieces fell together, resulting in the brief but great success the factory had. Certain devices, such as the electric carpets, could be ordered as late as the 1950s. Oh, for a time-machine! It really was something out of a wild fantasy, as if Rube Goldberg and the Marquis de Sade were given brief but gloriously free rein as business partners.

Clockwise from top left: The three DeMoulin brothers; the "Trick Bottom Chair"; the factory sewing department, circa 1915

    The factory produced never-ending, wildly ingenious, and heretofore unknown, hilariously nightmarish initiation devices of an often seemingly innocent but usually torturous nature. It is hard to imagine the atmosphere of constant merriment and invention that must have filled the office factories. What guffaws must have echoed down the vast walls, punctuated by machines, as newer, more outlandish and unapologetically sadistic devices were proposed. In the tradition of the best practical jokes, an innocent-looking, ordinary chair instantly transforms into a back-breaking, literally *shocking* device! The company was hell-bent on producing a vast array of beautifully crafted devices specifically designed to terrorize would-be initiates in dozens of fraternal organizations.
    Greenville, Illinois is a peaceful, sleepy little Midwestern town, an hour outside of St. Louis. Those fascinated by this book may want to visit this rural and quaint 'burg some day, if for no other reason than to see the DeMoulin Museum, founded in 2010 by local historian John Goldsmith. Here, a number of very rare pieces of DeMoulin Brothers initiation, burlesque, and side degree paraphernalia may be viewed.

The image and misconception that would-be Masons and initiates in other esoteric groups were forced to actually ride a wild goat as part of their initiation ceremonies goes back to the early 19th century. The connection was a vivid part of the anti-Masonic movement. Just as the greek god Pan's aquiline imagery was appropriated by the Church and conveniently turned into the devil, so too the goat was linked with the potentially frightening and unknown secrets of America's great fraternal orders.

Innumerable postcards, and even paperweights, link Masonry with goat riding. This is 100% inaccurate, for no such activity has ever occurred in a Masonic lodge. The legendary appearance of a black goat during the height of the medieval witches' black sabbath, another form of initiation, was borrowed by anti-Masonists. As early as 1845, a tract was published, *A True Key to Off Fellowship*, linking that group with goat riding.

The ancient stigma of the goat remains so strong to this day that initiates in actual Masonic lodges might be off-handedly asked if they like "the smell of goat" before more serious matters begin. It is repeated, because it was whispered to them—like an urban legend, or a Xeroxed piece of office humor. In a way, this helps battle the negative link between the goat and fraternal groups. It is an unfair link that judges the methods and traditions of private groups. The connection with the randy beast, even humorously, will forever be eerily efficient at setting the candidate on edge. He has no idea what to expect.

What's with the goats? In his insightful essay, "Riding The Goat: Secrecy, Masculinity and Fraternal High Jinks in the United States, 1845-1930," Professor William D. Moore (who generously provided a new essay especially for this edition) suggests that the goat, originally a tool used by the anti-fraternal to symbolize the debauchery and link to the diabolic, in time became a creature that was the joyful center of many late Victorian and early 20th century fraternal initiation rites. Moore suggests that goat riding helped define a new form of 20th century masculinity. Goat-riding became an escape from the restrictive, Victorian culture that would have found such behavior unthinkable. Slowly, even gentlemen began to view the physical and the earthy, as something to be respected.

The goat conveniently becomes a barrier against the idly curious public, as well as a subconscious example of future-thinking illumination. The very idea of the goat evokes the forbidden rites of Dionysus and the great god Pan. A single look, legend had it, into the eyes of the goat god during his surprise appearances at hot and high noon would result in instant madness. This side effect of illumination is only natural, for the human mind cannot contain *all* that there is to know, and Pan is *all*. Some survivors of the old goat-herding religions remained in Tuscany as late as the mid-19th century. A D.H. Lawrence-style social paganism was brewing. Men could now take part in a vaudevillian version of a mystical, witchy initiation rite, in the kind of skull-laden dens their grandmothers used to speak of in their terror tales. Robert Bly, eat your heart out. Many items in the catalog take a jibe at the trappings of the church or lodge. Devilish imagery prevails, hints of brimstone and hellish trials straight out of Dante.

An innocent prayer altar is anything but. A grim, papier-mâché skeleton pops out suddenly, reminding the humble candidate of his mortality (if he hasn't already dropped dead from a heart attack).

John Goldsmith, whose mother worked at the factory for 50 years and passed her historical interests down to her son, observed that these experiences led "men of all ages and backgrounds to gather and share a common experience. They could talk about the news of the day and then proceed to watch a fellow member fall off a DeMoulin goat."

"WHEN FATHER RODE THE GOAT"

The house is full of arcana, and mystery profound;
We do not dare to run about or make the slightest sound.
We leave the big piano shut and do not strike a note;
the doctor's been here seven times since father rode the goat.

He joined the lodge a week ago; got in at 4:00 a.m.—
And sixteen brethren brought him home, though he says that he brought them.
His wrist was sprained and one big rip had rent his Sunday coat—
There must have been a lively time when father rode the goat.

He's resting on the couch today! And practicing his signs—
The hailing signal, the working grip, and other monkeyshines;
He mutters passwords 'neath his breath, and other things he'll quote—
They surely had an evening's work when father rode the goat.

He has a gorgeous uniform, all gold and red and blue—
A hat with plumes and yellow braid, and golden badges too.
But, somehow, when we mention it, he wears a look so grim;
we wonder if he rode the goat—or if the goat rode him!

FLYING MACHINE
IT'S A STUNNER. A PUZZLE. A NEW SENSATION

On this aerial navigator the candidate clings to the rudder like grim death The fan with the clattering attachment and the rain sprayer in front chase the breezes and misty clouds against his anatomy with the sound and feeling of a huricane—he surges, he lurches and bobs, he ascends and descends, now and then passing through a cloud which sprays his brow—he occasionally thinks he is going to make a parachute leap, but cannot cut loose from the pesky thing. Thus it is one continual round of torture until he is again on terra firma.

See suggestions for introducing, page XIV in back of catalog.

The Flying Machine is substantially built and well finished. The oscilating and up and down movements of the platform driven by an eccentric from the main axle produce a good flying or swinging motion; the rocking spring pendulum from which the seat and handle bar are pivoted gives the victim all the flying sensation necessary to impress him that he is traveling at a high speed; the rain spray which may be turned on or off at will, makes him realize that he occasionally dashes right through a cloud. The wheels have rubber tires. The machine packs in a small chest. Shipping weight, 225 pounds.

3539 Flying Machine, including chest with lock and key..........................$40.00

5377 Costume for candidate, consisting of coat and trousers, as shown above... 2.60

5378 Costumes for manipulaters, consisting of robe and large papier mache donkey or goat head; each... 2.25

A few items that made it into the final catalog were so far-fetched that it is debated as to whether they were actually constructed (unless ordered). One such creation was The Flying Machine.

It *must* be emphasized once more that the Freemasons have never used, and would never use, any such comical or potentially dangerous "burlesque paraphernalia" in their organization. The study of such an odd aberration of the American psyche is both a fascinating and rib-tickling entertainment. By embracing a mockery of "secret society" antics, the participant was still energized and thrilled, without having to do the real, enlightening work. The only thing that got enlightened here was his rear end. Most often, he gleefully joined knowing he'd get to watch someone else traverse a similar rough road. It's only human nature.

Although one might cast doubts as to the spiritual effectiveness of such crude stunts enacted by ancient-sounding, short-lived organizations... who is to say what impact even an unintentional parody, or mock-ritual, might have on the vulnerable and eager psyche?

A treasure trove of fraternal humor may be found in *The Lodge Goat: Goat Rides, Butts, and Goat Hairs* (Cincinnati: C.B. Pettibone, 1902). The publisher was one of several competitors of the DeMoulin Brothers, even selling identical lion-head seals! This lushly illustrated tome is jam-packed with every imaginable type of fraternal goat and gag, fully embracing that which once was a threat.

The truth is that the goat served as a false lead, throwing the ignorant public even further off the track, shielding the truth with a wry wink and an ancient nudge.

The goats were the tip of the tormenting iceberg. Collapsible chairs fired off a blank cartridge when they hit the ground. The inductee was challenged to hold onto the handles of a "lifting machine" and pull with all his might, trusting his brethren. In fact, in an instant a board flew up on a spring and swatted his rear end with a mighty force. Simultaneously a cartridge exploded and water was shot in his face. HA! When the unwary fellow blew with all his might into the "lung tester," a .32-caliber cartridge exploded and a secret hole on the machine's fake dial blasted flour into his face. You could purchase a gold-framed mirror that shot water and made a loud BANG! A large, and very imposing looking, guillotine was easily obtained. For an extra fee one could purchase a severed head and a blood-spattered drop-cloth. The items were beautifully crafted out of wood, in the style of the day, so authentic-looking that they really fooled the would-be user.

Some of the amazing items for sale in this catalog appear to be upscale versions of classic novelty shop gags: The "Lung Tester" is a fancy upgrade of the black-eye viewing scope; the "Squirt Camera" appeared in S.S. Adams and Johnson-Smith novelty catalogs; the "Glad Hand" was a super-charged, electrified version of the classic "Joy Buzzer" that could almost knock a man out, so great was the electric shock. Also, very wonderful, and not to be over-looked, is "Fun in The Lodge Room," located at the back of the catalogue. This consisted of "directions and suggestions for introducing and using our burlesque and side degree paraphernalia." Here we have 30 pages of theatrical suggestions, complete with scripted dialogue and ironic, deadpan humor, to assist the jaunty yet somber brethren in how to use their newly purchased Goats-on-wheels, collapsible chairs, electrified and spiked carpets, and so forth. It is virtual book within the catalogue, and an arsenal of laughs for the modern reader who wants to relive a night of hair-raising stunts.

DeMoulin published one of the pocket sized editions of *Jack's Stunt Book*, a comical, cartoon-illustrated guide full of further tips and tricks to amuse the fellows at lodge. The fourth edition was much larger, and is crammed with wild ideas. It is unimaginable to perform many of these today, as well. These jokes and stunts were *dangerous*!

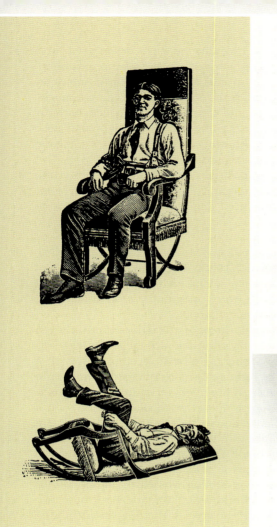 

several serious collectors of DeMoulin props and gadgets exist, many of them in the professional magicians' community. Magic historian, magician, collector, and writer Mike Caveney states that the work of the DeMoulin factory is "...still pretty unknown in the magic world." Caveney stumbled upon a DeMoulin chair, buying it after experiencing the collapsing effect first hand. He has the chair set up in his home and all new visitors are asked to innocently sit in it. A chain is yanked and the chair flips the sitter backwards, a picture is snapped simultaneously—and the victim remains trapped on the floor in the cleverly designed chair. When David Copperfield visited the magic historian's home with his girlfriend at the time, Claudia Schiffer, they witnessed the super-model being unceremoniously dumped to the floor in a DeMoulin chair, much to their mutual delight! Caveney has a scrapbook of photos depicting virtually every great magician in the world, feet flying up in the air, as he receives a dose of DeMoulin-style humor!

The appeal here is in the ingenuity and similarity of DeMoulin inventions to actual magical devices. The aforementioned magician, David Copperfield, is known to cherish the odd work of the factory, and paid a personal visit to the factory when on tour in 2002. His collection of DeMoulin side-degree paraphernalia is said to be extensive.

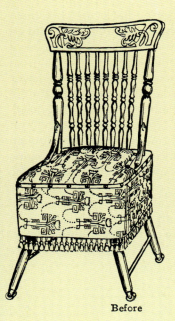

Before   After

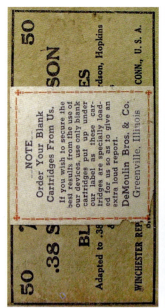   

Explosive .38 blanks to load into your "combined lifting and spraying machine." Just forty-five cents for a box of fifty!

Please do not be so foolish as to attempt to recreate these devices or stunts. You will end up burnt, bruised, and with a severely fractured spine—*if* you survive. The publisher is not responsible should you choose to be so absurdly foolhardy.

All of these devices were lovingly illustrated and described in a series of catalogs released over the course of about twenty years. The hand of two artists can be discerned: Ed DeMoulin, whose drawings ran for decades; and a woman, an anonymous member of the art staff for years. Both artists capture the key magical, explosive moment, the *instant* a gag has been sprung. This milks the merriment factor, and makes one want to see the tables turned on one's own esoteric associates. It was proved that these eccentric initiation ploys greatly increased lodge memberships. After going through a shocking ordeal, one could hardly wait to see another would-be member go through the exact same series of exotic, mystical trials and mechanical frights. This would help heal the bruised ego (as well as the posterior).

The number of pages devoted to increasingly outrageous, hilarious and downright sadistic devices and stunts increased with each catalog. The three DeMoulin Brothers must have spent an enormous amount of time simply sitting around devising their latest, never-before-created initiation machines. The catalog you are about to plunge into is the great #439, the version that the brothers threw the kitchen sink into. It has more devices and crazy ideas jammed into it than all the previous editions. This catalog is the holy grail amongst the cult of DeMoulin fanatics waiting to be born. Let's hope this reprint sows the seed.

Reading through the catalog for the first time is a jaw-dropping experience. The very existence of such a bible of practical jokes, stunts, and pranks is amazing. Here we have an armchair Baedeker for the gentle sadist. Many of the DeMoulin brothers' creations took some of the basic ritualistic aspects of various fraternal societies, perhaps known or suspected, spoken of in hushed whispers, and filtered these through

LIFTING AND SPRAYING MACHINE

D350

A candidate is always ready to display his strength to show that he is an able-bodied man, and it takes but a suggestion relative to his physical weakness to get him to prove that he can lift just as much as any other man of his weight and size.

See suggestions for introducing, page XX in back of catalog.

The machine has a dial to register the number of pounds lifted and when the candidate has lifted about 50 pounds, an automatic cartridge device is sprung, discharging a 32-calibre blank cartridge with a loud report; the startling effect causes candidate to release his hold, and then he gets a "free bath" by the spraying device concealed in the dial.

D350—Lifting and Spraying Machine, including box of 50 blank cartridges and full directions for operating....$14.00
(Weight, packed, 20 pounds)

Extra Blank Cartridges (not mailable), loaded specially for us to give an extra loud report; per box of 50.... .45

a pulp-colored lens of luridness, and made them come alive. The props came straight out of an 18th Century Gothic novel, Victorian Penny Dreadful or a *"weird menace"* pulp, replete with many a poised and glowing branding iron, creating a startlingly macabre and individualistic vision.

One of the greatest pleasures of the catalog is the *sotto voce* that runs through it by way of the promotional copy describing each machine, and each unique creation's potential for mental mayhem. The copywriter vividly places you in the experience. Additional testimonials from satisfied customers brought the "paraphernalia" vividly to life. Few more entertaining and chuckle-provoking books have ever been produced, and now it is back in print to stun and dazzle future generations of thrill-seekers. In this unintentional grail of American culture we see, all at once, the brilliance, maliciousness, endless invention, enthusiasm, bullying, beauty, grotesquerie, and embracing of the shadowy side of ourselves that has made this country unique. So sit back in the safety of your non-collapsible, non-electrified, non-explosive chair and celebrate a time when such incredible contraptions were actually built and used, to the tittering delight and shuddering terror of generations of eager gentlemen.

This edition of the catalog represents the end of a magical era. The threat of lawsuits continued. The spread of the automobile made men less transient, the lure of radio and movies distracted men from lodge life. The very real mustard gas horrors of World War I made the idea of simulated near-death experiences in a gentleman's lodge less attractive to young vets. Then, the Great Depression. These and other elements forced the DeMoulin company to focus on marching band uniforms and fraternal supplies. The wild days of their mirth-machines had ended.

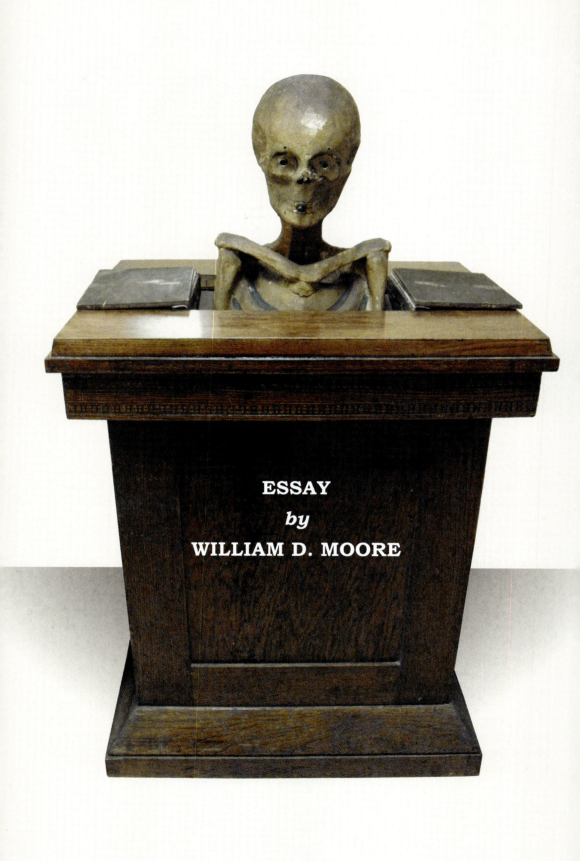

ESSAY
by
WILLIAM D. MOORE

Canned Snakes, Mechanical Goats, and Spitting Skeletons

Making Sense of the 1930 DeMoulin Bros. & Co. Catalog

In the first years of the twenty-first century, opening the pages of the DeMoulin Bros. & Co.'s *Catalog No. 439: Burlesque Paraphernalia and Side Degree Specialties and Costumes* may seem like falling down the rabbit hole, or slipping through the looking glass, in Lewis Carroll's famous Alice books. This catalog transports readers to a world that is similar to theirs, yet remarkably distinct. Some goods offered for sale within its pages continue to be available to American consumers. Item D14 on page 113, for instance, is almost identical in conception to the spring-loaded snakes hidden in potato-chip canisters that currently can be purchased at Spencer's Gifts novelty stores found in shopping malls in over 600 communities in the United States.[1] Other items, however, exhibit an alien sensibility profoundly dissimilar from that of our own time. The altar marketed on page 48, for example, concealing a mechanical skeleton that jumps out and spits in the eye of an unsuspecting dupe, brings together a constellation of symbols to express a form of irreverence which does not resonate for most in the present. Similarly, even if readers skip over the racist and stereotypically exaggerated costumes of African-Americans, Jews, Irish immigrants, and other ethnic groups, the devil's costume illustrated on page 136, featuring a long pointed nose and bizarrely curled toes, horns, and tail, simply appears curious, if not odd. Similarly, what are we to make of the fact that the firm offers a range of options for those seeking to purchase a mechanical goat?

Initially, the DeMoulin Brothers Co.'s *Burlesque Paraphernalia* catalog, with its seemingly idiosyncratic merchandise, may strike readers as an isolated, aberrant publication. This document, however, actually is compelling evidence of a largely

---

[1] Spencer's Gifts, "About Spencer's" http://www.spencersonline.com/about-spencers/ (accessed March 4, 2010). For an example of a Depression era snake in a can, see Mark Newgarden and Picturebox, Inc., *Cheap Laffs: The Art of the Novelty Item* (New York: Harry N. Abrams, 2004), 106.

forgotten industry and speaks to the vitality of the American economy on the brink of the Great Depression. The items illustrated here offer insight into the world in which our grandparents, great-grandparents, and possibly great-great-grandparents earned a living, raised families, and made their way in the world. Understanding why one would want to purchase an expectorating mechanical skeleton provides us a deeper understanding of the forces that have shaped the society in which we live today.

By analyzing the outrageous goods offered for sale within the pages of this trade catalog as products of American cultural and economic transformations taking place in the late nineteenth and early twentieth centuries, this introduction attempts to make sense of this apparently nonsensical publication. More specifically, the items offered here will be discussed in relation to the growth of American fraternalism, the increased prosperity created by industrialization, and shifts in American masculinity. As a result, we may be able to understand better why our forbears purchased mechanical goats, and why it made good economic sense for a firm in Greenville, Illinois to manufacture them.

AMERICAN FRATERNALISM

Fraternal organizations were pervasive in American society at the end of the nineteenth century; vast numbers of American men joined organizations such as the Freemasons, the Odd Fellows, the Knights of Pythias, the Modern Woodmen of America, the United Order of American Mechanics, the Benevolent and Protective Order of Elks, the Fraternal Order of Eagles, and hundreds of other more obscure societies. In an article in the *North American Review* from 1897, the writer H. S. Harwood reported that fraternal groups claimed five-and-a-half million members, while the total adult population of the United States was approximately nineteen million.[2] At about the same time, Albert C. Stevens, the compiler of the *Cyclopedia of Fraternities*, estimated that 40 percent of adult males maintained membership in a fraternal order.[3]

American fraternalism employed ceremonial initiations to bind individuals together in brotherhood, using a model developed by Freemasonry during the eighteenth century in Britain.[4] Fraternal groups shared cultural commonalities, including regalia, handshakes, and grandiloquent and imposing titles for officers, as well as progressively more complex rituals.[5] These characteristics distinguished fraternal societies from other voluntary organizations. Although often referred to as "secret societies," these groups maintained visibility in the public sphere by participating in civic parades, displaying symbols on the exterior of their meeting places, and wearing lapel pins and symbols of membership.

The fraternal model was so pervasive in American society during these years that it was adopted by a wide range of organizations promoting disparate agendas. For example, the Grand Army of the Republic initiated Union Army veterans into local camps to promote patriotism and to organize political support for government benefits. The Patrons of Husbandry, better known as the Grange, was founded

---

[2] W. S. Harwood, "Secret Societies in America," *North American Review* 164 (May 1897): 619-23.

[3] Albert C. Stevens, *The Cyclopedia of Fraternities* 2nd ed. (New York: E.B. Treat and Company, 1907), xvi. Women also participated in fraternalism, but to a lesser degree. See Mary Ann Clawson, *Constructing Brotherhood: Class, Gender, and Fraternalism* (Princeton, NJ: Princeton University Press, 1989), 178-210.

[4] For a popular overview of the history of American Freemasonry, see Mark A. Tabbert, *American Freemasons: Three Centuries of Building Communities* (New York: New York University Press, 2005).

[5] Noel P. Gist, *Secret Societies: A Cultural Study of Fraternalism in the United States* (Columbia: University of Missouri Press, 1940).

as a mutual support network for agricultural communities, whereas the Sons of Temperance used the organizational schema to fight the evils of alcohol, while Terence W. Powderly led the Knights of Labor in the struggle for the rights of workers.[6]

The initiation of new members comprised the primary activity of many fraternal groups. Men were incorporated into the fraternal body and simultaneously introduced to the organization's tenets and ideologies through the performance of secret rituals. These rites drew upon biblical and classical narratives to inculcate members with supposedly timeless systems of morality and ethics. Freemasonry, for example, was based upon an allegorical understanding of Solomon's Temple.[7] The Odd Fellows enlisted the lives of biblical patriarchs to exemplify correct behavior.[8] The Knights of Pythias used the story of Damon and Pythias to teach friendship and model interpersonal relations.[9]

During the late Victorian era, men joined these groups, in part, because they provided supposedly unchanging models of masculinity at a time when Americans were experiencing profound and threatening financial and cultural transformations. As the United States went from a rural nation grounded in an agricultural economy to an urban, industrial country, men eagerly pursued symbolic ceremonial identities that seemed to remain fixed and ageless. As W. C. Atwood, the Masonic grand orator of Missouri claimed "The principles of Freemasonry are as unchangeable and eternal as God Himself. They are hoary with age; they have endured the crucial tests of generation succeeding generation."[10] Not surprisingly, the most prominent of the fraternal organizations promoted teachings that resonated with the dominant world view of the Protestant majority and the values of Victorian middle-class America; the Masons promoted piety, honesty, sobriety, and self-restraint.[11] A period commentator on Odd Fellowship claimed that his group taught "loyalty to God, to man, to country, and to law."[12]

Because fraternal societies were organized around ideas of brotherhood and ceremonial kinship, they also provided a degree of economic stability in the volatile new industrial economy. Masonic brothers vowed to care for each others' widows and orphans, and established homes to fulfill these obligations. The Odd Fellows claimed "mutual relief" as a central tenet.[13] Some groups developed this informal system of brotherly assistance into incorporated "mutual assessment" or insurance fraternities. The Ancient Order of United Workmen, or AOUW, was among the earliest to offer life insurance to its members.[14] Joseph Cullen Root, a Freemason, established the Modern Woodmen of America in 1883 specifically as an insurance organization to serve white men in the Midwest.[15] Another group, the Woodmen of the World, founded in 1890, similarly mixed fraternal ritual with insurance coverage.[16] The Knights of Columbus, organized in 1882 in New Haven, Connecticut, provided fraternal insurance coverage to Catholic laymen.[17]

---

6 Barbara Franco, *Fraternally Yours: A Decade of Collecting* (Lexington, MA: Museum of Our National Heritage, 1986), 19-31.
7 For an analysis of the narrative of the Masonic ritual, see William D. Moore, *Masonic Temples: Freemasonry, Ritual Architecture and Masculine Archetypes* (Knoxville: University of Tennessee Press, 2006), 1-14.
8 Thomas G. Beharrell, *The Brotherhood: Being a Presentation of the Principles of Odd-Fellowship* (Indianapolis, IN: Brotherhood Publishing Co., 1875), 87-163.
9 John Van Valkenberg, *The Knights of Pythias Complete Manual and Text-book*, rev. ed. (Canton, OH: Memento Publishing, 1892), 60-64.
10 W. C. Atwood, *New England Craftsman* 3, no. 5 (Feb. 1908): 179.
11 Lynn Dumenil, *Freemasonry and American Culture, 1880-1930* (Princeton, NJ: Princeton University Press, 1984), 72.
12 Henry Leonard Stillson, ed. *The History and Literature of Odd Fellowship* (Boston: Fraternity Publishing Co., 1897), 814.
13 Beharrell, 19-22.
14 Clawson, 139.
15 Clawson, 226-27.
16 Alan Axelrod, *The International Encyclopedia of Secret Societies and Fraternal Orders* (New York: Facts on File, 1997), 264-65.
17 Christopher J. Kauffman, *Faith and Fraternalism: The History of the Knights of Columbus, 1882-1982*

By the end of the nineteenth century, fraternalism had become an omnipresent component of American life. Across the nation, men spent evenings practicing solemn ceremonies to initiate one another in a range of symbolic identities. These groups provided a form of community theater while also teaching values and providing economic security.

THE GREAT DEFLATION

In the decades after the nation's Civil War during which fraternalism blossomed, Americans experienced expanding prosperity. Through industrialization, mineral exploitation, and improved transportation, corporations expanded production. Wholesale prices decreased while the Gross National Product simultaneously expanded. Because consumer goods became cheaper at the same time that more money was available, economic historians have called this period the "Great Deflation."

As a result of their real income increasing by nearly 50 percent between 1877 and 1900, Americans simply could afford more consumer goods. Manufacturing firms introduced a spectacular array of goods to the marketplace.[18] Firms like Sears, Roebuck & Co. and Montgomery Ward published huge catalogs to harness the country's burgeoning industrial output and exploit the American consumer's purchasing power. Railroad corporations developed new technologies, while agreeing upon a standard gauge of track throughout the country, thus creating improved efficiency in transportation and contributing to decreasing prices.

Across the country, entrepreneurs established businesses to supply materials to fraternal organizations. Although regalia firms existed in antebellum cities such as New York, Boston, and Philadelphia, these companies were dwarfed by the growth of enormous Midwestern fraternal supply houses in the 1870s and 1880s. M. C. Lilley & Company of Columbus, Ohio, was possibly the largest of these firms that prospered in the late nineteenth century. Lilley manufactured and sold everything a fraternal organization required; from elaborate costumes and uniforms to elegant flags and draperies, and from costume jewelry and theatrical weapons to preprinted stationery and ceremonial furniture. The firm shipped goods to cities on the East and West coasts, but also to destinations as far away the Hawaiian Islands, South Africa, and India.[19]

Lilley's competitors included the Pettibone Brothers Manufacturing Company, of Cincinnati, Ohio; the Henderson-Ames Company of Kalamazoo, Michigan; and the Ward-Stilson Company of Anderson, Indiana, among numerous others.[20] DeMoulin Bros. & Co. was a minor player within this larger fraternal supply industry. The ballot boxes, gavels, hoodwinks, seals and other supplies offered on pages 105 through 112 of the catalog indicate the firm's place within this trade.

Fraternal supply houses succeeded by offering essentially the same merchandise to diversified markets. They sold slightly modified ceremonial goods to the Masons, the Odd Fellows, and other secret societies. Uniforms were sold to fraternal precision marching teams, National Guard units, marching bands, and taxi and limousine services.[21] Furniture of the same design could be ornamented with a cross for use in a church, a square and compass to outfit a Masonic temple, or an elk head for sale

---

(New York: Harper & Row, 1982).
    18 Regina Lee Blaszczyk, *American Consumer Society 1865-2005: From Hearth to HDTV* (Wheeling, IL: Harlan Davidson, Inc., 2009), 20.
    19 William D. Moore, "Masonic Lodge Rooms and Their Furnishings," *Heredom* 2(1993): 107-09.
    20 John D. Hamilton, *Material Culture of the American Freemasons* (Lexington, MA: Museum of Our National Heritage, 1994), 282-87.
    21 The Lilley Co., *Uniforms for Bands and Drum Corps Catalog No. 275* (Columbus, Ohio: The Lilley Co., n.d.).

to the Benevolent and Protective Order of Elks. Page 2 of this catalog illustrates that DeMoulin Bros. & Co. published dozens of catalogs targeted at groups as diverse as carnival workers, band directors, college faculty, firemen, Army officers, theatre owners, and circuses, beyond the numerous secret societies specifically enumerated.

With the availability of specialized ceremonial equipment, fraternal rituals became increasingly elaborate. Initiations, which previously had been conducted in business clothes, subsequently were performed in elaborate costumes and robes.[22] Lodges collected fees to initiate new members and used those fees to acquire ever more spectacular costumes and props.

The Scottish Rite of Freemasonry erected elaborate neo-classical cathedrals containing theatrical spaces outfitted with scenery and special effects for the presentation of degrees. These buildings comprise the ultimate expression of this fraternal inflationary impulse.[23] The Scottish Rite Masons of St. Louis, Missouri, for example, constructed a cathedral in 1924 that cost more than $2 million and could seat 2,950 people. Within these cathedrals, Scottish Rite Masons enacted ceremonies in ornate costumes while standing before spectacular backdrops that depicted biblical scenes, subterranean treasure vaults, ancient cities, and even the fiery confines of Hell. Participants conceived of scenery, props, and costumes as tools to increase the efficacy of their rituals in inculcating messages of respectability, industry, and sobriety.

BURLESQUE SIDE DEGREES AND A NEW MASCULINITY

Fraternalists distinguished between what were considered "regular" degrees and "side degrees." Ceremonies recognized and regulated by an organization's governing body were described as regular. Any ritual that did not have a group to regulate its performance was a "side degree."[24] The line dividing these two categories, which at first appears distinct, was extremely permeable in practice as fraternal organizations, while easily organized, often proved ephemeral. Enthusiasts wrote a ritual, formed an organization to promulgate it, and then lost interest. In other instances, individuals revived moribund side degrees and then created an organization to regulate them and established a means to make money by charging initiation fees. Dr. Darius Wilson of Boston, Massachusetts, for instance, founded the Royal Arcanum insurance fraternity in 1877, but also made a career of revitalizing esoteric Masonic degrees, a practice for which he was derided by many Masonic authorities as an unscrupulous peddler of meaningless certificates.[25]

Although many side degrees proved short-lived, others attained permanent institutional status. For example, a group of New York City Freemasons established the Ancient Arabic Order of the Nobles of the Mystic Shrine, commonly known as the Shriners, in a bar room in New York City in 1872 with no intention that it would evolve into one of the nation's most recognized providers of free medical care to the needy.[26] Similarly, the Order of the Arrow started as an informal fraternal ritual offered to members of the Boy Scouts of America, but later was regularized and fully integrated into the organization's corporate practices.[27]

---

22 See Moore, *Masonic Temples*, 34-38.
23 See C. Lance Brockman, *Theatre of the Fraternity: Staging the Ritual Space of the Scottish Rite of Freemasonry, 1896-1928* (Minneapolis: Frederick R. Weisman Art Museum, University of Minnesota, 1996).
24 "Side Degrees," *American Freemason* 1 no. 5 (May 1858): 385.
25 Stevens, 186-87; "Troubling the Masons," *New York Times* (Jan. 30, 1885): 8.
26 For an analysis of the history of the Shriners, see Moore, *Masonic Temples*, 93-117.
27 J. C. Halter, "The Order of the Arrow Turns 75," *Boys' Life* 8 no. 5 (May 1990): 19.

In the final years of the nineteenth century, fraternalists practiced a new series of side degrees which ridiculed, or burlesqued, the pieties of fraternal initiations. These innovative ceremonies inverted the ritual form and used it to teach a set of values which contrasted with the earlier emphases upon industry, reverence, and rectitude. In some cases, burlesque degrees became regularized and associated with the larger fraternal organizations. The Imperial Order of Muscovites and the Oriental Order of Humility and Perfection, for example, were affiliated with the Odd Fellows.[28] Members of the Knights of Pythias could join the "Dokies," more formally known as the Dramatic Order of the Knights of Khorassan.[29] Freemasons could choose from the Shriners, the Mystic Order of Veiled Prophets of the Enchanted Realm, or the Tall Cedars of Lebanon, or join all three.[30]

By burlesquing the earlier staid, solemn rituals, these associations specialized in horseplay and stunts intended to deflate "stuffed shirts." In quoting a Shriner publication, the journalist Charles W. Ferguson reported that in their prescribed undertakings "pomposity is punctured, pride is laughed to scorn, and dignity is bedeviled."[31] The Shrine trumpeted that it was "the playground" of Freemasonry while the Imperial Potentate of the organization asserted that the organization promoted "legitimate frivolity."[32]

In response to the success of these organizations, other fraternal societies incorporated roughhousing into their practices as a competitive means of making their meetings equally entertaining. In 1894, for example, the Modern Woodmen of America introduced a new section to its ritual which included blindfolding the initiate, placing him on a mechanical goat, and riding him around the hall.[33] Although the Sovereign Camp of the Woodmen of the World did not require a mechanical goat to be used during initiation, local affiliates voluntarily placed supplicants upon these devices.[34]

The fraternal supply firms embraced burlesque and side degrees because they offered the opportunity for new categories of sales. Around the turn of the century, many companies started featuring slapstick items such as mechanical goats and collapsing chairs in catalogs. W. E. Floding, of Atlanta, Georgia, as one instance, offered such materials in its 1910 Odd Fellows catalog.[35] Other suppliers, like M. C. Lilley and C. E. Ward, of New London, Ohio, instituted separate catalogs of burlesque goods.[36]

A few firms, including notably the Pettibone Brothers Manufacturing Company of Cincinnati, Ohio, made novelty items a particular specialty. In its *Catalogue No. 718: Burlesque Paraphernalia* published around 1902, this firm claimed to be the first to produce fraternal burlesque equipment and stated that some groups were still using materials purchased fifteen years previously.[37] Pettibone illustrated many props that are interchangeable with offerings in the 1930 DeMoulin catalog including gag guillotines, "harmless" electric faux branding irons, an electrical punch bowl that

---

28 Stevens, 261; Axelrod, 177.
29 Axelrod, 152.
30 Tabbert, 127-31.
31 Charles W. Ferguson, *Fifty Million Brothers: A Panorama of American Lodges and Clubs* (New York: Farrar & Rhinehart, 1937), 244.
32 James E. Chandler, 'Legitimate Frivolity' is Taught by Shrine," *Square and Compass* 2 no. 10 (June 1925): 9.
33 Modern Woodmen of America, *Revised Ritual of the Modern Woodmen of America* (Rock Island, IL: Head Camp, 1894), 34.
34 See "Lodge Goat is Shown in Court," *Freemason and Fez* 10 nos. 5-6 (May and June 1902): 42; "Secret Societies and the Law," *New England Craftsman* 2 no. 12 (September 1907): 452-55.
35 W.E. Floding, *Everything for the Lodge I.O.O.F. Catalogue, No. 54*. (Atlanta, GA: W.E. Floding, 1910), 59.
36 Burlesque items offered by M.C. Lilley & Co. are illustrated in "Your Money Will Cheerfully Be Refunded if Not Satisfied," *American Heritage* 23 no. 1 (Dec. 1971): 111. Catalog 66- Burlesque Goods is listed in on the back page of C. E. Ward Company, *Catalogue Number 104: Commandery Knights Templar Uniforms Costumes & Supplies* (New London, OH: C. E. Ward Company, n.d.).
37 Pettibone Bros. Mfg. Co., *Burlesque Paraphernalia* (Cincinnati: Pettibone Bros. Mfg. Co., 1902), n.p.

shocked the candidate when he tried to drink, and a range of mechanical goats.[38] Pettibone also supplied numerous side degree scripts which organizations could use to entertain themselves and their guests, including presentations entitled "The Daughters of the Sphinx," "The Queen of the Sahara," "The 20th Century Orient," and "The Disorganized Order of Gorillas."[39] Pettibone's copy writer described the latter production as "a burlesque, comical in the extreme; all sorts of indignities are heaped upon the candidate while passing through the 'wilderness,' and he is scared a 'powerful' sight. Nevertheless it is a harmless amusement, and the candidate comes out of the 'jungle' smiling and serene."[40]

The DeMoulin Brothers firm was the industry leader in burlesque and side degree paraphernalia. Founded in 1892, the company not only sold this material, it also consistently invented new forms of what were described on patent applications as "initiation apparatus for secret societies." On March 3, 1896, the U.S. Patent Office awarded Edmund and Ulysses S. DeMoulin a patent for the "Traitor's Judgment Stand" illustrated on page 31. In their application, the inventors explained, "The object of the present invention is to provide for secret societies an initiation apparatus which will be simple and inexpensive in construction, and which will be capable of surprising a candidate without the least danger of injuring him in any wise (sic), and which will present an appearance that will not arouse his suspicion or in any wise (sic) warn him of its operation."[41] The DeMoulins similarly were awarded patents for trick chairs, water guns, fake scales, dummy lung-testers, and the "combined lifting and spanking machine" illustrated on page 74.[42]

Each of these items is meant to surprise initiates by subverting expectations of fraternal ceremonies. The devices thus employ the symbolic vocabulary of the staid, establishment fraternal organizations, such as altars, skeletons, and ceremonial chairs, but employ them to overturn Victorian respectability. During Scottish Rite rituals, images of Hades reminded participants of the shortness of their sojourn here on earth; during burlesque initiation stunts a man in a devil suit symbolized the capriciousness of fate and of one's fellow men. Rather than teaching gentility, self-reliance, and restraint, the DeMoulins' inventions schooled American men in physical toughness, humor, and appropriate demeanor under stress. The initiate knelt at the altar expecting a lesson in morality and mortality; instead, he received a face-full of water from a mechanical skeleton. The test was whether he could laugh at himself and carry on.

The new playfulness within fraternal lodge rooms expressed in these stunts was a manifestation of changing gender relations within American society. Industrialization, urbanization, and the rise of corporate capitalism had profoundly reshaped American society at the end of the nineteenth century. Constructions of gender shifted in response. American men found that the old artisanal and agricultural ideals of character based upon self-restraint and Victorian gentility were unsuited to the emergent urban industrial order.

In the new economy of the twentieth century, men had needed to learn to laugh at themselves and their troubles. They had to be able to get up off the ground and chuckle

---

38   For an explication of fraternal goat imagery, see William D. Moore, "Riding the Goat: Secrecy, Masculinity, and Fraternal High Jinks in the United States, 1845-1930," *Winterthur Portfolio* 41 no. 2/3 (Summer/Autumn 2007): 161-188.

39   Pettibone Bros. Mfg. Co., *Select Catalogue of Plays for Use in Amateur Theatricals* (Cincinnati: Pettibone Bros. Mfg. Co., 1914).

40   Pettibone Bros. Mg. Co., *Catalogue 916: Descriptive Catalogue of Plays* (Cincinnati; Pettibone Bros. Mfg. Co., n.d.), 5.

41   U. S. Patent 555,499, filed by Edmund DeMoulin and Ulysses S. DeMoulin June 12, 1895 and issued March 3, 1896.

42   U. S. Patent 920,837, filed by Ulysses S. DeMoulin September 12, 1908 and issued May 4, 1909.

when thrown from the goat, so that they would have the opportunity to humiliate the next initiate. Participants were encouraged to "win friends and influence people," in the words of self-help writer Dale Carnegie, even after receiving an eyeful of skeleton spit.[43] Some scholars have called this transition in masculinity a shift from character to personality.[44] Sociologists like David Riesman have described it as a shift from an inward orientation to an outward focus.[45] However it is described, American men created a new paradigm of manhood that rejected Victorian respectability and replaced it with salesmanship and presentation of self.

The DeMoulin Bros. & Company catalog is not a rabbit hole, or a looking glass, or an entrance into an alternate reality. Instead, it is a type of time machine; a portal into the past that reveals an America enriched and reshaped by industrialization. Through this prism we can see a nation of men attempting to fit into a new world of corporate capitalism in which the older models of respectable masculinity no longer serve their purposes. These men work furiously to acclimate themselves to novel societal demands by riding mechanical goats, shocking their friends with electricity, and laughing hilariously at their own pranks.

---

[43] For Dale Carnegie, see Lynn Dumenil, *The Modern Temper: American Culture and Society in the 1920s* (New York: Hill and Wang, 1995), 87-88.
[44] See Frederick Lewis Allen, *The Big Change* (New York: Harper, 1952).
[45] David Riesman, *The Lonely Crowd* (New Haven: Yale University Press, 1961).

Catalog No. 439

CATALOG
NO.439

OUR FACTORY

is equipped to manufacture anything included in the following arts and crafts:

Church Furniture
Church Pews
Lodge Furniture
Furniture and Woodwork
Varnishing and Painting
Upholstering
Dies and Patterns
Iron Machine Work
Iron Forgings
Iron, Brass and Aluminum Castings
Swords
Metal Stamping
Jewelry
Plating
Leather Work and Special Footwear
Uniforms
Caps and Special Hats and Head Gear
Costumes, Regalia and Banners
Art and Scenic Painting
Art Bullion and Silk Needle Work
Printing Cuts
Printing and Lithographing
Badge Embossing
Button and Celluloid Novelties

Our factory represents an investment of over a half million dollars. We are located in a small city with excellent shipping facilities, cheap fuel, natural gas and low taxes.

Our factory is thoroughly equipped with the very best machinery; is excellently lighted and ventilated, and is managed by competent stockholding managers. Our stock of materials is very heavy and complete.

We were established in 1892 and have enjoyed a constant growth since. You are assured of our stability through a successful record of more than 38 years in the business.

With these natural advantages, which reduce our fixed expense to the minimum; with such excellent manufacturing facilities; with such complete stock of materials, we are enabled to manufacture in the highest quality, economically and without delay, every article listed.

Such an establishment at your service should be sufficient assurance that all orders will be filled promptly and that you will receive the greatest possible value for the amount expended.

DeMoulin Bros. & Co.
Greenville, Ill.

Printed in U. S. A.

OUR CATALOGS

Below we give a partial list of catalogs that we issue. Doubtless you are interested in some of these organizations and can tell us what supplies are needed by them. We solicit correspondence from, and information concerning, prospective purchasers.

A. A. O. N. MYSTIC SHRINE ....
A. E. O. OF SCIOTS ....
ALIANZA HISPANO AMERICANA ....
AMERICAN LEGION ....
ANCIENT MYSTIC ORDER SAMARITANS ....
ANCIENT ORDER UNITED WORKMEN
ARMY OFFICERS' UNIFORMS AND EQUIPMENTS ....
BALL THROWING GAMES AND DEVICES ....
BAND UNIFORMS AND EQUIPMENTS ....
BANNERS, BADGES, FLAGS, ETC. ....
B. P. O. ELKS ....
BROTHERHOOD OF AMERICAN YOEMEN ....
BROTHERHOOD OF L. FIREMEN AND ENGINEMEN ....
BROTHERHOOD OF RAILROAD TRAINMEN ....
CARNIVAL SUPPLIES ....
CHURCH FURNITURE ....
CHURCH PEWS ....
CHURCH PULPIT GOWNS ....
CHOIR GOWNS, CAPS, ETC. ....
CIRCUS EQUIPMENT ....
COLLEGE FRATERNITIES ....
COLLEGE AND UNIVERSITY BAND UNIFORMS ....
COLLEGE GOWNS AND CAPS ....
COLLEGE PENNANTS, CAPS, ETC. ....
DEGREE OF POCAHONTAS ....
DRAMATIC ORDER KNIGHTS OF KHORASSAN ....
ENCAMPMENT I. O. O. F. ....
FIREMEN UNIFORMS AND SUPPLIES ....
FRATERNAL ORDER OF EAGLES ....
FRATERNITIES (COLLEGE AND UNIVERSITIES)............
FORTY HOMMES ET EIGHT CHEVEAUX ....
HAYMAKERS (IMP'D O. R. M.) ....
HIGH SCHOOL GOWNS AND CAPS ....
HIGH SCHOOL BAND UNIFORMS ....
IMPERIAL ORDER OF MUSCOVITES ....
IMPROVED ORDER OF RED MEN ....
INDEPENDENT ORDER OF ODD FELLOWS ....
JOB'S DAUGHTERS ....
KIWANIS CLUBS ....
KNIGHTS TEMPLAR UNIFORMS ....
LETTER CARRIERS' UNIFORMS ....
LIONS' CLUBS ....
LODGE FURNITURE ....
LOYAL ORDER OF MOOSE ....
MASONS ....
MASONIC CLUBS ....
MASONIC CONSISTORY ....
MACCABEES ....
MINSTREL ....
M. O. OF VEILED PROPHETS OF THE E. R. ....
MODERN WOODMEN OF AMERICA ....
MYSTIC WORKERS OF THE WORLD ....
NATIONAL GUARD UNIFORMS AND EQUIPMENTS ....
ORDER OF DEMOLAY FOR BOYS ....
ORDER OF EASTERN STAR ....
PLAY GROUND EQUIPMENT ....
REBEKAH I. O. O. F. ....
ROYAL ARCH MASONS ....
ROYAL NEIGHBORS OF AMERICA ....
SECURITY BENEFIT ASSOCIATION ....
SIDE DEGREE PARAPHERNALIA, COSTUMES, ETC. ....
TALL CEDARS OF LEBANON ....
THEATRE UNIFORMS ....
THEATRE COSTUMES ....
UNIFORM RANK K. OF P. ....
UNIFORMS FOR COLLEGES AND UNIVERSITIES ....
UNITED COMMERCIAL TRAVELERS ....
USHERS' UNIFORMS ....
WOODMEN OF THE WORLD ....
WOODMEN CIRCLE ....

DeMoulin Bros. & Co.   Greenville, Illinois

ORDER BLANK

DeMoulin Bros. & Co.
Lodge Supplies, Uniforms, Banners, Badges,
Lodge and Church Furniture, Etc.
Greenville, Ill.

Gentlemen :—

Find enclosed ....
Draft or Money Order

for $............. for goods selected from

Catalog No. .... Please ship by

.... to
Freight, Express or Mail

Please do not write in above space.

....
Name of Person and Shipping Point

Would like for goods to reach destination not later than ....
Give Date

By order of .... No. ....
              Name of Lodge   Name of Order

Located at .... State ....
Location of Lodge or Organization

Name ....
Person Ordering

Street or R. F. D. ....

Post Office .... State ....

Date .... (Fill in all blanks correctly.)

Detach Order Blank Here

Quantity	Article No.	Name of Article	Price
		Total carried forward......	

Every Order, Large or Small, Will Receive Careful Attention

Quantity	Article No.	Name of Article	Price	
		Amount brought forward......		
		Total.....		

REMARKS:

OUR CREDENTIALS

C. E. HOILES.
PRESIDENT

J. M. DANIELS.
VICE PRES.

G. J. McCUNE.
CASHIER

FRED E. MARTIN
ASS'T CASHIER

STATE BANK OF HOILES & SONS
GREENVILLE, ILLINOIS

Sept. 15, 1930

To Whom It May Concern:

It is with pleasure that we testify to our good opinion of the integrity, responsibility and business ability of DeMoulin Bros. & Co.

Their factory is well equipped, they have ample capital to conduct their business, and have excellent good standing in this community. They command our full confidence and, we believe, can be relied upon to do exactly as they agree.

President.

Making a purchase from a manufacturer without reputation and responsibility is like lending money without security.

Our reputation for fair dealing, the personal interest we show in each transaction, the uniformly satisfactory relations existing between ourselves and our customers—what stronger arguments can we present in favor of your purchasing from us?

INDEX

ARTICLE	Page
Aeroplane	14
Alcohol, Wood	105
Altar and Pedestal	158
Altar, Pledge	48
Animal Heads, Papier Mache	117–119
Animals	123, 124
Auto-mul-ti-pede	75
Baby Doll	33
Baby Bouncer	54
Bad Egg Test	47
Badges	157
Baloon Ascension	27
Ballot Boxes and Ballots	110
Balls, Large Rubber	98
Band Uniforms, Burlesque	103
Banners	156
Baseball Stunt	75
Batons for Marshal	154
Batteries, Electric	39
Belts, Candidates	67
Belts, Sword	153
Benches, Electric	21
Binding Straps	67
Bird Heads, Papier Mache	117
Bird Cage	55
Blank Cartridges	106
Blanket, Electric	51, 87
Blarney Stone	96
Bleeding Test	96
Boat, Ocean Wave	75
Bomb Stunt	20
Branding and Whirling Table	77
Branding Outfit	63
Bridge, Falling	87
Bridge, Swinging	46
Bucking Couch	93
Burlesque Band Instruments	103
Burlesque Band Uniforms	103
Burlesque Costumes	125–138
Burlesque Rituals, Plays and Drills	107
Burning Brands, Deceptive	63
Burnt Cork	114
Camels	123, 124
Camera, Trick	22
Camp Fires	105
Cane, Electric	47
Cane	149
Cannon	85
Caps	149
Carpet of Tacks	40
Carpets, Electric	40–41
Cases for Books and Papers	111
Chair Covers	150
Chairs, Trick and Surprise	16–18, 22
Charleston Girls	57
Cigar Box, Trick	113
Cigars, Trick, Loaded	70
Clubs, Stuffed	71
Clubs, Policeman	53
Coats, Parade	149
Coffee Urn, Trick	70
Coffin Stunt	52–53
Colored Fire	109
Comb and Brush, Trick	37
Cones, Red Fire	109
Continental Uniforms	152
Costume, Devil	136
Costumes, Lodge	143–146
Costumes, Burlesque	125–138
Costumes, Race	139–142
Crepe Ribbon	104
Cross Bones	122
Current Affair	45
Dater	106
Deceptive Burning Brand	63
Deceptive Glasses	99
Decorations	104
Desk Phone, Trick	28
De Stink	47
Devil's Slide	86
Dog Show Stunt	65

ARTICLE	Page
Doll, Baby	33
Drinking the Goat's Blood	32
Dummy Man	33
Electric Attachment for Chairs	16
Electric Batteries	39
Electric Benches	21
Electric Branding Iron	63
Electric Blanket	51, 87
Electric Cane	47
Electric Carpets	40–41
Electric Chair	18
Electric Fountain	69
Electric Lavatory	69
Electric Portieres	75
Electric Razor	58
Electric Runways	40
Electric Sandals	90
Electric Saw and Buck	97
Electric Spanker	71
Electric Skeleton	51
Electric Spiked Pathway	45
Electric Stretcher	56
Electric Stuffed Club	53, 71
Electric Teeter-Totter	64
Electric Trident	38, 61
Electric Tunnel	80
Electric Wheel Barrow	60
Electric Wooden Shoes	45
Electrified Smoke	66
Embalmed Meat Test	47
Face Paint	114
Falling Bridge	87
Fencing Contest	43
Flags, U. S.	155
Flash Torches	92
Flying Machine	75
Fountain, Electric	69
Furniture	158
Gavels, Block and Case	112
Glad Hand	60
Goats	9–13
Goat's Blood	32
Golf Stunt	59
Gongs	160
Grease Paint	114
Greased Pole	72
Guillotine	29
Guns, Trick	24
Heads, Papier Mache	117–119
Home Brew Stunt	75
Hoodwinks	108
Hornet's Nest	75
Hose and Sandals	146
Hula Hula Bull Dance	83
Human Centipede	50
Human Heads, Papier Mache	117–119
Ice Cream Table	95
Ink Pad	106
Iron Test	26
Invisible Paddle Machine	73
Jag Producer	23
Jewish and Swiss Naval Battle	84
Judgment Stand	31
Kettle	105
Knife, Emblematic	107
Knife Throwing Stunt	76
Ladle Lead Test	67
Lanterns, Magic	159
Lavatory, Electric	69
Lead Test, Molten	67
Letter File	106
Lifting Machine	68, 73, 74
Lighting Transparency	109

(Continued on Next Page)

INDEX—Continued

ARTICLE	Page
Lion's Roar	102
Liquid Air Tank	35
Loaded Cigars	70
Lung Tester	30
Lycopodium Flash Torch	92
Magic Lanterns and Slides	159
Masks, Wigs, Beards, etc.	109, 113–121
Masquerade Goods	113–121
Maul, Striking	72
Minstrel Chair Covers	150
Mirror, Trick	37
Molten Lead Test	67
Moral Athletics	34
Moss Paper for Decorating	104
Muscular Test	68
Musette	102
Napkins, Emblematic	105
Naval Battle	84
No Man's Land	62
Noise Producers	101
Nose Putty	114
Ocean Wave Boat	75
Paddle Machines	73, 74
Page of Suggestions	8
Paints, Face	114
Papier Mache Heads	117–119
Palls	122
Parachute Leap	27
Parade Costumes	149
Parade Umbrellas	154
Parliamentary Books	107
Pedestals	158
Pie Table	94
Pillory	92
Pillow Fight	91
Plate Breaking Stunt	25
Plates, Banquet	104
Plays and Drills	107
Pledge Altar	**48**
Plumes	104
Pointed Affair	19
Policeman's Club	53
Portable Battery	39
Portieres, Electric	75
Race Costumes	139–142
Raiding the Hornet's Nest	75
Rain Box and Spray	102
Rattles	100
Razor, Electric	58
Receptacle for Cones and Colored Fire	109
Red Fire Cones and Torches	109
Rejuvenating Machine	78
Revolver	106
Ribbon, Crepe	104
Rickety-Rackety	100
Robes	143–145
Rocky Road	46
Roller Pathway	90
Rooters	100
Rouge, Grenadine	114
Rubber Stamp	106
Rubber Tubing	105
Runways, Electric	40
Sandals and Hose	146
Sandals, Electric	90
Sashes	151
Saw and Buck, Electric	97
Saw Mill	97
Say It With Flowers	82
Scene Cases	122
Screens, Magic Lantern	159
Sea Serpent	49
Seals	111
Shoes, Devil	61
Shoes, Wooden	45
Shoot the Chutes	75

ARTICLE	Page
Skeleton, Electric	51
Skeletons and Skulls	122
Slap Sticks	71
Slide, Devil's	86
Slide for Life	87
Slides, Magic Lantern	159
Sliding Stairs	89
Smoke, Electrified	66
Song-o-Phones	103
Spankers	71
Spanking Machine	73, 74
Spears	112
Spiked Pathway, Electric	45
Spikey Block	89
Spikey Stool	19
Spirit Gum	114
Spraying and Lifting Machines	68
Squirt Guns	86
Stairs, Sliding	89
Stereopticons	159
Stick-em-up Car	42
Stretcher, Electric	56
Stuffed Clubs	71
Submarine	15
Surprise Chair	22
Swinging Bridge	46
Swords and Sword Belts	152, 153
Table, Branding and Whirling	77
Table Cover	104
Telegraph Call	100
Telephone, Trick	28
Terms and Conditions	7
Theatrical Hair Goods	114
Throne of Honor	88
Thunder Sheet	102
Tom-Tom, Chinese	102
Toss Up	91
Tooth-Pulling Stunt	36
Traitor's Judgment Stand	31
Treadmill	69
Trick Camera	22
Trick Chairs	16–18
Trick Cigar Box	113
Trick Coffee Urn	70
Trick Comb and Brush	37
Trick Guns	24
Trick Loaded Cigars	70
Trick Mirror	37
Trick Telephone	28
Trick Tray	81
Trident, Electric	38, 61
Trilby Feet	79
Tripods	105
Trip Thru a Stormy Desert	79
Tug of War	44
Tunnel, Electric	80
Tunnel of Trouble	90
Umbrellas, Parade	154
Uniforms	147–149
Upward, Onward, Downward	87
U. S. Flags	155
Water Cooler	35
Wet Stool	19
Wheel Barrow, Electric	60
Whirling and Branding Table	77
Whistle	100
Whiz Bang Base Ball	75
Wind Machine	99
Wireless Trick Telephone	28
Wooden Drum	101
Wooden Shoes	45
Wreaths	104
Zig Zag Road	35
Zouave Uniforms	148

Let us develop your ideas on any novel or distinctive stunts. Write us about them. That's a part of our service as well as to manufacture and supply them economically.

OUR POLICY

Always buying the best materials possible, in large quantities, at the right prices and for cash.

Taking advantage of every means to improve our goods and manufacture them economically.

Not expending one cent unnecessarily or where it will not add to the value of the merchandise.

Shipping supplies on approval. See our liberal conditions, offering you the opportunity of subjecting the goods to an actual test or examination before paying for them. You will receive reliable goods —that is certain.

OUR SALESMAN

This catalog is our silent salesman. Acting in this capacity, it permits you to study our goods and methods intelligently—without feeling hurried—makes it easy for you to order at your convenience.

This silent salesman incurs no expense such as salary, commission, carfare, hotel bills, incidentals, etc., which expense usually averages from fifteen to twenty-five per cent of the sales of the average concern. Just think what a saving this means. It goes to our customers, either in lower prices or higher qualities in the goods.

We have been selling lodge supplies, uniforms, lodge and church furniture, etc., by mail for many years. These goods can be purchased from us by correspondence as safely and with as much satisfaction as if a salesman called on you. Thousands and thousands of lodges and other organizations have been convinced of this fact.

You will find it easy, pleasant and profitable to order by mail from our catalog.

DeMoulin Bros. & Co., Greenville, Ill.

DeMoulin Bros. & Co., Greenville, Ill.

TERMS AND CONDITIONS

All Prices in This Catalog Are Net and Subject to Change Without Notice

All orders for banners, badges, or any goods with name and number of Lodge engraved or printed thereon, or goods made to order, **must be accompanied by at least one-fourth cash.** Such goods can not be returned if they are as represented and order has been filled correctly.

All other goods sent on approval if ordered under seal of Lodge, or if order is signed by a committee of three who have been appointed and authorized to purchase, provided persons ordering agree to prepay express or freight charges in case goods are returned. Unless these conditions are complied with, goods will be shipped C. O. D., subject to examination.

If goods are to be sent by mail, proper allowance must be made for postage and amount included when remittance accompanies the order. Surplus postage will be returned. We make this requirement in order to obviate the necessity of opening accounts for very small amounts.

We make no charge for boxing or drayage.

We cannot stand responsible for delays of freight shipments. Freight is usually uncertain and can not be depended upon, therefore we recommend that all goods, except furniture and heavy paraphernalia, be shipped by express, or insured parcel post.

Always write your name, town, county and state plainly, and specify how you want goods shipped. **If there is no express or freight office at your place, do not fail to give correct shipping point.**

Make all remittances preferably by **draft, post office money order or express money order.**

Fraternally and courteously,

Catalog 439.

DeMoulin Bros. & Co.,
Greenville, Ill.

INSURE MAIL PACKAGES

We cannot stand responsible for loss of mail. Valuable packages should be insured—the fee is only five cents for value not exceeding $5.00; eight cents for value not exceeding $25.00; ten cents for value not exceeding $50.00, and twenty-five cents for value not exceeding $100.00. **Packages not insured will be mailed at purchaser's risk.**

DeMoulin Bros. & Co., Greenville, Ill.

A PAGE OF SUGGESTIONS
To Aid in Putting Life and Pep Into Your Side Degree Work

LOTS OF NOISE AND ACTION—that's what makes side-degree work interesting. As noise producers use; Spankers (page 71); Rattlers (page 100); Rickety-rackety and Rooters (page 100); Wind Machine (page 99); Rain Box and Thunder Sheet (page 102). Keep things moving—fast and furious—something doing every minute—that's what the members enjoy.

BURLESQUE COSTUMES—Dress the candidates in burlesque costumes. You will find this a mighty amusing feature of the initiation. We list a great variety of costumes, making it possible for you to have many different characters and natinoalities represented by the candidates. The greater the variety the greater the fun. Try it. See pages 125-138.

ZOBO BAND—Made up of candidates dressed in burlesque costumes. See pages 103 for instruments; pages 125-138 for costumes.

PARADE OF CANDIDATES—Representing animals, funny characters, celebrities, etc. Use camel, elephant, horse, donkey, etc., with two men inside; large animal and human heads; burlesque and race costumes, etc. See pages 123-138.

ROPE CLIMBING CONTEST—Use large size electric carpent. Suspend large rope from ceiling to hang over center of carpet. Several candidates are brought in, barefooted and hoodwinked, and commanded to take hold of the rope, which they are to start climbing when the attendant counts three. At "three" turn on the juice and watch them climb.

WRESTLING CONTEST—Have eight or ten candidates lie down on large electric carpet, in pairs, with arms around each other. Count three, turn on the juice and witness the liveliest wrestling match you ever saw or read about.

HOT SPOTS—Make the candidates step lively by having a number of "hot" spots around the hall. This can be arranged in various ways. Have a series of small electric carpets. A long run-way of white or brown duck with electric spots in it concealed. A run-way with connections so the current can be shot to any place desired. A covering for the entire hall with series of small electric mats under the cover. Tell us what arrangement you want or what results you wish to produce and we'll work out the details for you.

CHI-RO-GYM-NAS-TICS—After candidate has undergone several severe tests his condition may call for a little chiro treatment. Place electric carpet on table, with a sheet over the carpet. Place candidate on table, on his stomach, his head off the table. After the doctor has "tickled" his backbone a little, turn on the juice. Candidate will leave the table posthaste and thoroughly revived.

HOW DRY I AM—Suspend a paper sack of water from the ceiling. Place a table under the sack and have several candidates seated around the table to be served with drinks. They are first required to demonstrate their vocal ability and some one suggests that they sing "How Dry I Am." After they have sung a few lines release the sack and—splash—down comes the water on the table. It's quite a surprise for the candidates. This stunt can be made more "effective" by placing the table and chairs on a large electric carpet and giving the candidates the juice just as the sack hits the table.

PRESENTATION RING—The fellows will get up and dig when there is some incentive—a prize to be won. Announce that the winner of some contest will be presented with a nice (give name of organization) ring. The winner is escorted to the station of the presiding officer, where he is presented with the ring which consists of a loud rap on a gong. For gongs and strikers see page 160.

DEVIL CHASING THE CANDIDATES—Have one of the candidates dressed in devil costume, armed with a portable battery and electric cane. Dress the candidates in burlesque costumes. Let the devil chase the candidates into and around the hall, goading them with the electric cane. See page 47.

Book of Stunts. See page 107.

For Suggestions and Directions for Introducing and Using Our Side Degree Paraphernalia, See Ritualistic Section in Back Part of Catalog.

DeMoulin Bros. & Co., Greenville, Ill.

A LOW-DOWN BUCK

D760

We thought we had about reached the limit when it came to inventing goats, but out of the realm of our imagination and ingenuity we have produced another specimen of the goat family. Though probably more applicable to his construction than to his conduct, yet we believe this animal is deserving of the title "A Low-Down Buck".

This goat is entirely different from any other we have ever invented—different not only in construction but in action as well. The action is not mechanical but is produced by the man at the handle, and he can sure make it rough for the candidate. As the weight is all on and directly over the large wheel, the goat is light on his feet and very easy to manipulate. The four small wheels keep the goat "right side up".

Only the large wheel runs on the floor. The small wheels might be compared to the four hoofs of a goat in action—they hit the floor, occasionally. When this goat is hustled into the hall, these four wheels produce a clatter that sounds like a gallopin' horse, and the candidate does not have to work his imagination overtime to believe that he is to be given a ride on a real live prancin' steed.

We haven't space here to tell about all the good (?) points of this goat and how he will perform, but we do say that your Lodge will find him to be a rip snorter. No matter what experience you might have had with other goats, you cannot afford to miss the big show which this low-down buck will produce.

Goat is packed in a chest with hinged cover, lock and key. Weight, packed, about 165 pounds.

D760—A Low-down Buck, with rubber tires and goat blat $53.00

D761—Rough Rider or Cowboy Outfit, consisting of hat, shirt trousers with fringe on outside seams, belt and handkerchief, complete...... 7.50

Horse, Donkey, Tiger or Camel Body, instead of goat body, extra 10.00

Convict Costume, see Page 127.

For Electric Stirrups and Fountain Attachment, see Page 12.

THE ROLLICKING MUSTANG GOAT

D175-D176

One way to get the candidate's goat is to watch where he ties it. A better way is to give him a ride on this rollicking, frolicking mustang. When it comes to kicking, bucking, wabbling, rearing and other antics peculiar to the goat family, this mustang has 'em all beat. The candidate experiences all the thrills of a cross-country ride in a "lizzie." Don't let any candidate get by without taking a ride on this wild beast. See suggestions for introducing, page II in back of catalog.

We recommend this noiseless goat as the most substantial and effective made. Our many years of practical experience has enabled us to build it with all points of merit, combining the greatest variety of motions with strength, perfect safety, compactness, simplicity and light running.

The eccentric front wheel serves as a safeguard against the candidate taking a "header" but does not rest on the floor except when "Billy" takes a notion to buck. Then the handle-bar is raised until the frame runs on all three wheels. As the hubs are out of center, the irregular motions produced are indeed very realistic and characteristic of the goat family. The peculiar arrangement of wheels and the strong spiral spring pivoted to body, together with the up-and-down motion of the handle-bar, produce the desired results. The body is well upholstered with best tanned wool skin, and has horns and eyes. Goat packed in a chest with hinged cover, lock and key. Weighs about 140 pounds.

D175—Goat, with rubber tires $53.00

D176—Goat, without rubber tires 49.00

Horse, Donkey, Tiger or Camel Body, instead of goat body, extra 10.00

For Electric Stirrups, Fountain Attachment and Goat Blat, see page 12.

To create more amusement, we suggest that goat be manipulated by persons wearing burlesque costumes. Costumes listed on pages 125-138.

THE FUZZY WONDER
The Champion of His Species

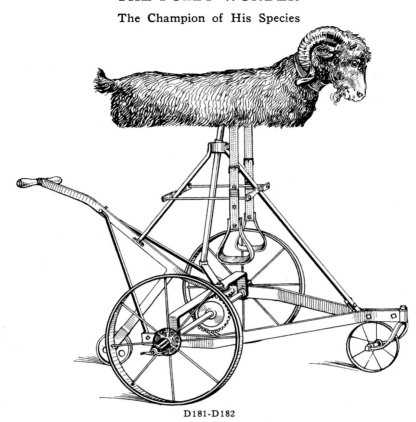

D181-D182

Kipling wrote: "The female of the species is more deadly than the male." If judged from this viewpoint, this Fuzzy Wonder must be a she-goat instead of a he-goat. While it might appear ridiculous to attempt to establish any relationship between Fuzzy Wonder and a wild western bronco, yet our suspicion is confirmed by the fact that a bronco is tame compared with this goat.

"Fuzzy Wonder" is a spectacular Goat in every respect. Every part is substantially made of steel and so constructed that it affords less resistance in order to bring about the desired results than any other Goat on the market. Attendants do not have to exert themselves to demonstrate the galloping, rearing, wobbling, kicking and bucking antics by the up-and-down motion of the handle-bar. This is all brought about by merely pushing on the handle-bar. The frame remains in a normal position at all times, but the body is arranged so that a special centrifugally designed mechanism, automatically produces a series of maneuvers peculiar to no other Goat but "Fuzzy Wonder."

See suggestions for introducing, page II in back of catalog.

The same qualities characteristic of our other Goats may well be applied to this one also. The body is well upholstered with best tanned wool skin, and has horns and eyes. Goat is packed in a chest with hinged cover, lock and key. Weighs about 200 pounds.

D181—Goat with rubber tires $82.00
D182—Goat, without rubber tires 79.00
Horse, Donkey, Tiger or Camel Body, instead of goat body, extra 10.00

For Electric Stirrup, Fountain Attachment and Goat Blat, see page 12.

To create more amusement, we suggest that goat be manipulated by persons wearing burlesque costumes. Costumes listed on pages 125-138.

THE BUCKING GOAT

D187-D188

We call this the Bucking Goat because that common trait can be so easily and effectively demonstrated. Hubs of wheels are out of center to produce the side motion. Goat can be made to gallop and buck by working the handle-bar up and down.

We suggest the use of tossing blanket (listed on page 91) with this goat for the purpose of throwing the candidate and letting him experience the thrills of a "Double-header."

This goat is strongly built with steel frame and wheels. Body is upholstered with good wool skin, and has horns and eyes. Shipping weight, 100 pounds.

See suggestions for introducing, page II in back of catalog.

D187—Goat, with rubber tires on wheels, frame and wheels finished in aluminum, chest with hinged cover, lock and key $37.00
D188—Goat, same as D-187, but without rubber tires 34.00
Horse, Donkey, Tiger or Camel Body, instead of goat body, extra 10.00

To create more amusement we suggest that Goat be manipulated by persons wearing burlesque costumes. Costumes listed on pages 125-138.

FOUNTAIN ATTACHMENT

D177—Fountain Attachment, can be attached to any of our Goat bodies to produce spray of water from back of goat where candidate sits; extra ....$ 3.00

ELECTRIC STIRRUPS

D178—Electrically Wired Stirrups, for either magneto or jump spark battery; extra ....$ 2.00
D179—Magneto Battery and Cord; extra 11.25
D213—Jump Spark Battery and Cord; extra 23.00

GOAT BLAT

D180—Goat Blat, can be attached to any of our Goat Bodies; extra ......$ 3.00

FERRIS WHEEL COASTER GOAT

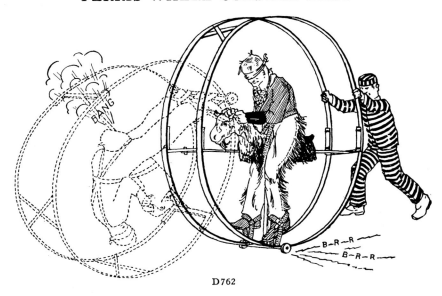

D762

This is the Ferris Wheel Goat with several new features added which make it a much more exciting stunt. See the two small wheels. These enable the attendant to coast the ferris wheel on the floor with the candidate right-side-up. About the time the candidate has relaxed and has kidded himself into believing that he is to enjoy a smooth ride—over he goes right on his head. The firing of a blank cartridge adds to the consternation. A ba-a-a attachment also makes this goat more goaty.

D762—Goat, including cartridge firing attachment under body, goat blat and 50 blank cartridges (weight packed, about 190 pounds) $58.00

Extra Blank Cartridges (not mailable), loaded specially for us to give an extra loud report; per box of 50 .... .45

Rubber Tires on above goat, extra 15.00

Horse, Donkey, Tiger or Camel Body, instead of goat body, extra 10.00

Every Member Looks Forward to Meetings

"Our Legion one year ago had only forty-six members and owed plenty of money. I was elected Master of Burlesque. Received one of your catalogs and got busy with an order; consequently, today we have over 400 members all paid up and money in the treasury. Every member looks forward to something new at each one of our meetings. Everything we ever bought from you has more than made good, and I can recommend your house in the highest degree."—George E. Garland, Paul Revere Legion, No. 28, M. L. of the W., 24 Warren St., Roxbury, Mass.

"Enclosed you will find a check for $79.10 for bill of recent date. We are well satisfied with the goods and wish to thank you for the prompt and courteous treatment your company has given us."—Harold L. Kremser, Phi Epsilon Frat., Emaus, Pa.

WHIZ BANG AEROPLANE

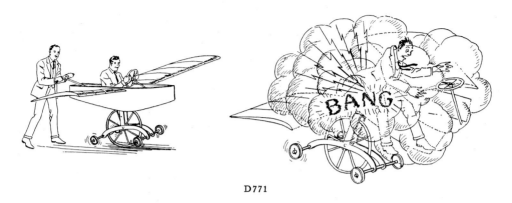

D771

Darius Green would look with envy upon this worthy successor to his crude old flying machine. And why not? This whiz bang aeroplane is a thriller from the word go. The action is not mechanical but is controlled by the man at the handle, and he can produce all kinds of thrills such as the figure eight, tail spin and nose dive.

Sometimes a piece of machinery does not perform as well as it looks. The air currents seem to have a disastrous effect upon this aeroplane or perhaps the aviator has engine trouble. Anyway, there is an explosion and one wing drops off; another explosion and another wing off; a third explosion and the sides fall out. The candidate is stranded in mid-air and his only hope is to glide to the earth, which he does with considerable difficulty.

D771—Aeroplane, with rubber tires, fire-proof compartment in which fire-crackers are fired, cartridge-firing attachments, 50 blank cartridges and seat wired for electricity with connections (battery not included); weight, packed, about 180 pounds $125.00

MORE THAN GOOD

"With reference to paraphernalia received, will say that they are more than good. We had one of the best nights ever. Have a half dozen more for next meeting. Some fun. Just beginning—wait until we get some more. Watch for orders."—Brooklyn and L. I. Milk Square Club, Brooklyn, N. Y.

"The equipment has been exceptionally satisfactory. Quite recently Voiture Locale No. 1, La Societe des 40 Homes et 8 Cheveaux, was awarded first prize at the American Legion Pennsylvania State Convention, conducted at Reading, Pa. At that time your products played a very conspicuous part. Of course, being used only during the secret work."—Samuel G. Stauch, Voiture Locale, No. 1, Germantown, Philadelphia, Pa.

THE SUBMARINE

 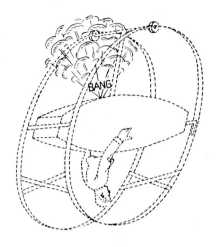

D770

Sailing over the deep blue sea may be an enjoyable pastime, but a ride in this submarine is an entirely different proposition. Just one thrill after another, first on top of the water and then down he goes head first into the deep. All goes well until the engine misses and then—Bang—an explosion and a smoke screen that will convince the candidate that his craft has been hit by a submarine chaser.

D770—Submarine, including clatter attachment on small wheels, cartridge firing attachment, fire-proof compartment in which firecrackers are fired and large compartment for tin cans, rocks, sand, etc., which serve their purpose to good advantage when submarine turns over (weight packed, about 300 pounds) $77.00

Extra blank cartridges (not mailable), loaded specially for us to give an extra loud report; per box of 50 .... .45

Attendance at Meetings Never So Great

"The 'Skee' Degree of the Erie Railroad Square Club written and directed by myself is becoming more famous every day. The attendance at our meetings has never been so great in the history of our club prior to this side-degree, and all of this is accomplished by the use of the costumes, paraphernalia and stunts which we bought from you. We have right now more invitations to other clubs than we can take care of."—Fred H. Blom, Erie Railroad Square Club, 71 W. 23rd St., New York City, N. Y.

"Goods received in ample time for our big meeting on 19th inst. Everything was O. K. and made big impression on visiting lodges as well as candidates. We will want some more side-degree stuff a little later. Thank you for favor of sending on approval."—W. R. McCoy, Lexington Council No. 179, Jr. O. U. A. M., Lexington, Va.

TRICK BOTTOM CHAIR

D193

Even the floor will rise up to greet the candidate; at least that is the impression he gets when the bottom of this chair suddenly drops from under him. And if, as we understand it, an impression means a dent in a soft place, we are inclined to believe that the impression will be well defined.

The Candidate always welcomes an opportunity to sit down and rest. This chair will look mighty good to him, especially after he has become fatigued from other tests. He sees himself, comfortably seated here and watching the other candidates get what's coming to them. But, alas, he suddenly starts on a quick descent to the lower abyss of chaos, until the floor offers resistance to his impetuous precipitation.

This chair is similar to the regular folding chair used in lodge rooms. At the will of attendant, the bottom drops and a blank cartridge is exploded. It is a sure catch, not for candidates but for members who don't get around to the meetings very often.

D193—Trick Bottom Chair with 50 blank cartridges .... $ 9.50

Extra blank cartridges (not mailable), loaded specially for us to give an extra loud report; per box of 50 .... .45

We suggest placing electric carpent on floor under chair upon which candidate is dropped, listed on page 40.

ELECTRIC ATTACHMENT FOR CHAIRS
Read "Electric Batteries," page 39

D194—Electric Attachment, complete, with magneto and cord $13.25

D195—Electric Attachment, without magneto and cord, otherwise same as **D194** 2.00

D196—Electric Attachment, complete, with jump spark battery and cord; far superior to **D194**; electricity will penetrate the clothing without the use of conductors 25.00

D197—Electric Attachment, without jump spark battery and cord, otherwise same as **D196** 2.00

TRICK CHAIRS
Down He Goes!

Before   After

What goes up must come down. This old adage can be forcibly impressed upon the candidate by the use of this trick chair in connection with the electric chair shown on page 18. He will be thoroughly convinced that life is a see-saw of ups and downs.

The trick chair is made of oak, nicely finished and upholstered to represent a parlor chair. It may be used as an ordinary chair by a locking device which prevents it from falling. At the will of the attendant the legs automatically separate, the chair collapses, and a blank cartridge is exploded. Imagine the candidate's surprise when, after picking himself up, he looks around and finds the chair standing just as it was before he took a seat. The mechanical or trick part of chair is operated by the best tempered steel springs.

D202—Trick Chair, as described above, complete with locking device and cartridge attachment, including 50 black cartridges $23.50

D203—Trick Chair, same as **D202**, but not upholstered and without locking device 21.50

D204—Trick Chair, same as **D203**, but without cartridge attachment 19.00

(Weight of chair, packed, 37 pounds.)

Water attachment, to produce spray of water from seat of chair; extra.... 2.00

Extra Blank Cartridges (not mailable), loaded specially for us to give an extra loud report; per box of 50 .... .45

See suggestions for introducing, page II in back of catalog.

ELECTRIC ATTACHMENT FOR CHAIRS
Read "Electric Batteries," page 39

D196—Electric Attachment, complete, with jump spark battery and cord; electricity will penetrate the clothing without the use of conductors. $25.00

D197—Electric Attachment, without jump spark battery and cord, otherwise same as **D196** 2.00

ELECTRIC CHAIR
Up He Goes!

D199

The candidate did not at first realize how much it was to mean to him to become a member of the lodge; that he was due for a sudden "rise" in the world. He is asked to be seated for a few moments while other details are arranged. The "rise" comes sooner than he expected. It is a rather warm situation in which he finds himself and he would like to knock the "sit" out of situation.

This electric chair is one of our latest and best inventions. It is arranged with electric battery concealed beneath the seat. An important and attractive feature is the switch, which can be turned off so that no shock is received by the person sitting on the chair. The switch can be turned on and off without the knowledge of those whom it is desired to "catch." A good plan is to post a few members who are to sit on the chair when the switch is off. Then along comes a member or candidate who is not next to the scheme. He takes a seat and he gets it good and plenty, and he wonders how in the world he happened to get stung when others sat on the chair without any "emotion" whatever. The chair is a positive deceiver and never fails to work at the proper time. It may be placed anywhere in the lodge room and any member as well as a candidate, can be made a "victim".

D199—Electric Chair, complete $28.50

"Barrel of Fun"

"Received all goods recently ordered from you in the very best shape and desire to thank you for the prompt service rendered. I am sure we will have a barrel of fun out of the new members from now on. I am perfectly satisfied with the goods. Again thanking you, I am."— W. C. Wiehman, Chiropody Society of West Virginia, Huntington, W. Va.

A POINTED AFFAIR

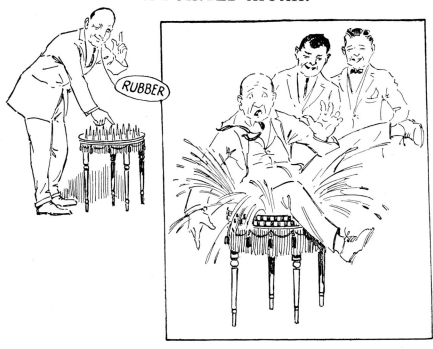

D225

Some times when a candidate cannot see the point he might be excused for refusing to yield in an argument. In this case the "points" are very clear, yet it only makes him remonstrate all the more. But if he carries the argument too far, the points involved might be driven home by forcibly seating him upon what appears to be sharp-pointed spikes. Naturally the candidate is not very keen about having his anatomy punctured. It may tax the physical ability of several attendants to clinch the argument, but—how silly the candidate will look when he finds that the thing is perfectly harmless.

See suggestions for introducing, page XI in back of catalog.

D223—The "Spikey Stool" is strong and well made; the top is filled with large, sharp-pointed (flexible rubber) spikes. This stool has a penetrating aspect, calculated to appear extremely uninviting ....$ 5.75

D235—"Spikey Stool", same as **D223**, but with electrical attachment, battery and cord not included 7.75

D213—Jump Spark Battery and Cord 21.25

D224—"Spikey Stool", with real steel spikes; otherwise like **D223** 5.75

D225—"Spikey Wet Stool," with a double spring bottom. The lower bottom is in the form of a pan that holds water, and when the candidate attempts to sit on the upper, or rubber spiked bottom, it springs down and is telescoped into the lower one, thereby causing the water to flow over the seat. This is indeed a "pointed wet affair," and forms a suitable seat (?) for the smart lodge-joiner who thinks he knows it all 19.50

D226—Wet Stool, same as Spikey Wet Stool, but with spikes omitted. May be used to seat candidate after he has been "there" and is longing for one blissful moment of rest 17.50

BOMB STUNT

This harmless though highly exciting ceremony will not encourage the bolshevik spirit or the bomb-throwing habit. On the contrary, it will teach the candidate not to fool with bombs and infernal machines.

This stunt consists of a chair, fake bomb and garbage can. The chair is arranged to fire a blank cartridge and turn on electric current at the same time, any jump spark battery being used. The bomb is an iron ball with a fuse which does a good deal of sputtering when lighted but throws off no sparks. The can is made with a firing device on the inside which explodes a blank cartridge.

Candidate is seated on the chair and the lighted bomb is handed him by a bolshevik or attendant, or candidate might be compelled to light the bomb himself. Of course, he expects the infernal machine to go off and he can be made to believe it has, any time the attendant sees fit to shoot on the juice and fire the cartridge. The attendant then suggests that he throw the bomb into the garbage can, and this strikes the candidate as being a good way out of his precarious situation. As he raises the lid and is in the act of throwing in the bomb, the explosion in the can occurs, and candidate thanks his stars that he got rid of the bomb just in time to escape being blown into atoms.

D405—Bomb Stunt Outfit Complete, consisting of Chair, Fake Bomb and Garbage Can, including extra fuses and box of blank cartridges, (battery not included) $30.50

D406—Chair 10.50

D407—Fake Bomb 5.00

D408—Garbage Can 14.00

Extra Blank Cartridges (not mailable), loaded specially for us to give an extra loud report; per box of 50 .... .45

ELECTRIC BENCH

D211

Josh Billings sez: "Anatomikally konsidered, laffing is the sensashun ov pheeling good all over and showing it principally in one spot." We would hesitate to say that these candidates feel good all over but, whatever the "sensashun", it seems to have affected them in one "spot" of their anatomy. As a laugh producer (that is, for the members) the electric bench cannot be beat.

This bench is a very innocent loking piece of furniture, but it possesses wonderful possibilities. With it your Lodge can raise money—also candidates. After candidates have been initiated, let them be seated on the bench. The presiding officer then brings up the business left over from the previous meeting—that of raising funds for a new hall or some other fictitious project. Some one moves that the members be given an opportunity to subscribe to the fund. "All those who will donate $100.00 please rise." Immediately the philanthropic candidates jump to their feet, with exclamations indicating that they want to head the list. Or a member moves that the candidates be raised to the next degree. The person in charge of "current events" does his duty and the candidates are raised in short order. We repeat—this is one of the very best stunts used.

D211—Electric Bench, 6 feet long; substantially constructed of plain solid oak; rich golden oak or any other finish; gloss or varnished and rubbed; seat covered with leatherette; completely wired for jump spark battery $35.00

D212—Electric Bench, 6 feet long; no back or arms; substantially constructed, completely wired for jump spark battery 15.00

D213—Jump Spark Battery and Cord 23.00

THE TRICK CAMERA AND SURPRISE CHAIR

It is perfectly natural for the Lodge to want the candidate's picture to keep on file for identification or for advertising in case he should show up missing. But if the candidate knows how near he is to his "down-fall," he might have a suspicion that his picture is intended for the rogues' gallery.

The negative slide carrier which is inserted in rear of camera is provided with twelve comic photos—among which a picture can be found suitable for most any character or profession.

The Trick Camera is a clever device, having the appearance of a real camera. The photographer takes focus through peep hole in lens, and asks the candidate to sit perfectly quiet, to smile, etc. He then presses the bulb, which sends a spray of water with a strong force into the candidate's face. At the same time, if surprise chair is used, the attendant pulls it off, causing it to rock backward and fire a blank cartridge.

See suggestion for introducing, page IV in back of catalog.

The Surprise Chair may be used very effectively alone. It has the appearance of a nice upholstered lodge chair and may be so used, as nicely finished in polished oak and upholstered in imitation leather. At the will of the operator, the chair may be caused to suddenly rock backward and at the same time a blank cartridge is automatically exploded with a loud report. It does not complete the fall with a jar and at no time attains a fixed stop. When the chair has fallen, the candidate finds himself in such an awkward position (since the high arms prevent his rolling out to one side and he cannot move the chair) that his usual method of escape is to actually loop-the-loop (turn a back somersault).

See suggestions for introducing, page II in back of catalog.

D208—The Trick Camera, perfect imitation of a genuine photo camera, with polished lens. Size 8x8 inches. Price, including focusing cloth, folding tripod and 12 comic photos $16.00

D209—Surprise Chair, including 50 blank cartridges, weight packed, 65 lbs.. 33.50

Extra Blank Cartridges (not mailable) loaded specially for us to give an extra loud report; per box of 50 .... .45

THE "JAG PRODUCER"

D365

With the advancing H. C. J. (high cost of jags) we predict increasing popularity for our artificial jag producer. It has the "kick" and candidate fully expects the contraption to fly up any minute and kick him in the face. As a producer of that feeling of unsteadiness and uncertainty it is a dandy. The candidate being hoodwinked, he cannot watch his step, so must take things just as they come. He has no idea whether he must reach for the bloomin' thing with his foot or whether it will meet him halfway.

See suggestions for introducing, page XIX in back of catalog.

In connection with the Jag Producer, we would recommend the Rocky Road, Electric Carpet and Electric Spiked Pathway. Have them joined together and start the candidate on his journey. The result is hysterically funny.

D365—The Jag Producer is built in such a way that it is impossible for candidate to walk over it steadily, the sections being arranged as illustrated. It is built in the best manner and can be folded into a small space (weight, packed, 70 pounds) $16.00

If desired, can add any number of cartridge exploders to Jag Producer, which fire when candidate steps on different sections; extra, per exploder 2.00

Extra Blank Cartridges (not mailable) loaded specially for us to give an extra loud report; per box of 50 .... .45

"MORE THAN PLEASED"

"We have received paraphernalia in fine shape and tried it out last night. We sure did have a good time. The boys are more than pleased. It is the life of the Lodge."—Harry Rasche, B. P. O. E. Lodge No. 1457, 29 W. Post Road, Mamaroneck, New York.

DeMoulin Bros. & Co., Greenville, Ill.

THE DeMOULIN TRICK GUNS
ONE-TWO-THREE, SHOOT!

ACT I
"He Really Doesn't Expect It"

ACT II
"But—Twice He Gets Hit"

THERE'S A BARREL OF FUN TO EVERY GUN

HERE IS MONEY VERY WISELY INVESTED

If there is any thing that will get a fellow excited it is to be "double crossed." You will notice that the candidtee with the black coat is the goat both times, although in the second act he thinks he is to have the joy of seeing the other fellow get what he (the candidate) got in the first act. See full instructions for introducing, page VI in back of catalog.

This is a mighty clever trick. There's a barrel of fun to every gun. Order a pair of these and you'll see the members go "gunning" for candidates. A number of pairs can be used with great effect by a "firing squad."

D718—Pair of Guns as described $15.00
D719—Front-Action Gun, shoots water forward 6.50
D720—Back Action Gun, shoots water backward 8.50
D721—Target, 12 inches in diameter .... .75

"The goods reached us in ample time and in fine condition. They are entirely satisfactory. The back action gun was the hit of the 'Fun Night' of our convention. We appreciate the prompt service you gave us on this order. Check will be mailed under separate cover."—M. S. Chism, Purina Mills, St. Louis, Mo.

PLATE BREAKING STUNT

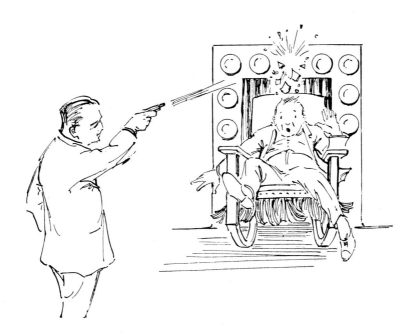

No doubt the Candidate has a lot of confidence in his future Brothers, but when one of them starts taking pot shots at the plates in his immediate vicinity (a little too immediate for his comfort) the extent of his confidence is severely tested. His mind isn't eased at all when the sharp-shooter (?) makes a couple of wild shots at first, shattering an electric light bulb or disturbing some other nearby object.

Our surprise chair supplies the climax of this hair-raising stunt. At the last shot it is tripped, and the Candidate makes a very abrupt and ungraceful exit through the curtain.

A novel effect, and an additional surprise for the victim will result if the gun only clicks on the last shot but the plate is shattered anyway.

D284—Plate Breaking Stunt, consists of frame with attachments for six plates, curtain in opening, 60 plates and striker for breaking plates from rear by attendant $25.00

Extra Plates, in lots of 60 .... 1.00

Our **D209** Surprise Chair listed on page **22** will operate very nicely with this stunt, as opening in frame is proper size for this chair to fall through.

IRON TEST

D286

Here's a severe test of a man's courage. It takes nerve to even stand behind a cannon and fire at the enemy, but when it comes to pulling the trigger and letting a cannon ball drop from the ceiling and hit you in the region of the diaphragm—well, if that does not require courage, then there is no such animal. Believe us, this stunt is a dandy and will jar the candidate's slats. Chances are he will absolutely refuse to pull the rope, in which case the attendants should be in readiness to hold him down while someone else does the pulling.

See suggestions for introducing, page XIV, back of catalog.

The Iron Test consists of two large balls exactly alike (in appearance); one is of solid cast iron and the other of thin hollow rubber; a grab hook is also provided with a cartridge exploder attached, iron pulley and several feet of rope. When the ball is released from grab hook, a trigger automatically fires a blank cartridge.

D286—Iron Test, complete .... $ 9.60
D287—Iron Test, without cartridge attachment, otherwise the same as **D286** 8.75
Extra Blank Cartridges (not mailable) loaded specially for us to give an extra loud report; per box of 50 .... .45

HOW IT MAY BE INTRODUCED

The candidate may be asked to lie on the floor just below the pulley, which has been previously attached to ceiling; the iron ball is then attached to hook and handed to him, that he may satisfy himself that it is solid iron. Just at that moment a member moves that candidate be blindfolded so he cannot see the torture. As soon as blindfolded the hollow rubber ball is hung on hook in place of the iron one and is drawn to ceiling. Motion is then made and carried that the candidate be allowed to see and that he also be compelled to pull the rope and cause the ball to drop. The blindfold is then removed; the results can better be imagined than described.

BALLOON ASCENSION
Or the Parachute Leap

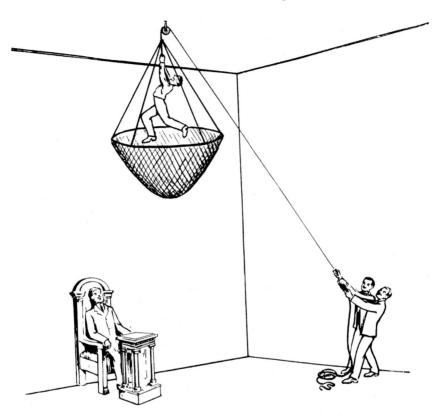

In this new age when aeroplanes and dirigibles are being put to practical use in the conveying of passengers, no candidate will have any serious objection to taking such a ride through the air. But when it comes to hanging on to the rope of a balloon, to be drawn up above the clouds—and in the dark at that—well, that's a horse of another color. To cap the climax, when up a mile or more the balloon takes fire and the rope becomes so hot that the candidate can hold on no longer. He lets go, thinking it's all over. To his great surprise and unspeakable joy he is caught in a net, the parachute opens and he lands safely but exhausted.

The candidate should be drawn up a few feet, then quietly lowered, then drawn up again, etc. He will finally imagine he has been carried very high. This effect can be produced by speaking thru paper tubes while he is being drawn up, gradually lowering the tubes till they point down.

D283—Balloon Ascension, consisting of net and all necessary ropes; rope from which man is suspended being wired for electric current; complete $55.00

D214—Magneto and Cord, extra 11.25

DeMoulin Bros. & Co., Greenville, Ill.

TRICK DESK PHONE

HELLO! HELLO! HELL—O! ! !

D763

Here is another new stunt and a dandy. As a deceiver and a sure catch this phone has the world beat. We say with all the emphasis we can command that this is one of the best stunts we have ever offered. They'll all fall for this one—candidates and members alike.

This is a regular desk phone. Nothing about it to indicate any trick. The bell rings. The officer at the desk or anyone who is "next" answers and calls Mr. So-and-So to the phone. He takes the receiver to his ear, when all of a sudden there is an explosion of a blank cartridge (this firing device is not in the phone itself). At the same time a stream of water is squirted through the receiver against the ear and face of the victim.

D763—Trick Desk Phone, complete outfit, with full instructions for installing and operating $35.00

Extra Blank Cartridges (not mailable) loaded specially for us to give an extra loud report; per box of 50 .... .45

"Desk Phone great stuff—check enclosed."—Fred M. Walker, Capitol Council, No. 95, U. C. T., 511 S. Lincoln Ave., Springfield, Illinois.

DeMoulin Bros. & Co., Greenville, Ill.

THE GUILLOTINE

D264

The headsman's axe is not in it compared with this heathenish invention. The very sight of this horrible instrument with its huge glittering steel blade, will make the candidate shiver; and when he sees the block and blade spattered over with blood and a few locks of human hair, which have been left over from the last execution, he will be convinced that it is no "dream" but the "real thing." When his head is laid across the chopping block he will beg, he will resist, but he is held in position by being bound with handcuffs and with a strap over his chin. When the knife is dropped it accidentally (?) gets stuck in the slots and stops within several inches of his neck, exploding a blank cartridge with a loud report. How fortunate for the poor victim that it failed to work, for just at this moment of anxiety a friend comes to his rescue. See suggestions for introducing, page XII in back of catalog.

D264—The Guillotine is built of wood to look like a massive structure. The knife is covered with smooth bright tin to look like polished steel. There is a positive stop arrangement in the slots (invisible to candidate) so knife cannot drop lower than within several inches of the neck. It is perfectly safe and harmless. Weight, packed, 100 pounds. Price, including 50 blank cartridges $37.00

D265—Cloth spattered with blood and showing signs of struggle, on which to place guillotine and candidate. Not essential, but very desirable. 3.75

D266—Decapitated Head, or papier mache, realistic. Not essential, but very desirable 3.50

Extra Blank Cartridges (not mailable), loaded specially for us to give an extra loud report; per box of 50 .... .45

Executioner's Robe and Cowl 4.20

DeMOULIN'S PATENT LUNG TESTER

D352

The candidate will resent any suggestion that he is not chesty enough to become a member of the Lodge. On the other hand, he does not want to be accused of being a big "blow." He may say there are three sides to the question—his side, your side, and the right side. The only way to settle the argument is for him to test his "blowing" capacity on this lung tester. He does not have to blow his head off to get results, but when the thing goes off, he will imagine he has been dealt a knock-out blow right between the eyes. This is a dandy stunt which should be introduced by every Lodge.

This lung tester has the appearance of a high price surgical instrument. Case is 5½x6½x 10½ inches, nicely covered with leatherette; nickel plated base, trimmings and mouthpiece. The dial, which makes the deception complete, is in plain view of the person blowing into the lung tester and is supposed to register the pressure of air blown into the instrument. The interior contains a mechanism ingeniously constructed, so that when a person blows into the mouthpiece, a 32-calibre blank cartridge is exploded, and flour is blown with a strong blast squarely on the end of the "blower's" nose and is scattered over his face. With the lung tester we furnish blanks, arranged with questions pertaining to the candidate's health, age, etc., so as to lead him on to the test without his suspecting any joke. (Weight of lung tester, packed, 14 pounds.)

See suggesions for introducing, page XX in back of catalog.

D352—Lung Tester, complete, including 50 blank cartridges and 25 question blanks $22.50

Extra Question Blanks, per hundred .... .75

Extra Blank Cartridges (not mailable), loaded specially for us to give an extra loud report; per box of 50 .... .45

TRAITOR'S JUDGMENT STAND

D354

Explanations are now in order. The candidate has committed some offense which cannot be tolerated, even in the midst of the hilarity caused by the initiatory work. He must be made to understand that while the stunts are productive of considerable fun and amusement, each one teaches a lesson, his appreciation of which should be shown by proper decorum on his part. When the lodge has a case against any candidate this stand should be used. At the proper time the attendant presses a lever, causing the top to fall flat to the floor. A blank cartridge is exploded. This is one of the best stunts ever introduced.

See suggestions for introducing, page XXI in back of catalog.

When trap is sprung, the top falls FLAT (not one side first) because all four sides are released simultaneously Also exposion of cartridge cannot cause injury for the discharge is inside the stand and entirely separated from the candidate at all times. It is solidly built and will not get out of order. We guarantee it to work properly and give complete satisfaction

D354—Judgment Stand, woodwork well finished, polished and varnished; upholstered in fine velour carpet, packed in stained chest with hinged cover, lock and key; including 50 blank cartridges..........$23.50

D355—Judgment Stand, same in all respects as **D354**, but cheaper carpet and no fringe on edges; packed in stained chest with hinged cover, lock and key; including box of 50 cartridges 22.00

D356—Electric Carpet for judgment stand, complete, with jump spark battery and cord 28.25

D357—Electric Carpet for judgment stand, without jump spark battery and cord, otherwise as **D356** 3.00

Extra Blank Cartridges (not mailable), loaded specially for us to give an extra loud report; per box of 50 .... .45

Weight of **D354-D355**, packed, 98 pounds.

DRINKING THE GOAT'S BLOOD

D422

Whether it be the Camel, Tiger, Elk, Eagle, Moose, Owl or Goat, there can be no more appropriate ceremony than serving the candidate with the blood of the animal, in order that he might be thoroughly imbued with the spirit and life of the organization. When the invitation is first extended, the candidate smacks his lips and even has thoughts of some "home brew," but when he takes a look at the contents of the tub, his stomach turns upside down. He sees the "blood" adulterated with old shoes, rags, feathers, leaves, sticks, etc. And as the attendant draws a glass of the "blood" for the candidate, some of the members spit into the tub, others throw in cuds of tobacco, others cigar butts. It is needless to say that the candidate is extremely reluctant about taking the drink which is offered him and it may be necessary for several attendants to help serve the refreshments. The liquid is actually drawn from separate container in bottom.

D422—Drinking the Goat's Blood, complete, table not included $12.50

TESTIMONIAL

"The paraphernalia that we have received has been very satisfactory in all ways and has proved very successful to this organization. We always look forward to putting it in action and we also have increased our membership with the articles that we have received from your Company."—Thos. Goughler, Amurath Siesta Princes of Bagdad "77", Pittsburgh, Pa.

BABY DOLL
(Woman Suffrage Beauty)
"Hush little baby, don't you cry;
Mother will be comin' bye and bye."

With the adoption of the Nineteenth Amendment to the Constitution we deem it advisable to encourage Lodges in the adoption of one or more of our Baby Dolls, in order that the men might be given some training in caring for the children. When mother is attending the club or is engaged in a political campaign, father will be left in charge of the infants. He must know what to do and when to do it. Baby Doll will afford him an opportunity to learn, as it has the failing of the youngest and "wettest." It even cries for mamma and must be fed. If the candidate can master the situation he is fully qualified to act as nurse at home.

"GO TO SLEEP, MAMMY'S LITTLE PICKANINNY"

Baby Doll is a very obliging child. Having no racial prejudice, she (he or it) consents to being furnished in either white or black.

Josh Billings sez: "If a man kan't laff, there iz sum mistake made in putting him together; and if he won't laff, he wants az much keeping away from az a bear-trap when it iz sot." If you want to find out whether there are any "bear-traps" in your Lodge, just introduce this Baby Doll stunt. It's a "scream."

See suggestions for introducing, page XXII in back of catalog.

D216—Baby Doll; life size; arranged with attachment which, at the proper time, causes lukewarm water to flow freely from under the doll's clothing, much to the discomfort of candidate; also an arrangement which by moving body causes Doll to produce an exact imitation of a baby's cry, "Ma-ma"; including diaper; complete $14.50

D-218—Colored Baby Doll, otherwise same as D216 .... 14.50

D217—Grotesque Nursing Bottle, with long rubber attachment and nipple .90
Mama Cry, to be distributed among spectators, produces an exact imitation of a baby's cry "Ma-ma," each .... .35

DUMMY MAN
D319—Dummy Man, made of extra heavy duck, well stuffed, life size, not dressed 13.50

MORAL ATHLETICS

"A Square Deal"

Your lodge should stage this bout as it is 'bout the best stunt ever introduced. If any of the candidates show pugilistic tendencies, here is a chance for them to go in for a try-out. Each pugilist will wonder why it is that he is getting so many blows, yet cannot reach his opponent. Should either contestant fear a knock-out blow, he will find it impossible to retreat, so all he can do is to run up the white flag and signal for the dove of peace.

The "Champions" are blindfolded and their "prize belts" are buckled around them. By means of a long rope, one end attached to the back of belt and the other securely fastened to the floor with strong rings and heavy screw eyes, both candidates are tied so they cannot get within reach of each other. If there is objection to use of screw eyes in floor, each rope can be held by an attendant. One short rope with snaps is also provided to hook to the front of each belt so they cannot separate from the referee, who does all the striking while the candidates fan the air. While this "Fake Punch and Judy Show" is innocent and perfectly harmless, yet there is more real fun in connection with it than one can ever imagine.

See suggestions for introducing, page XIV in back of catalog.

D291—"Moral Athletics" Outfit consists of three pair of boxing gloves, (one pair extremely large), two strong belts with strong rings at front and back, also one rope to keep candidates together and two to fasten to floor or for attendants to hold. The ropes are provided with strong snaps, rings and screw eyes. Complete outfit..$ 9.60

The addition of an electric carpet to the above test will have marked results. Any size desired can be obtained. See page 40. Much hilarity can be had by using our "Dummy Man" as a fake candidate for the real candidate to box. See page 33.

DeMoulin Bros. & Co., Greenville, Ill.

LIQUID AIR TANK

Attempting to draw a glass of water   The Result

After his strenuous initiation, the candidate will appreciate a cool, refreshing drink. He approaches the tank without any fear or trembling, for who would suspect that innocent looking water cooler will blow up like a depth bomb? The candidate attempts to draw a glass of water and he gets the water all right, but not in the glass. His face is cooled by a spray sent forth with a strong pressure from the tank. He is convinced that it contains water, but his next thought is that it contains liquid air. For, when he releases the faucet, a blank cartridge is exploded within the tank, causing the cover to be blown five or six feet in the air. Candidate wonders what the infernal machine will do next. This is a fine stunt and perfectly harmless.

See suggestions for introducing, page XXV in back of catalog.

D446—Liquid Air Tank, including 50 blank cartridges (weight, packed, 25 pounds)......$23.00
    Extra Blank Cartridge (not mailable), loaded specially for us to give an extra loud report; per box of 50 .... .45
D447—Liquid Air Tank, without water attachment, otherwise same as D446 .... 16.50

ZIG-ZAG ROAD

If there ever was a time when a fellow wishes he didn't have any feet, it's when he has been led on this "zig-zagged affair." Seems like he is all feet and a burdensome botheration at that, for they are continually in the way—either being stepped on or knocked unmercifully hard by some vexatious obstructions.

This stunt produces all the thrills of crossing a swollen stream in the dark on floating logs. About the time candidate plants his foot on a log, he feels it slipping from him. It requires some close and rapid calculation on his part to step from one log to another and to keep from getting his feet wet. But he makes progress, not only across but down stream as well, and finally reaches the other shore.

Use in connection with the jag producer and electric carpet and you can give the candidate an interesting journey.

See suggestions for introducing, page XXV in back of catalog.

D448—Zig Zag Road, substantially made of very strong material, 27 inches wide, three yards long; hummocks securely fastened; strong rope at each of the four corners..$10.00
D449—Zig Zag Road, same as D448, but 5 yards long 16.00

DeMoulin Bros. & Co., Greenville, Ill.

TOOTH-PULLING STUNT

D774

This is a mighty keen set-back for the candidate who thinks he is wise to all the lodge tricks. Just pull a wisdom tooth or two; let him spit out the pieces and the blood. He'll be ready to admit that even after the loss of his wisdom teeth he is wiser than he was before the operation.

The impression which this stunt produces upon the candidate is the nearest possible approach to a real tooth-pulling ordeal. He hears the tooth crack; he feels the spurt of the warm blood in his mouth; he spits out the blood and the pieces of his broken tooth. Seeing is believing—sometimes.

D774—Tooth Extractor ....$ 4.00

Let us develop your ideas on any novel or distinctive stunts. Write us about them. That's a part of our service as well as to manufacture and supply them economically.

TRICK MIRROR

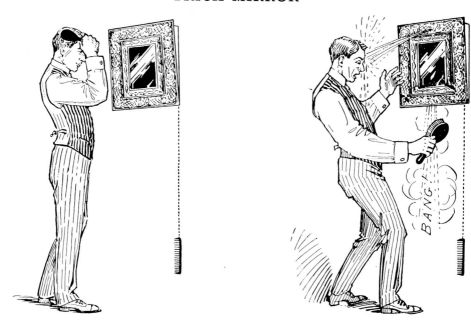

If the candidate could always see himself as others see him, he might be somewhat embarrassed at times. But he begins to feel like himself once more when he is given an opportunity to go to the mirror and "doll up." He thinks he needs it after having gone thru such a lively initiation, and he likes the idea of being able to slick up and make himself presentable. But it's all a mistake. Even the mirror is loaded. The candidate intended to comb his pompadour dry but (at the will of attendant) he gets a strong spray of water in his face and a 32-calibre blank cartridge is exploded. If he sees himself at that particular moment, he will be struck by the sudden change in his countenance. This mirror is an ornament to a lodge room and may be used for toilet purposes.

See suggestions for introducing, page XXVI in back of catalog.

D470—Trick Mirror, including comb and brush, also 50 blank cartridges.$14.00

Extra Blank Cartridges (not mailable), loaded specially for us to give an extra loud report; per box of 50 .... .45

TRICK COMB AND BRUSH

To be used just after candidate has been shaved. May also be used just before the banquet, or before he goes home to his wife, to make himself presentable.

D471—Trick Comb and Brush, arranged so the operator may cause water to squirt from them at will ....$ 5.00

See Electric Razor listed on page 58. This, with Trick Comb, Brush and Mirror, will make a complete tonsorial outfit. We suggest placing Electric Carpet listed on page 40 on floor below mirror.

PORTABLE JUMP SPARK BATTERY

This battery produces a strong jump spark current which will penetrate any part of clothing. It is very substantial and compactly put up in a box shaped to fit closely to body, so it can be carried by a shoulder strap and concealed under coat or costume.

The picture shows some of the devices with which the portable battery can be used. It is especially adapted for use with such articles as the Electric Cane (page 47), Wooden Shoes (page 45), Glad Hand (page 60), Cigar Box (page 66), Electric Attachment for Chairs (page 16) and Devil's Trident.

D215—Portable Jump Spark Battery $23.00
D388—Devil's Electric Trident, wired for electricity, with connections..... 10.50

BATTERIES AND MAGNETOS

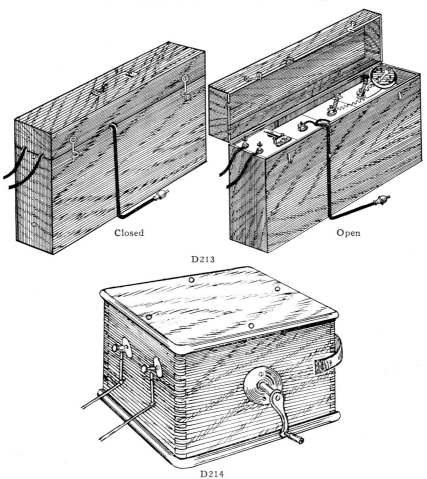

Closed   Open

D213

D214

D213—Jump Spark Battery; very strong pump spart current having three different degrees of intensity which can be regulated by the operator; very substantial and neatly put up. The electricity will penetrate any part of the clothing. It can be used with any of our electrical appliances. Price, including cord $23.00

D215—Portable Jump Spark Battery; very strong jump spark current which will penetrate any part of clothing; very substantial and compactly put up in box shaped to fit close to body; carried by shoulder strap, concealed under coat. It can be used with any of our electrical appliances. Price, including cord 23.00

D402—Transformer Spark Coil, suitable for alternating current only, can not be used with direct current, provided with a plug which is attached to an ordinary electric light socket. The current is reduced to proper strength for any of our electrical appliances. There are three degrees of intensity (four, eight and twelve volts; equivalent to three, five and eight dry cells, respectively), which are regulated by means of a switch. This arrangement is perfectly safe, as the voltage is absolutely fixed. It is substantial and will not get out of order. Complete with cord and plug 23.75

D214—Magneto; entirely mechanical and no cells to wear out; strong current which can be regulated by the operator; very substantial and neatly put up. It is made special for and can be used with any of our electrical appliances where our Jump Spark Battery is not specified. The electricity will not jump, however, as in our Jump Spark Battery, must follow a circuit. Price, including cord 11.25

D219—Magneto; produces current double the strength of D214; otherwise same as D214... 15.00

ELECTRIC CARPETS

The mother of Achilles dipped him in the River Styx in order to render his body invulnerable. But she overlooked the heel by which she held him, and that was thereafter his one and only vulnerable spot. The candidate might well have longed for an opportunity to dip his pedestrial extremities in the Styx before being compelled to travel this road. He experiences all the woes of the hot desert sands, aggravated by corns, bunions and ingrowing toe nails.

See suggestions for introducing, page XV, in back of catalog.

The improved Electric Carpet is very substantial, made of insulated waterproof material, color of sand. Our manner of construction does away with all wires, buttons, etc., hence short-circuiting is impossible; nothing to get out of order by broken connections or by buttons coming off. Candidates receive full "benefit" whether he stands on one foot or both. Occupies but little space; three-yard length can be rolled up in roll four inches in diameter. Usually ordered in lengths of three to five yards.

D292—Electric Carpet, 25 inches wide, for magneto; running yard ....$ 3.25
D293—Electric Carpet, 50 inches wide, for magneto; running yard 6.25
D294—Electric Carpet, 25 inches wide, for jump spark battery; running yard 3.25
D295—Electric Carpet, 50 inches wide, for jump spark battery; running yard 6.25
D242—Electric Carpet, any size desired, per square foot .... .45
D214—Magneto and Cord 11.25
D213—Jump Spark Battery and Cord; far superior to D214; electrically penetrates sox or clothing without use of conductors 23.00

Carpet is preferable 50 inches wide, which prevents candidate from striding it to get away from current.

ELECTRIC RUNWAYS

D296—Electric Runways for the Lodge room, made of white canvas, 29 inches wide, with invisible electric connections; can be used only with No. D213 Jump Spark Generator; per running yard ....$ 3.60

In lengths of ten yards or more; per running yard 3.30

CARPET OF TACKS

D297—Carpet of Tacks, 3 feet square, can be used with electric carpet. Ask candidate to prove his courage by walking upon these long sharp tacks. Then while he is being hoodwinked by the attendants, remove the Carpet of Tacks and substitute the electric carpet ......$ 3.25

See suggestions for introducing "The Tack Test," page XV, in back of catalog.

ELECTRIC CARPETS

An electric carpet is the prize stunt, and will furnish more action than any other one. If you are having trouble in making a selection from the number of stunts listed, just order one of these carpets—you can't go wrong.

D242—Electric Carpet, made of insulated waterproof material, color of sand; any size above 9 square feet, per square foot (small sizes quoted on request) ....$ 0.45

Note—We can furnish Electric Carpet in any size and shall be glad to furnish quotations on special arrangements for Lodge room use. If interested, send us a diagram of your hall or state size of carpet desired.

Meeting Was a Riot

"Our January meeting was a riot. It was the first time our Club had a Degree Team of their own and, being well advertised among our members, a great many came to the meeting out of curiosity and also prepared to criticize, as they were positive that we could not produce anything worth while. But what a surprise! It would have done you good to have listened to all the flowery remarks and words of praise from the biggest grouches in our Club. There was but one decision, the best degree work they had ever seen—original, clean, instructive and entertaining for members and candidates alike. Six candidates had to travel, and you never can tell—one darn thing after another. There were present quite a number of members from out of town, and the result is that on Saturday we are going to Port Jervis, N. Y., a city 100 miles from here, to hold our meeting there, and entertain out-of-town Square Clubs, Blue Lodge, Chapter, Commanders and Shriners."—Fred H. Blom, Erie Railroad Square Club, New York City, N. Y.

"The jump spark battery is very satisfactory. Our electric carpet has not been used for over a year, but is now the most popular of our paraphernalia. We wish to thank you for your kind suggestions and excellent service."—G. J. Groskrenz, Railway & Steamboat Clerks Benevolent Association, Milwaukee, Wis.

Let us develop your ideas on any novel or distinctive stunts. Write us about them. That's a part of our service as well as to manufacture and supply them economically.

STICK-EM-UP

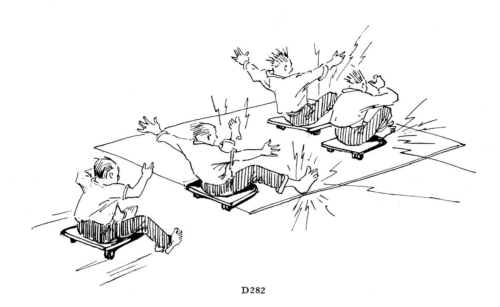

D282

One might at first wonder "what's in a name," and not see the connection between the title of this stunt and the stunt itself. But, believe us, the connection is there and becomes very evident when the candidates attempt to steer these "Stick-Em-Up" cars across the hot desert. This race has all other marathons beat a city block and is one of the most exciting contests you ever witnessed. The larger the race course (electric carpet) and the more contestants there are, the greater the fun.

The "Stick-Em-Up" car consists of a platform, just large enough for candidate to sit on; well made and finished, provided with three insulated castors. The candidate must manipulate and guide the car with his hands and bare feet. You can imagine the result when the juice is applied and the candidates feet and hands alternately touch the carpet. He will sure "stick-em-up" or he can be left there until he "chooses to run,." and indulge in a wild alternating performance which will make the race a prolonged though mighty interesting affair.

D282—Stick-Em-Up Car .... $ 5.00

Several cars should be used. For electric carpet see page 40.

Let us develop your ideas on any novel or distinctive stunts. Write us about them. That's a part of our service as well as to manufacture and supply them economically.

DeMoulin Bros. & Co., Greenville, Ill.

FENCING CONTEST

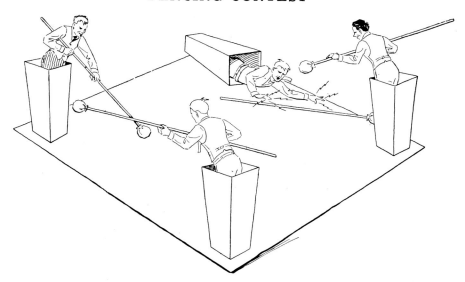

You may have read about the "Man on the Box," but here is where you learn about the man IN the box. And yet this is not a boxing match—it is simply a revival of that old art of fencing. The results are far-reaching; that is, one contestant may not only feel for the other fellow, but if he is real handy with the pole he may also reach him. And when one or more of the contestants take a tumble, the fun just begins, because they land on something "hot" and there is a wild scramble to get out of the desert.

These boxes are proper height and there is just about enough room at the bottom for a man's feet. This makes it rather difficult for the contestants to maintain their equilibrium when warding off attack and reaching for their opponents.

Boxes are made of insulated fibre and are very light, yet strong, shaped to permit resting; in fact, strong enough that you can invert boxes and candidates stand on bottom if preferred to use in this manner.

The best way to put on this fencing contest is to use four boxes and an electric carpet sixteen feet square. Place the boxes at the corners about four feet from each edge, so there will be room for the fencers to land on a warm spot, no matter which way they fall. Two boxes might be used with one width of electric carpet, but four boxes make the contest more interesting and call for more skill, as each contestant can be attacked from two sides.

D241—Fencing Outfit, consists of four boxes and four poles; boxes are light and can be nested so as to take up little room in shipping and storing. Price $23.50

D242—Electric Carpet, any size above 9 sq. ft., per square foot .... .45

D295—Electric Carpet, 50 inches wide, per running yard 6.25

D213—Jump Spark Battery, for use with Electric Carpet; electricity penetrates sox or clothing without use of conductors 23.00

TESTIMONIAL

"Our attendance has been on an average of about 40 to 50, but since we received your paraphernalia and worked up a side-degree for entertainment purposes, our attendance has increased for the last six weeks to about 175 to 200 members. We also have increased our membership to the extent of 65 new members, and I must say that this side degree has certainly been a big booster for our Lodge. If other Lodges have an outfit like ours, and will get the members to co-operate and get up a good side degree, they will have no trouble in increasing their membership, also their attendance."—H. E. Brewster, Pomona, Cal.

DeMoulin Bros. & Co., Greenville, Ill.

TUG O' WAR

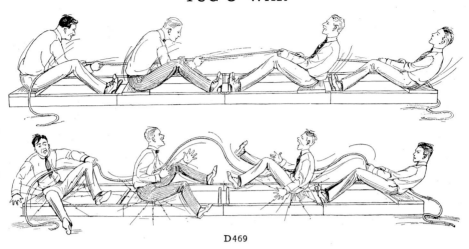

D469

Here is a real contest, in which the candidates receive a valuable lesson in team work—maybe. They learn that when two sides pull against each other they get nowhere. And it isn't always the fellow with a big pull who lands in a soft place, for when the juice is shot into the tug they forget all about the pull and they land—well, there's no telling where. They let loose of the rope but they seem to hold to one opinion and that is that it's time to go. Take it from us, this stunt is a dandy, full of action.

D469—Tug o' War, fourteen feet long; made to fold in four sections, thus occupying but little space when not in use; substantially constructed, four seats and foot braces, wired for **D213** Battery.......$48.00

D213—Jump Spark Battery and Cord 23.00

NOTE: We can make the Tug o' War to seat any number of persons. The more, the merrier. Four on each side makes a battle royal and a wild scramble when the "pep" is applied. Figure about three feet additional length and $12.00 extra for each additional seat.

THEY HAD TO MOVE TO A LARGER HALL

"The paraphernalia which we ordered and are using in our Lodge has resulted in a great increase in attendance. We have a big crowd every Thursday night now. It has meant so much to us that we have to get a larger hall and are on the lookout for one now. We have lots of work to do every meeting night and every man who takes our Degrees works hard to get someone else in to take them. We are highly pleased with paraphernalia and cannot say too much for it. It took me a long time to get the Lodge to agree to purchase these few things, but I just kept dinging at them until they agreed with me, and now they would not take twice the price that the paraphernalia cost."
—Geo. H. Parrish, Henderson, N. C.

ELECTRIC SPIKED PATHWAY

D302

Generally we are permitted to choose the road we travel and our companions for the journey. In this case the candidate must be guided by strange hands, but he can see all the "points" of interest along the way if he will only look down. When he gazes upon this pathway of sharp-pointed steel (?) spikes, he gets no joy out of anticipation, and when he has started down the path, he is soon convinced that there's a hot time in the old town tonight, with himself as one of the chief actors. His experience makes an impersonator of him, changing the expression of his "Phiz" from that of a polished gentleman to the resemblance of a terrified monkey.

See suggestions for introducing, page XVII in back of catalog.

D302—Electric Spikey Pathway, substantially made; rubber spikes, an exact imitation of steel; securely fastened; short circuiting absolutely impossible; 22 inches wide; per running yard $10.00

D214—Magneto and Cord 11.25

WOODEN SHOES

D303—Wooden Shoes, extra large to make them awkward and inconvenient. Arranged to fasten securely to feet, so cannot be kicked off. Very amusing to see candidate escorted through the degree work with these shoes; per pair ....$ 2.75

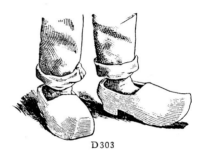

D303

D304

A CURRENT AFFAIR

Electric Wooden Shoes

It is very evident that the candidate is not suffering from locomotor-ataxia. He has no trouble whatever in getting over the ground in quick-step fashion. The shoes are put on and he is requested to demonstrate that he is fleet of foot and able to run to the assistance of a brother in distress. An occasional injection of the electric current will send him down the avenue in double quick time. A race between two or more candidates furnishes all the excitement of a real Marathon. See further suggestions for introducing, page XVII in back of catalog.

D304—Shoes, Magneto and Cord, complete $16.75
D305—Electric Wooden Shoes without magneto and cord, per pair...... 5.50
D306—Electric Sandals, magneto and cord, complete 14.75
D307—Electric Sandals without magneto and cord, per pair 3.50

CROSSING THE SWINGING BRIDGE

The candidate has often been admonished not to cross the bridge until he comes to it. In this instance he will not care to borrow any trouble, as he will have plenty of his own. He will find it a rather difficult task to reach the other side, and, although he hears the roar of the water below and the lashing of the waves against the rocks, he will be convinced that not all of the "current" is beneath the bridge. He will feel some of it flowing through the rails to which he is obliged to hold in order to be able to walk.

See suggestions for introducing, page XVIII in back of catalog.

The Electric Swinging Bridge is a substantial and handsome piece of paraphernalia. The posts and rails are of gas pipe finished in aluminum. The floor is of wood and metal, nicely finished and ornamented, and is suspended from the rail posts so it will readily swing with each step which the candidate takes. This motion creates a peculiar sensation and causes him to repeatedly grasp one or both of the side rails, each time giving him an electric shock. This swinging motion may be made more uncertain by the attendance. The Bridge may be quickly taken apart, occupying but little space for storing, and may be as quickly set up for use. Weight of **D308**, packed, 235 pounds; **D309**, 170 pounds.

D308—Electric Swinging Bridge, 14 feet long, three posts on each side....$65.00
D309—Electric Swinging Bridge, 8 feet long, two posts on each side..... 47.50
D214—Magneto and Cord 11.25

THE ROCKY ROAD TO DUBLIN

The Rocky Road to Dublin will make even a son of the old sod shed tears of joy (?). It reminds the candidate of his boyhood days when he walked barefooted over the clods and stubbles. His feet ache from the bruises and he curls up his toes in an effort to relieve the pressure on his tender trilbies. He proves to be a real tenderfoot, and, although he tries to step lightly over sorrow, his ludicrous facial expressions and awkward, jerky gestures bear evidence of the roughness of the road.

See suggestions for introducing, page XVIII in back of catalog.

The Rocky Road is a mat of double canvas with irregular articles sewed between same. Can be rolled up in small space when not in use. Carpet is made 22 or 44 inches wide, and can be furnished in any length; (usually ordered in lengths of three to five yards).

D312—Rocky Road, 22 inches wide, per running yard ....$ 2.35
D313—Rocky Road, 44 inches wide, per running yard 4.00

For very rocky road, see Electric Carpet, page 40.

ELECTRIC CANE

D210

An ordinary walking stick in the hand of the attendant looks perfectly harmless to the candidate, but when the end of the cane touches him on the north side of his bay window or any other part of his anatomy, he imagines that he has come in contact with the ends of a red hot poker. This electric cane is "hot" stuff—just the thing to goad the candidates and make them step lively around.

D210—Electric Cane Outfit, consists of a portable battery and cane; complete $33.50

EMBALMED MEAT OR BAD EGG TEST
"DE STINK"

After the candidate has had a few "whiffs" of this triple extract of "stink," he will long for a piece of Limburger to take the taste out of his mouth, and if a piece is held to his nostrils he will consider it a sweet perfume, so great is the improvement over "De Stink" that emanates from the atomizer.

See suggestions for introducing, pages III and IV in back of catalog.

D206—Atomizer consists of receptacle, rubber bulb, etc., in which a few drops of "De Stink" fluid are placed, and the horrible fumes arising from it are blown into the face of the candidate; price, including bottle of odor..$2.75

D207—Extra 2-ounce bottle of "De Stink" (not mailable) ...... .85

THE PLEDGE ALTAR

 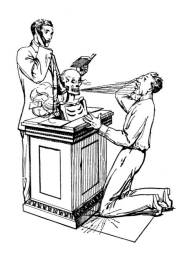

Things Are Not Always What They Seem

The candidate kneels before the altar, in all meekness and sincerity, to take the obligation. How thankful he is that it is all over; that all he has to do is to pledge himself not to reveal the secrets of the sublime degrees through which he has just passed. When lo! the room is darkened; up before him jumps a skeleton with large, illuminated, glaring eyes; a blank cartridge is exploded; a stream of water hits him in the face; an electric shock is shot into his knees.

This altar is not tricky, but is ornamental and useful. It is a regular lodge room altar such as every lodge should have. Made of solid oak, top and panels of built-up veneered quartered oak; rich golden oak finish carried in stock—other finishes to order. We highly recommend this altar, not only for its usefulness but as the culmination of surprises.

See suggestion for introducing, page IX in back of catalog.

D267—Pledge Altar, 33 inches high, top 22x27 inches; with electric mat and 50 blank cartridges $76.00

D213—Jump Spark Battery and Cord 23.00

D268—Pledge Altar, same as **D267**, but without electric mat 73.00

Extra Blank Cartridges (not mailable), loaded specially for us to give an extra loud report; per box of 50 .... .45

We recommend the above Battery; however, our Magneto at $11.25 may be used if the candidate's bare skin comes in direct contact with the mat.

SEA SERPENT

The idea of the Sea Serpent is to keep the class of candidates in line, in spite of obstacles such as electric carpets which otherwise tend to cause some confusion in the ranks.

D736—Sea Serpent, consists of heavy canvas body 20 feet long, well stuffed, and having grotesque head with squak attachment, supporting straps every five feet $30.00

Additional length, $0.75 per foot.

For Electric Carpet, see pages 40 and 41.

TESTIMONIALS

"Shipment reached us in due time and wish to take this opportunity to thank you for so promptly and efficiently filling out order. It sure is hot stuff."—E. B. Terrell, El Nomad Temple, No. 239, D. O. K. K., Knoxville, Tenn.

"Yama Yama Costumes made quite a hit at our ceremonial. We used them on the candidates in the parade and also in the side-degree or ruff stuff."—Geo. A. Davis, Samis Grotto, Richmond, Va.

DeMoulin Bros. & Co., Greenville, Ill.

THE HUMAN CENTIPEDE OR NIGHT MARE

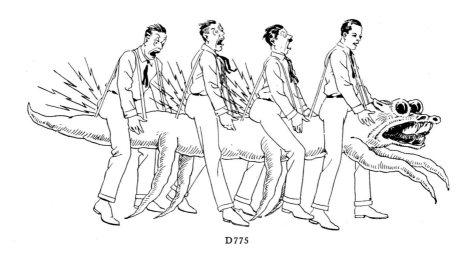

D775

Did you ever have a night mare? Well, if you did, you can sympathize with the candidates who are compelled to ride this animal. A "night mare," or any old "day horse," for that matter, is not one-two-three compared with this wild and woolly centipede. The mere thought of having to mount and hold fast to this uncanny beast is enough to make anybody want to stick to the tow path.

This mare is controlled by the man in front. At any desired time he can shoot the "animal heat" into the candidates and make the mare go in a way that will terrify them.

D775—Human Centipede or Night Mare, grotesque head with squak attachment, completely wired, including jump spark battery and connections $52.00

"It Is the Only Thing"

"We are well pleased with the paraphernalia we are using, and it is the only thing to keep up the attendance. We have a fairly good assortment of paraphernalia and we have probably put on the work in more neighboring towns than any other Camp in Northeastern Iowa. Perhaps some may ask why. Well, simply because the interest is kept up the year 'round and they always know there is a good time in Edgewood when we have a meeting, and when some other Camp gets some members, they say, 'Let's get Edgewood to come down and bring their stuff and put them through'."—C. S. Todd, Edgewood, Iowa.

"Greater Interest and More Enthusiasm"

"The result of the use of the side-degree paraphernalia obtained from you is very satisfactory. Since we introduced the side-degree work the attendance at our meetings has increased, and there has been greater interest and more enthusiasm among the members. We used the paraphernalia at our last initiation and it proved all that is claimed. I cannot but express my entire satisfaction at the quality and condition of the goods."—Jos. Gunville, Freda, Mich.

FAMILY SKELETON TURNED LOOSE AND ELECTRIC BLANKET

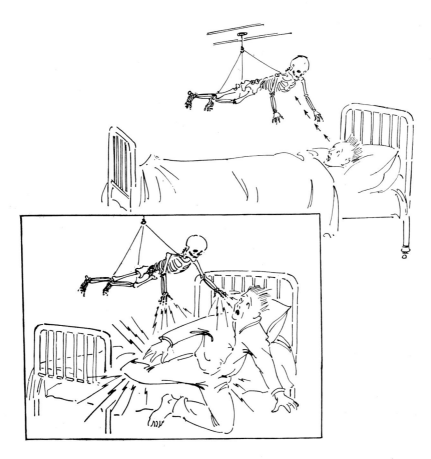

To go to sleep with the firm belief that the family skeleton is securely locked in the closet; to awaken suddenly and behold the aforesaid party floating over your bed with fire in his eyes—well, how would YOU enjoy (?) such an experience? No wonder the bed gets rather "warm" and the candidate loses all desire for sleep.

To the guilty candidate it is a "shocking" reminder of wild oats sown in younger days, but to the unsophisticated it is a warning which he is sure to heed.

D734—Electric Skeleton, consists of full size skeleton, substantially constructed of papier mache, colored electric light eyes, with pulley wire for manipulating feet and hands (electric blanket not included).$37.00

D301—Electric Blanket, size 3½x5 feet 8.75

D213—Jump Spark Battery 23.00

COFFIN STUNT OR FUNERAL OF AL. K. HALL

See Next Page for Description

DeMoulin Bros. & Co., Greenville, Ill.

COFFIN STUNT OR FUNERAL OF AL. K. HALL

This is one of our latest and very best.

The stunt consists of a coffin with electric bottom, and top arranged so it will fly into pieces and create a great deal of clatter; a special keg with exploding device; costumes for "Al. K. Hall", pallbearers, chief mourners, etc.

HOW STUNT IS USED

Candidate is dressed as a white mule with a white mule head and is placed in the coffin and the lid put on. On top of coffin is placed the keg labeled "Al. K. Hall At Rest."

The pallbearers and chief mourners consist of Drunkard, Convict, Thug, Wild Wild Woman, Skeleton, Disease, Poverty, Lust,, the Devil, Indian, and a large bottle with man inside—all dressed to represent these different characters.

Stage is set to represent a funeral scene and the digging of a grave. Near the grave the floor is prepared with a bare spot where coffin is to be placed and an electric runner on each side.

The scene opens on the stage with the grave diggers digging a grave, throwing out real dirt and singing an appropriate song. After throwing out a good size pile of dirt, the diggers depart, leaving the stage dark.

A red light is lighted in the grave and the devil appears, as if looking for the victim.

A funeral march is played and the funeral procession enters. They march up to the grave and place the coffin on the floor on the bare spot. The pallbearers and chief mourners are asked to kneel on either side of the coffin (on the electric runners) and assist in the ceremony.

An appropriate eulogy is given by one of the members who has charge of the funeral ceremony and who may use, if desired, statistics showing the record of "Al. K. Hall." He may make any kind of a talk he sees fit and which is most appropriate for the community.

At the words, "The dead shall rise again," the juice is turned on and the white mule kicks the entire top out of the coffin. The keg also explodes, scattering staves in all directions.

The pallbearers and chief mourners likewise get the juice when the white mule kicks his way out of the coffin and they scramble away in wild confusion. If desired, a policeman with an electric club may be on hand to take after the white mule and place him under arrest or run him out of the hall. Or he may be pursued by the devil with an electric trident.

Being a new stunt, you may, after having used it, be able to suggest ways of improving the ceremony. Any suggestions you have to offer will be appreciated.

THE PRICES

D384—Coffin, completely wired, with connections $60.00
D385—Keg, collapsible, cartridge attachment 17.00
D386—White mule costume with head 8.00
D244—Devil's Costume, good quality red cotton knit material, including cape and head with mask 10.00
D388—Trident, wired for electricity, with connections 10.50
D387—Convict Suit, of good quality striped material, the trousers without fly front but with draw-string at waist, one patch hip pocket; including cap, blouse and trousers, complete 6.30
D389—Skeleton Costume, including headpiece of black cotton knit material, anatomy in white felt applique on front 18.00
D390—Skeleton Costume, same as D389 but anatomy on both sides—front and back 22.50
D391—Black Gloves, with anatomy of white felt applique 1.75
D631—Ghost; white robe with black cross-bones on front, white hood and waxed linen skull mask 5.60
D622—Policeman, coat, trousers, belt, club, star, mask with headdress 6.70
D392—Electric Policeman's Club, made of wood; wired for electricity, with connections ... 11.00
D452—Stuffed Club, substantial material, tightly stuffed .... .75
D456—Electric Stuffed Club, wired complete with connections 5.00
D336—Large Bottle, papier mache, for man inside 20.00
D550—Grease Paint, set of eight colors; per box 1.25
D393—Nose Putty, per stick .... .50
D245—Two electric runners, each fifty inches wide and three yards long, for placing on floor at sides of coffin; price for the two 37.50
D213—Jump Spark Battery, in carrying case 23.00
D215—Portable Jump Spark Battery, for use with electric club, arranged to carry under front of policeman's coat, answers for stomach pad; also caried under devil's cape for use with electric trident 23.00

BABY BOUNCER
For Use With Electric Carpet

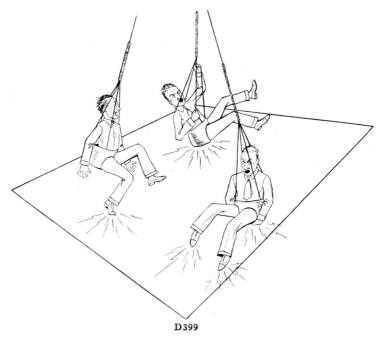

D399

Baby Bouncer—there are always a few smart babies in the bunch—show 'em off.

Consists of a harness and a spiral spring 30 inches long, suspended on a rope which goes through a pulley above the stage or in the ceiling; each baby is handled by an attendant; the carpet contains real sparks of laughter.

D399—Baby Bouncer, very substantial, including spiral spring, each ......$ 6.00

Electric Carpets listed on pages 40 and 41.

MEMBERSHIP INCREASED FROM 20 TO 200

"Up to last fall our Camp of about 700 members was as dead as they make them; always broke, trying to take care of our sick and needy neighbors; no interest taken in the meetings (if we had 20 members present we thought we had a good showing).

"A few of us got together and organized a drill team (that has turned out to be the best in the State), then we organized a drum and bugle corps, forming a club on the side, giving dances and doing other things to make a little money. This money was used to buy equipment to use in putting on the work. All candidates are given the whole works, ritualistic and funny, and the rougher we use them the more come back with other candidates to see them get a dose of the same medicine.

"Today we have a first-class set of officers, a good team, a fair drum and bugle corps (good enough to have the invitation to lead the parade in Benton Harbor on April 16th). The club has between five and six hundred dollars in cash, the Camp has about eight hundred dollars in the general fund.

"Our last few meetings we have had from one to two hundred members present. Does it pay to buy equipment for the camps and put on the work in full? I SAY IT DOES."—Alex Fuller, Clerk, Camp 1075, M. W. A., Muskegon, Michigan.

BIRD CAGE

D396

Bird Cage—a few birds hung around the hall help keep up the chip and chatter; if they pant, give them a dose of electric tonic.

Substantially built and arranged with electric bottom; collapsible; can be used with any jump spark battery; completely wired, with connections; including necessary rope and pulley, also a good bird whistle.

D396—Bird Cage, half length, sitting size $20.00

D397—Bird Cage, full length, standing size 25.00

Jump Spark Battery listed on page 39.

MEMBERSHIP AND ATTENDANCE INCREASED

"Paraphernalia we purchased from you recently arrived in fine order. We believe the burlesque side degree plays a large part in the success of our Club. It stimulates interest, creates enthusiasm, causes larger attendance and naturally increases membership. We not only use this degree work in our own Club, but take it to our Brother Lodges to help to increase for them. Recently we went a distance of eighty miles to put on this degree."—Howard M. Miller, B. P. O. E. No. 569, Iola, Kansas.

ELECTRIC STRETCHER

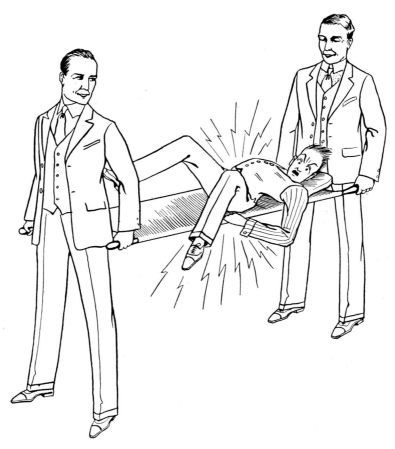

D395

Electric Stretcher—this is a good one to use on the chicken livered one who applies for admission to the hospital squad.

Electric Stretcher, substantially built, rolls up and packed in small space; size of canvas body 21x66 inches, not including carrying poles; completely wired, including connections.

D395—Electric Stretcher, each ....$ 8.00

Jump Spark Battery listed on page 39.

VERY MUCH PLEASED WITH PARAPHERNALIA

"We are very much pleased, indeed, with all the paraphernalia received from you and have had a great deal of fun and amusement. All the paraphernalia received worked nicely and without a hitch; in fact, we wish to compliment you very much on all received.

"Any time we can be of further service to you we will be glad to have you write us."—Dr. A. S. Vance, Master of Revels, St. Petersburg, Florida.

CHARLESTON GIRLS

D394

Charleston Girls—tall ones, short ones, thin ones and fat ones; all dressed up and ready to go; they are the clinging vine type; the fellows that draw them are sure to step high, wide and handsome.

The girls are built up like the old-fashioned rag doll; the arms are attached around the shoulders, and the feet are attached to the feet of the dancer; use them on a large electric carpet; no instructions necessary to the lounge lizard that draws one; they are a scream.

D394—Charleston Girls, each $22.00
Electric Carpets listed on pages 40 and 41.

Larger Attendance at Lodge

"The paraphernalia we received from you is all right. We certainly have had a good time with them and all the members are anxious to use them. The articles all work good and we are well pleased with them. We are having a larger attendance at Lodge, and I think the paraphernalia is a benefit to the Lodge."—Jakie Brensing, Clerk, Camp 5190, M. W. A., Hudson, Kansas.

"We received our paraphernalia O. K. and put on a good initiation. It increased our attendance 200 per cent."—Malcolm L. Griffin, B. P. O. E. No. 795, Fernandina, Florida.

"I would like to voice the approval of every member of Crisfield Lodge No. 1044. They have placed the O. K. on every article which you were so kind as to ship to Crisfield. It has been the means of a marked increase in attendance of the Lodge and a more than wonderful increase in membership. We stand ready at any time to recommend your goods to any Lodge or person who is looking for real live stunts and want to say that we are very sorry that the Lodge did not consider earlier in securing the stunts that we have."—Charles H. Smith, Crisfield, Maryland.

THE ELECTRIC RAZOR

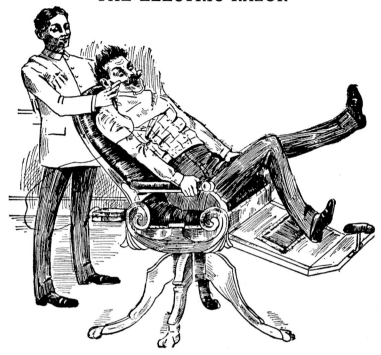

"Next gent!" The candidate who is next in order but not "next" to what's coming to him, takes his seat. He is asked whether he wants 'em shaved close or just the once over. The tonsorial artist may be a smooth guy, but this cannot be said of his shaves. His keen edge gets tangled up in the candidate's whiskers and he attempts to pull them out by the roots. The candidate's hair, in sympathetic action, stands straight up like the bristles on the barber's comb. When it's all over and he again hears the call, "Next gent," he is satisfied he had a close shave and is glad he escaped with his life.

See suggestion for introducing, page XVIII in back of catalog.

D433—Complete Outfit, consisting of an electric razor, bib, magneto and cord $15.75

D434—Razor and Bib, without magneto and cord 4.50

D435—Large Wooden Razor, burlesque pattern, black handle, silvered wood blade 1.50

D436—Large Burlesque Razor, wood handle, hollow bright tin blade 1.75

D437—Mug, of questionable character, properly decorated; also large brush 1.75

"Lots of Fun"

"I received trick guns and spanking machine and we put on some work with them and had lots of fun that we would not have had if we had not got them. We mailed out cards to all members and we had a large crowd and they all enjoyed the new stunts and I think that the candidates enjoyed it, too. I am enclosing money order for the full amount."—L. A. Alsobrooks, Washington Camp, No. 24, P. O. S. of A., Salisbury, N. C.

GOLFITIS

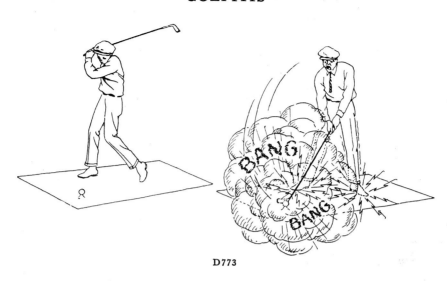

D773

Here is a stunt that will appeal to the candidate. If he indulges in that ancient and ever popular game of golf, he will welcome a chance to show what a splendid drive he can make. If he is a novice at the game, he will not object to a lesson, as he may have a beginner's luck.

The imitation golf ball used in this stunt is of hollow rubber and very light. No danger whatever in its use, but if preferred it might be driven at a screen or target, or the same results can be had by putting instead of driving.

The instant the candidate hits the ball the tee blows up, his feet begin to itch (?), and he will know he has had an attack of golfitis.

D773—Golf Stunt, including imitation golf ball, which is hollow rubber and securely anchored to tee, golf club, electric carpet with connections, cartridge-firing apparatus and 50 blank cartridges (battery not included) $22.00

Extra Blank Cartridges (not mailable), loaded specially for us to give an extra loud report; per box of 50 .... .45

Membership and Attendance Increased

"The side-degree has increased our Order both in membership and attendance, caused largely from the use of the paraphernalia received from you. We also have an electric chair which causes some interesting entertainment."—J. F. Gettig, Woodward, Okla.

"We were on the dead list for the past year, but since procuring your paraphernalia we have initiated ten members and have several more on the way. We have been having an average attendance of about forty."—F. H. Conroy, Easton, Ill.

DeMoulin Bros. & Co., Greenville, Ill.

THE GLAD HAND

If there is any one thing the candidate is anxious to receive, it is the grip. He welcomes the moment when the officer will extend to him the right hand of fellowship and with it the grip of the Order. To him it means that the initiation is all over. But he has another guess coming and when the officer gives him the "warm" hand he is completely taken off his feet. This is a fine stunt which can be used on members as well as candidates.

See suggestions for introducing under "Electric Wooden Shoes," page XVII in back of catalog.

D464—The Glad Hand Outfit consists of a small electric storage battery and induction coil with a spring push button concealed in the inside coat pocket with insulated wires running through the sleeve to a new improved arrangement which is concealed in the palm of the hand. When the officer grasps the candidate's hand, he places his left hand over his chest as if giving a warm greeting, and when he has a good grasp of the candidate's hand, he presses the button and the candidate does the jigging $12.00

ELECTRIC WHEEL BARROW

The candidate may have ridden in and on all sorts of contrivances, yet he gets a new thrill in this one-wheeler. It's a "shock" to his dignity and other parts of his anatomy to be compelled to ride in a wheel barrow, but he will recover from the shock in time to continue his journey by more modern methods. (Introduce Flying Machine, Balloon Ascensions, etc.)

See suggestions for introducing, page XIV in back of catalog.

The Electric Wheel Barrow is strongly made of best seasoned wood and has a rubber-tired steel wheel. The bottom and edges are wired so that no matter what position candidate may take he is bound to get all the "juice" he wants.

D465—Electric Wheel Barrow (wiring included) $12.50

D213—Jump Spark Battery and Cord (electricity will penetrate clothes without use of conductors) 23.00

DeMoulin Bros. & Co., Greenville, Ill.

THE DEVIL HAS 'EM ON THE RUN

Here is where the candidates have a "devil" of a time. If they ever questioned the existence of his satanic majesty, their doubts will fly—and they, too, will fly when the devil suddenly and unexpectedly rushes in on them. He makes his presence felt in a way that convinces the candidates that this is something else besides a wild goose chase. If it is desired that the candidates have the joy (?) of anticipation, the devil might announce his presence by showing his head through a curtain or at the door.

D777—Devil's Costume, including head, tights, forked tail and portable jump spark battery which is concealed in hump on back $32.25

D778—Devil's Costume, as **D777**, but without portable battery 9.25

D779—Devil's Shoes, good quality red leather with up-turned toes 5.25

D388—Devil's Electric Trident, wired for electricity, with connections.... 10.50

NO MAN'S LAND

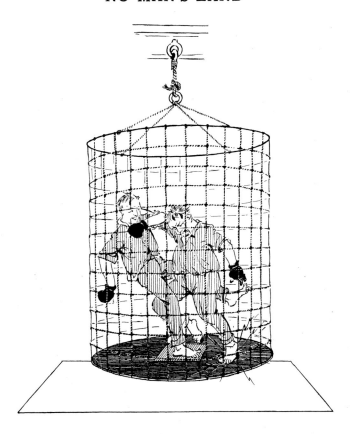

Here is the greatest test of Brotherly Love ever invented.

The bottom is solid and electric, with the exception of a spot in the center, which is not quite large enough to accommodate both candidates. Swings from pulley and when drawn up to clear the floor, makes it very difficult for candidates to keep their equilibrium.

If they have any Brotherly Love at all they will alternately enjoy a period of relief by standing on this "safety spot." On the other hand, it is highly probable that there will be a wild scramble in "no Man's land" as both victims will manifest a strong desire to reserve parking space on this oasis in the desert of hot sands and cactus. Their actions will be very much unlike those prompted by Brotherly Love. It's rather uncomfortable for the candidtaes but interesting and entertaining for everyone else.

D735—No Man's Land, consists of net made of heavy cotton twine, 9 feet high (ceiling should be 15 ft. to operate successfully) and 6½ feet in diameter, steel hoop at top and solid bottom, pulley and rope; also two pair boxing gloves to be worn by candidates............$48.00

ELECTRIC BRANDING IRON

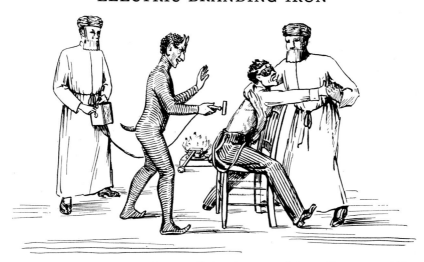

Because we show here the Devil in the act of branding a candidate, we would not have you construe this as an inference that every new member belongs to his Satanic Majesty. No, not by any means! But that is the impression the victim gets. When he has seen his adversary ready to perform this terrible (?) operation; when he has felt the hot (?) iron and smelt the odor of his own burning flesh, he will be thoroughly convinced that the infernal region is just around the corner and that he is able to take up his abode there. See suggestions for introducing, page VII in back of catalog.

D227—The Electric Brand is harmless in action, no objectionable features. The hot iron brand is only a bluff, the Electric Brand being the one applied. Burning sensation ceases as soon as brand is removed. Price, including magneto and cord, one iron brand, one electric deception brand, bottle of alcohol, alcohol stove $15.75

D228—Electric Brand without magneto 4.50

Complete Instructions With Each Outfit.

D229—Devil Costume, as illustrated above 9.25
D230—Costume for Attendants, consisting of robe and turban, including mask with curtain; per set of two 7.80

DECEPTIVE BURNING BRAND OUTFIT

D231—Deceptive Burning Brand Outfit, consists of two brands, alike in appearance—one a real iron burning brand, the other a deceptive brand of wood and rubber; ink pad, alcohol stove and half pint alcohol. The burning brand is heated and handed to candidate, so he may be convinced that it is really hot. Branding is done with deceptive brand, which has previously been inked on pad and bulb inflated with smoke, so that candidate may see it used on the one just before him. If this is worked correctly, the deception is perfect. Complete outfit ....$ 2.25

D232—Deceptive Brand only 1.00
D233—Ink Pad only .... .25
D234—Iron Burning Brand only .... .75
D238—Alcohol Stove only .... .35
D239—Pint Alcohol only .... .35

ELECTRIC TEETER TOTTER

D765

'Tis said that life is a see-saw of ups and downs. But, does the candidate appreciate that fact as he should?—that's the question. Needless to say, the Lodge is not willing to take his word for it, so the only thing to do is to give a practical demonstration. A personal experience on this teeter-totter will quickly remove any doubt the candidate might have had about this life and see-saw analogy.

D765—Electric Teeter-Totter complete, including collapsible buck, board with straps for securely attaching candidates and electric connections which turn on automatically as feet of one candidate touches floor causing him to spring up and bring other candidate down to get his (can be used with any style Jump Spark Battery, battery not included) $35.00

D213—Jump Spark Battery 23.00

Everybody Takes More Interest

"We have a good live Lodge of 160 members. We have just recently reorganized our Team and since receiving the paraphernalia the Team is doing some good work, and I can see that everybody seems to take more interest in the meetings. As one man said who has not been out to the meetings very often, 'I am coming out every meeting now as the boys are having too much fun and I can't afford to miss it.' So it goes, unless a lodge has a good live team and plenty to work with, the meetings grow tiresome and soon the attendance grows smaller and the lodge is a dead one."—C. T. Thurber, Highland, Kansas.

DOG SHOW STUNT

Hark! Hark! The dogs do bark. Take it from us, when this show is put on, the dogs will not only bark and howl; but there will be the "doggondest" scramble you ever saw, and the kennels will not hold the dogs. Try this stunt—it's a "howler".

Kennels are made of cardboard with names on them, and are placed on a large electric carpet. The candidates are provided with large papier mache dog heads and are assigned to the kennels. The show is now open. Each dog is required to demonstrate his barking ability, and each one will try to out-bark the other. About the time this show is in full swing—WOW! Enough said—don't fail to put on this show. We do not quote kennels as the shipping charge would be more than they are worth. These can easily be made of heavy cardboard.

D404—Dog Heads of papier mache, to be worn over head, each ....$ 3.85
D409—Electric Mat, fifty inches wide, four yards long 25.00
D213—Jump Spark Battery 23.00

Size of mat required will depend upon number of dog houses used. We can furnish any size at 45 cents per square foot.

AN ELECTRIFIED SMOKE

It's all right to talk about electrifying a railroad engine to do away with the smoke, but when it comes to electrifying a man's cigars, we doubt very much whether the movement will meet with popular approval. Be that as it may, here is one time when the smoker has no say-so in the matter. He will not hesitate a moment about taking (?) one of these cigars from the box. Oh, yes, he will hesitate all right; but his first intentions are good.

"Have a smoke?" "Yes, thank you." And why not? A box of choice cigars—nothing unusual about that. The unusual thing happens when Mr. Man reaches in and, instead of getting what he thinks is a choice cigar, he takes hold of a "fire brand." 'Nough said—Mr. Man concludes the performance. The stunt is perfectly harmless but productive of considerable action.

D243—Electrified Smoke consists of box of 50 trick smokes, the box being cleverly arranged and wired so that when Mr. Man reaches in for one he gets—well, he gets what he doesn't expect by any means. Price $12.30

D213—Jump Spark Battery, for use with Electrified Smoke, Electric Carpet and any of our electrical appliances 23.00

The Electrified Smoke can be used in different ways. It can be placed on a table or passed around, in either case the "juice" being turned on at the will of the person in charge. Trick or real cigars can be used. When the **D240** trick smokes are used, let several take theirs without giving them the "juice". After seeing others get a "hot" one, they will congratulate themselves on having escaped the shock, only to find a few minutes later that their smokes are loaded in a different way.

Testimonial

"We have received the Trick Guns and I assure you they were greatly enjoyed during the first initiation. We put four candidates through the paces and with the aid of the guns and your splendid catalog it was a proved success. I am enclosing draft for $313.50 to cover the cost and I assure you that we will be ordering other apparatus at a later date."—D. W. Rathford, Pit River Aerie, No. 2025 F. O. of E., Alturas, Calif.

THE MOLTEN LEAD TEST

When the candidate joined the lodge he might have had some hopes of getting his fingers "in the pie," but he did not dream that he would be expected to dip his hands in molten lead as an evidence of his bravery. This request will cause a display of his rebellious nature and it is necessary for the attendants to show their authority by assisting the candidate in this painful (?) performance.

This test is a great improvement over the small ladle test. Our dry mercurine powder is much cheaper than the liquid mercury and looks exactly like molten lead. It can be ladled up and poured back into the pot repeatedly in the presence of candidate, and the delusion is absolutely perfect. The contents of the pot is simply cold water, with a pinch of our new dry mercurine sprinkled in it.

See suggestions for introducing, page X in back of catalog.

D250—Complete Outfit, consisting of pot, tripod, ladle, alcohol stove, can of alcohol and a can of dry mercurine, sufficient for fifty or more trials, with full directions for using ....$ 4.75
Dry Mercurine, extra can, when wanted, by mail postpaid .... .75
Wood Alcohol, in tin screw-top can, per pint, 35 cents; per quart.. .60

ELECTRIC ATTACHMENTS FOR MOLTEN LEAD TEST

With this attachment the candidate will receive a shock when he plunges his hands in the molten lead, which will cause him to believe that the test is no "fake."

D251—Mat, properly wired and with connections for attaching to pot..$ 3.50
D214—Magneto and Cord 11.25

THE LADLE LEAD TEST

D252—Ladle, with can of Dry Mercurine and full directions for using.......$1.10

D253—Ladle, extra heavy and well made, with can of Dry Mercurine and full directions for using 1.30

BINDING STRAPS

D254—Straps for binding candidate $0.85

CANDIDATE'S BELT

D255—Belt of leather, 3½ inches wide; straps on sides with which to guide candidate; very strongly made; will fit any size man $3.75

LIFTING AND SPRAYING MACHINE

A candidate is always ready to display his strength to show that he is an able-bodied man, and it takes but a suggestion relative to his physical weakness to get him to prove that he can lift just as much as any other man of his weight and size.

See suggestions for introducing, page XX in back of catalog.

The machine has a dial to register the number of pounds lifted and when the candidate has lifted about 50 pounds, an automatic cartridge device is sprung, discharging a 32-calibre blank cartridge with a loud report; the startling effect causes candidate to release his hold, and then he gets a "free bath" by the spraying device concealed in the dial.

D350—Lifting and Spraying Machine, including box of 50 blank cartridges and full directions for operating....$14.00
  (Weight, packed, 20 pounds)

Extra Blank Cartridges (not mailable), loaded specially for us to give an extra loud report; per box of 50.... .45

D350

D351

THE MUSCULAR TEST

The Muscular Test is just what the strong, healthy candidate is loking for to enable him to demonstrate his strength, but when he attempts to lift this 200-pound (?) weight, he will be willing to admit that he is feeble, rather than grapple with a live wire.

See suggestions for introducing, page XX in back of catalog.

The Muscular Test is cast hollow and weighs but 50 pounds. There is an electrical contrivance in its interior ingeniously constructed to automatically produce a good strong electric current through the lifting handles as soon as it is lifted from the floor.

D351—Muscular Test $22.50

TREADMILL

D274

"Love's Labor Lost" is exemplified by this stunt. The candidate is very conscientious in his advocacy of the conservation of energy. He does not object so much to the hard-labor punishment which he must undergo, but he is chafed because there is no utilization of the power he creates. His scruples might be satisfied by attaching the mill to the fan or the elevator. Notice also that the candidate is getting rather nervous and finds it difficult to retain his hold on the bars of the Treadmill.

See suggestions for introducing, page XII in back of catalog.

D274—Treadmill, substantially constructed of the best seasoned wood; latest model with string of rollers under the entire length of platform, also tension screws permitting adjustment. Weight, packed, 175 pounds $62.50

D275—Electric Attachment, complete, including magneto and cord 14.75
D276—Electric Attachment, without magneto and cord, otherwise same as D275 .... 3.50

THE FOUNTAIN OF YOUTH

Had Ponce de Leon been privileged to drink from this fountain he doubtless would have declared it to be the fountain of youth. There can be no question about the invigorating effect upon the candidate. It makes him step around like a ten-year-old. And all the time he wonders how the others can drink from the fountain without feeling the same effects.

See suggestion for introducing, page XXV in back of catalog.

The Electric Fountain consists of a neat oak-finished and varnished stand, arranged with ornamental reservoir and large ornamental bowl, an air pump, a mat and six fancy cups. The stand has hooks upon which the cups can be hung.

D444—Electric Fountain, including magneto and cord $65.00
D445—Electric Fountain, without magneto and cord 53.75

DeMoulin Bros. & Co., Greenville, Ill.

TRICK LOADED SMOKES

This is a well made cigar, of very good appearance, and a fairly good smoke (while it lasts). It is made up containing a spring which is tied under pressure with a light string. When the cigar is about one-third smoked, the fire gets to the string and all to pieces goes the cigar, much to the surprise of the victim. Contains no explosive, nor anything that can cause the least injury. We do not furnish samples of this article nor accept orders for less than one box.

D240—Trick Smokes, box of 50 ....$5.00

TRICK COFFEE URN

This is not an illicit still, but when the candidate discovers what deception has been perpetrated on him, he may be disposed to think that such an act ought to be unlawful and that it does not evince the true fraternal spirit which he expected to find in the Lodge. Imagine his indignation when, after having partaken of a cup of fine Mocha-Java, he finds that the stuff has been made of limburger cheese, asafoetida, feathers, old shoes, dish rags, etc. Is it any wonder that his stomach rebels and that he has difficulty in warding off a serious attack of sea-sickness? Undoubtedly he will be impressed with the fact that he should practice no deception toward his fellow-men.

See suggestions for introducing, page XII in back of catalog.

D280—Complete Outfit, consisting of urn, tripod, alcohol stove and bottle of alcohol $13.50

Wood Alcohol in tin screw top can, per pint, 35 cents; per quart .60

D280

SPANKER

When it is desired to add a "personal touch" to the initiation, a few of these spankers will do the work in a manner which will greatly "impress" the candidate. If in proper position, he may receive an inspiration which will lead him to "jump" at conclusions as to what caused the loud report.

This spanker is the lightest weight made. The discharge is certain, no matter which part of spanker is struck. It is raranged with an automatic firing device so that when candidate is spanked, a 32-calibre blank cartridge is discharged, the concussion and fire of which is completely muffled by our new muffling attachment, thus avoiding any possibility whatever of accident. We include an attachment with which the empty cartridge shell is easily removed.

See suggestions for introducing, page XXVI in back of catalog.

D451—Spanker complete with 50 blank cartridges ....$ 5.00
Extra Blank Cartridges (not mailable), loaded specially for us to give an
    extra loud report; per box of 50 .... .45

See Striking Maul listed on page 72.

ELECTRIC SPANKER

D401—Electric Spanker, same as **D451**, but wired for electricity; for use
    with **D215** portable battery; price (not including battery) ....$ 7.50

You can add the "finishing touch" with this spanker. Just as it strikes the candidate, push the button. His imagination will work overtime, as he will sure think the shot has penetrated his anatomy.

SLAP STICKS

D450—Slap Sticks, sizes 2x28 inches; with shaped handles; made of good grade
    lumber:
    Less than 6, each $1.50
    6 or more, each 1.35
    12 or more, each 1.25
    25 or more, each 1.00
    50 or more, each .... .90

STUFFED CLUBS

D452—Stuffed Club, substantial material, tightly stuffed; just the thing for
    larraping candidate ....$ .75
D453—Stuffed Club, same as **D452**, but smaller size .... .50
D456—Electric Stuffed Club; wired complete with connections 5.00

THE STRIKING MAUL

As shown in the pictures, the striking maul has a "striking" effect upon the candidate; in fact, he imagines he is struck at both ends. The maul is a very close imitation of a lumberman's maul. Though somewhat larger and of light weight, yet it is realistic enough to deceive even the oldest forester. the firing mechanism is released by a slight jar, firing a 32-calibre blank cartridge. Absolutely safe and no danger whatever of an accident.

See suggestions for introducing, page XXII in back of catalog.

D454—Striking Maul, complete with 50 blank cartridges $12.50

Extra Blank Cartridges (not mailable), loaded specially for us to give an extra loud report; per box of 50 .... .45

GREASED (?) POLE

Greased Pole Outfit—pole waxed so that it is as hard to climb as the old familiar greased pole. How aptly this stunt illustrates the saying that "man is but a boy of larger growth." We all recall how we, when kids, tried to get the dollar from the top of the greased pole at the County Fair. At the top of this pole is placed a goblet of water, so that when the candidate has reached the top in an exhausted condition, he can refresh himself with a nice cool drink. The fun produced by this stunt will even warrant the placing of a coin at the top of the pole as an inducement for the candidate to try his "durndest." And if he lacks the energy, a little assistance applied at the rear with one or two hand spankers or a shot from a water gun will not be out of order. Here's how the candidate gets it "fore and aft."

D455—Greased Pole Outfit, complete (spankers not included) $26.00

INVISIBLE PADDLE MACHINE

D334

In this stunt the candidate is taught to paddle his own canoe, instead of depending too much upon the assistance of his brothers in the lodge. It is also a good catch for the smart fellow who thinks he knows all about lodge room tricks. The surprise is all the greater because the candidate is not hoodwinked. Even though he might have a suspicion that the front end of the blooming thing is loaded, yet it is absolutely certain that he will not anticipate an attack from the rear. With a stream of water hitting him in his face and a plank hitting him on his "rear," backed up by a thunder-bolt, the candidate will sure imagine himself between the devil and the deep blue sea.

See suggestions for introducing, page XIX in back of catalog.

The Invisible Paddle Machine is so ingeniously constructed that the results obtained by it are really wonderful. The paddle positively cannot be detected. This cannot be said, however, after the candidate pulls up on the handles, for by so doing he releases a trigger, and this in turn automatically causes the top of the machine to spring out of place from the rear end until it engages a device that reverses the course by throwing it in an upright position and in line with the seat of his pants. The moment the paddle strikes a blank cartridge is exploded and water is discharged in his face from a special spraying device concealed in the dial.

D334—Invisible Paddle Machine, with 50 blank cartridges (weight, packed 20 pounds) $21.00

D335—Invisible Paddle Machine, same as **D334**, but with an electrical attachment as used in our Lifting and Spanking Machine (weight, packed, 20 pounds) 33.50

Extra Blank Cartridges (not mailable), loaded specially for us to give an extra loud report; per box of 50 .... .45

LIFTING AND SPANKING MACHINE

D342-D344

With this machine the candidate cannot kick his own pants while wearing them, but can have them spanked where his mother used to apply the sole of her slipper, by simply testing his strength. The position in which he places himself causes a little strain in the seat of his pants, which is not objectionable, as it pulls up all the slack when he pulls up on the handles. Just about the time he gets well started lifting, a trigger is automatically released, which causes the spanking paddle to spring into place and strike him on the kazabo, at the same time exploding a 32-calibre blank cartridge with a loud report. (Paddle can be easily removed and used as a spanker.) That is not all; there is also an electric attachment concealed under the platform of the machine that turns on a good current of electricity at the same time the paddle hits his pants.

See suggestions for introducing, page XIX in pack of catalog.

Great improvements have been made in the electrical parts of this machine. We now use a special coil with dry batteries, which is almost impossible to get out of order. Each machine is guaranteed to give a good strong electric current, and will not get out of order, except for the occasional replacing of dry batteries. (Weight, packed, 55 pounds.)

The machine takes up but little room. Handles and paddle can be easily removed, so that it will fit in a box 22x34x5½ inches.

D342—Lifting and Spanking Machine, with 50 blank cartridges $32.50

D343—Lifting and Spanking Machine, same as **D342**, but without electric attachment 20.00

D344—Lifting and Spanking Machine, same as **D342**, but with special spraying device as used on our Invisible Paddle Machine 35.00

Extra Blank Cartridges (not mailable), loaded specially for us to give an extra loud report; per box of 50 .... .45

HOME BREW

The candidate is escorted into the hall wearing a hat (preferably an old straw hat), he is severely reprimanded for his ill manner by the Head Officer, who places the hat on a stand in front of his chair. He then orders the candidate to be searched and a flask is found on his hip.

The candidate doesn't realize how "potent" home brew may be, until the Head Officer takes a drink from his flask and spits it on the floor, where it explodes, sending up a cloud of smoke.

The Head Officer puts the flask under the candidate's hat on the stand, and —BANG—another explosion follows, blowing the hat to pieces.

A waste basket with a firing device arranged in the bottom is furnished when ordered, the bottle is thrown in it and an explosion follows.

D723—Home Brew, includes bottle, firing device for under hat and one on floor, 2 oz. powder in screw top tin can, and 50 blank cartridges...**$15.00**

D724—Waste Basket, with firing device and 50 blank cartridges 9.00

SOME VERY LIVELY STUNTS

Space does not permit illustrating them here. Write for sketches and prices on those which interest you.

Shoot the Chute
The Auto-Mul-ti-pede
Electro-Dropo Bench
Whiz Bang Baseball
Electric Blanket (putting the candidate to bed)

Electric Rocking Chair
Raiding the Hornet's Nest
Electric Portieres
Flying Machine
The Ocean Wave Boat

KNIFE THROWING STUNT

In the category of nerve-testing, hair-raising experiences, there are some that cannot be described. Unless you have gone through the ordeal yourself, you will never realize the feeling produced. It is so with this knife throwing stunt. Believe us, it's a dandy. Perfectly harmless, but a complete deception. The candidate firmly believes that the knives are being thrown by the Arab and each time one sinks (?) into the wall near his body, or when he receives an instant electric shock in one arm and at the same moment a knife lodges very near this point, his opinion as to the knife thrower's ability will be somewhat exaggerated.

To make the deception more complete, a spotlight should be directed from behind the knife thrower on the candidate. When the Arab's arm comes in the shadow of his body, the candidate, blinded by the light and not being able to follow the course of the knife, will think the Arab has thrown the knife and is in the act of reaching for another.

The knives are concealed back of the "wall" and are thrown out through slots with a thud by means of springs operated from behind. One of the straps around the arm has an electric arrangement so that when the knife nearest this point is sprung an electric current is automatically caused to pass through the arm for an instant only, giving the same sensation as if the arm had been cut by the knife.

D269—Knife Throwing Stunt Outfit, including knives (battery not included) $155.00
D213—Jump Spark Battery and Cord 23.00

Prices on Spotlight quoted on application.

COSTUME FOR KNIFE THROWER

D272—Costume, consisting of jacket, shirt, sash, bloomers, cape and turban. Jacket of red army duck with yellow braid border; shirt of white mercerized cashmere; sash of black and yellow striped galatea; bloomers of red army duck; cape of green mercerized cashmere; turban of yellow and green mercerized cashmere. Price, including brown, black and red face and arm paints $14.60
D273—Mustache, black hair on gauze, including a bottle of spirit gum for attaching .... .50

THE BRANDING AND WHIRLING TABLE

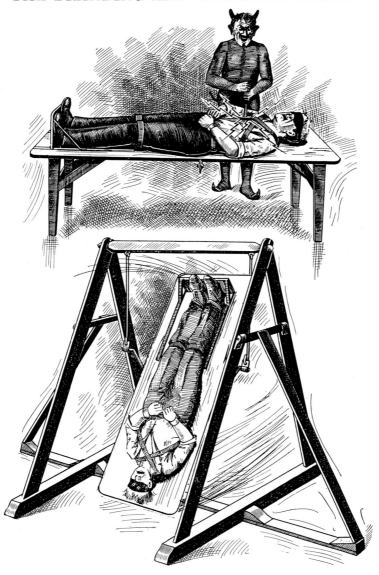

Here is the branding stunt with an added attraction. The devil shows the victim no mercy whatever. Not content with having made him suffer the torture of the brand, he whirls him into space, then drops him head-first into the deep abyss.

See suggestions for introducing, page VIII in back of catalog.

The Branding and Whirling Table consists of table which has legs that fold up out of the way when used to whirl, and substantial whirling frame which folds into small space for shipping and storing.

D260—Branding and Whirling Table (weight, packed, about 215 pounds)..$57.00

D261—Branding and Whirling Table without whirling frame, but **strong screw eyes** to be screwed in joist of ceiling from which table is to be suspended by ropes (ropes not included) 32.50

Branding Outfit listed on page 63.

REJUVENATING MACHINE

Steinnach's gland operation has nothing on this machine, the Rejuvenator DeLuxe.

Here is a stunt with plenty of action, an unusual climax, and a variety of possibilities.

The Candidate is lowered into the hopper with a rope and pulley. Even the prospect of being rejuvenated will not keep him from doing plenty of squirming when he comes in contact with the electric current while entering the hopper. While an attendant produces a terrific clatter by turning the crank, the Candidate disappears into the box and is rejected—a changed man. His clothing is in shreds; the rejuvenating process seems to have "gone wrong," but when the juice is shot to the carpet on which he lands, life instantly returns to him and he performs some highly entertaining antics.

The climax can be varied by ejecting another Candidate dressed in a monkey suit, instead of the one lowered into the hopper.

(Monkey costumes are listed on page 151.)

Another variation is the substitution of a younger man for the one who is "fed" into the Rejuvenator.

D726—Rejuvenating Machine, size 5x10 feet, is made collapsible and folds up compactly, occupying very little space when not in use; otherwise, as described above $57.00

TRIP THROUGH A STORMY DESERT

D288

It may well be said that the candidate is a victim of circumstances, which in this case are many. He will firmly believe that all the elements have conspired against him, but after he has come out of this terrible storm without a scratch, he will say he would not have missed the experience for anything.

This feature is almost a complete initiation by itself and with a little practice can be made exceedingly interesting. With the different articles furnished a perfect rain and electric storm can be imitated. Electric Sandals are provided for candidate's feet to remind him that even the ground seems to be electrified. When he attempts to drink from the well, which is an exact representation of the old fashioned rock well, a blank cartridge explodes, thus more than likely causing him to spill the water from the bucket all over his shirt and trousers.

D288—Trip Thru a Stormy Desert consists of one substantially constructed well with rope and bucket; one pair of electric sandals with battery and cord; one long mat upon which footprints are shown; one lightning transparency with lycopodium torch and powder; one thunder sheet, wind machine and rain drum; and five imitation snakes. Directions sent with each outfit to show how it should be set up. Price, complete $75.00

In case your Lodge should have a few of the articles used in the above outfit, deduct the following amounts from the price quoted: Rain Drum, $2.25; Wind Machine, $5.00; Thunder Sheet, $2.25; Lightning Transparency, $10.25; Lycopodium Torch and Powder, $7.00; Electric Sandals, $3.50; Battery and Cord, $11.25.

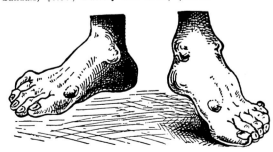

TRILBY FEET

D289—Trilby Feet, of waxed cloth; very large and grotesque; made to go over footwear; per pair..$1.50

HANDS

D290—Hands to match trilby feet; per pair ...$1.25

ELECTRIC TUNNEL

This tunnel, consisting of solid wood platform suspended from trestle which permits it to swing, making it difficult for candidates to keep their equilibrium, with side walls of heavy cotton cord, should be placed at the bottom of our slide, listed on page 95.

After the candidate has enjoyed (?) a nice long slide he would like to rest and regain his breath right where he lands, but he changes his mind rather abruptly when he is dumped into the tunnel.

Instead of a resting place for tired candidates, it becomes a scene of great activity as the victims strive to get through in "nothing flat."

D728—Electric Tunnel, consists of net made of heavy cotton twine, 20 feet long and 8 feet high, including necessary ropes, pulleys and frame (electric carpet, extra) $135.00

D729—Electric Tunnel, as **D728** except omitting trestles, in which case tunnel would be suspended from ceiling 95.00

D295—Electric Carpet, 50 inches wide and 20 feet long, for jump spark battery 41.50

D213—Jump Spark Battery and Cord 23.00

TRICK TRAY

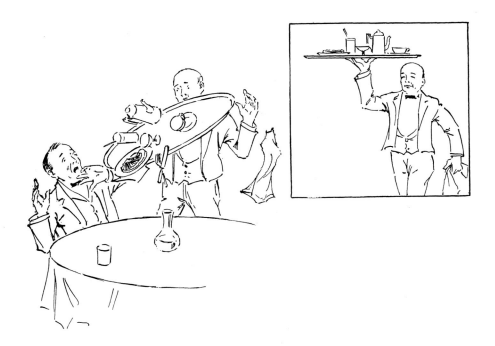

This is an ideal stunt to work at a banquet.

The waiter enters, balancing a large tray of dishes; apparently loses his balance, and everyone feels that sinking sensation in the region of their diaphragms. But the dishes are fastened to the tray and can fall only far enough to make the effect decidedly realistic and startling.

A handle beneath the tray enables the awkward (?) waiter to hold it securely.

D776—Trick Tray, includes tray and tableware usually carried on tray....$ 6.75

"Very Much Pleased"

"We wish to acknowledge the receipt of the goods recently ordered by us. On examination we find the apparatus all that you represent it to be and we are very much pleased with it. Kindly forward your invoice for this material so that we put in line for payment."—Robert Tenbrook, Stockton Pyramid No. 5, A. E. O. S., Stockton, Calif.

"Goods arrived in good condition and we found them very satisfactory and are pleased with them. In the future should we require goods, we shall be glad to place our order with you."—Edwin M. Kesterson, Court Friendship No. 4813, I. O. O. F., Baltimore, Md.

"Paraphernalia received and was used for the first time last evening and proved very satisfactory. Your electric mat surely has some pep."—Russell K. Patterson, Mahatma Sanctorum No. 242, A. M. O. S., Harrisburg, Pa.

SAY IT WITH FLOWERS

The bouquet of flowers cleverly conceals a device which at the proper time acts much like a young geyser.

When the candidates are drinking their beer and favoring the audience by singing "How Dry I Am" there is an explosion—the flowers, including a large quantity of water, blow up, and, like the rain referred to in the Scriptures, falls upon the just and unjust alike. Is automatically discharged by candidate or attendant pushing call button on table, or can be discharged by attendant at a distance.

D730—Say it with Flowers includes folding table, bouquet of imitation flowers and flower vase with automatic arrangement which fires blank cartridge and shoots water in all directions, also 50 blank cartridges $26.00

Extra Blank Cartridges (not mailable), loaded specially for us to give an extra loud report; per box of 50 .... .45

HULU HULA BULL DANCE

A novel stunt that is a whole show in itself can be worked up with this outfit. It consists of tuned cowbells to hang between the legs of the candidates, well up in the crotch, and appropriate costumes. The operator uses a bull prod to "play the bells." Each candidate represents a certain note and dances when prodded by the director thus producing his note. There are ten bells representing ten notes including F sharp and B flat, making it possible to play many simple airs, "How Dry I Am," etc.

D428—Hula Hula Bull Dance, consists of 10 suits of tights in assorted sizes and colors with note fastened on back, 10 imitation grass skirts, 10 cow bells tuned for one complete octave and including F sharp and B flat suspended by strap, also prod with which bull driver directs music from rear; complete $76.00

Can furnish trunks instead of tights on above outfit at a reduction of 22.00

If above outfit without trunks or tights, deduct 36.00

The Human Shimmy Bell Outfits (see illustration above) is somewhat similar but more effective on account of substituting tuned sleigh-bells in place of cowbells. These can be worn around the wrists, waist and ankles if desired, but sufficient music can be produced with the bells just on the wrists. We can elaborate on this outfit, to make the effect more deceiving to the spectators, by including a miniature piano with wires connected from each key to the candidate. These wires are attached to a waist belt which has a small electric light in front. The "musician" at the piano silently plays a familiar air—the lights immediately flash and the candidates respond with a shimmy, thereby producing the "real music." Prices quoted on request.

JEWISH AND SWISS NAVAL BATTLE

All the thrills of a canoe tilting contest right in your hall! The boats run on casters and are liable to go in almost any direction, which makes it no simple matter for the tilters to maintain their equilibrium. The sides of the canoes are low to prevent the participants from falling too hard.

A novel and entertaining race can be staged with the "canoes" piloted by candidates, who will experience some difficulty in controlling their course.

D731—Jewish and Swiss Naval Battle consists of two boats on casters, two fencing poles and two push oars with rubber tips $40.00

TESTIMONIALS

"We want to tell you that we took in a class and knocked them cold with the Pledge Altar. I do not think that you can improve on it."—J. Harry Williams, Valentino St., Bellefonte, Pa.

"I have used several of your items and have found them absolutely as described, and of excellent workmanship, and will not hesitate to recommend them to any Voiture."—C. Warren Reid, Gr. Cor. "Forty and Eight," Tacoma, Washington.

Let us develop your ideas on any novel or distinctive stunts. Write us about them. That's a part of our service as well as to manufacture and supply them economically.

BIG BUSY BERTHA

D772

If the candidate is to be shot at sunrise and the firing squad is otherwise engaged, just bring this B—B—B into action and do a good job of it. This extra large cannon fires a large shell and is a heavy smoke producer. With the cannon we furnish mask, glove and body protector, so that the baseball stunt can be pulled off in good shape. The action is intensified by the use of electric chair.

D772—Cannon, including mask, body protector and glove, also 50 blank cartridges, 4 rubber balls and 1 iron ball $78.50

Extra Blank Cartridges 38-calibre center fire (not mailable), loaded specially for us to give an extra loud report; per box of 50........... 1.25

D722—Electric Trick Chair, same as **D204** listed on page 17, except seat of chair having electric attachment (battery not included) 21.00

They Reached the 1,000 Mark

"Inclosed find check for $125.50 in payment of paraphernalia. We had ONE THOUSAND AT OUR Conclave on the 15th, and everything went fine. Everyone of the stunts we purchased from you went fine, and we received many compliments on the excellent Degree work we put on. To you people we give the credit for making this possible. You will hear from us again next year."—K. K. Stimson, Milford, N. H.

THE DEVIL'S SLIDE

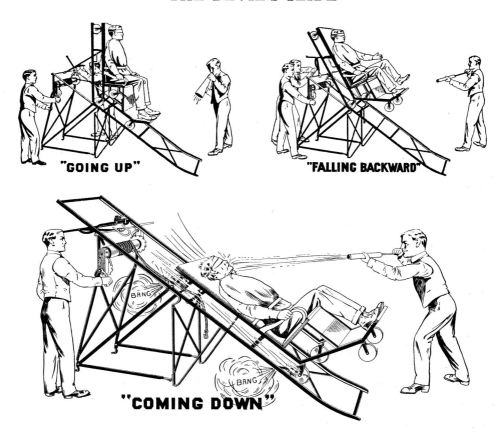

"GOING UP" "FALLING BACKWARD" "COMING DOWN"

Throw her in high! Put on the cut-out! Step on the accelerator! He's off! After having been drawn to what seems a dizzy height, the trigger is released and the candidate starts on his wild joy ride. It doesn't last long, but, take it from us, it's a thriller.

See suggestions for introducing, page V in back of catalog.

The Devil's Slide is substantially constructed, the framework being of steel. All parts are nicely finished and the chair is upholstered. It is quickly put up or taken down and folds compactly, requiring but little space. The chair is securely held in place by a trigger, which can be released at any moment, causing the chair to first fall backward and then precipitately plunge forward down the track. The clattering attachment under the chair gets in its noise-producing work as the chair goes down. When the candidate nears the bottom, the attendant uses the squirt gun with telling effect. The wheels have rubber tires and will run a short distance after reaching the floor.

D258—Devil's Slide, in chest having hinged cover, lock and key and including squirt gun and waterproof apron $155.00

D259—Extra Squirt Gun, for those desiring two 2.00

DeMoulin Bros. & Co., Greenville, Ill.

"UPWARD, ONWARD, DOWNWARD"
or Falling Bridge

D323

Here is where the candidate halts between two opinions. He starts up the incline at a speed rivaling that of a race horse, and in his opinion he has traveled miles, when he finally reaches the top and halts. Though it is only for a moment, he soons realizes that he who hesitates is lost, and that "pride goeth before a fall". Priding himself that he has risen to such a height in the race for worldly honor, his next opinion is that he has stripped a gear. He comes down with a bump that jars his false teeth and he completes the journey on his coat tail.

See suggestions for introducing, page XXII in back of catalog.

D323—"Upward, Onward, Downward," is strongly made of the best seasoned wood. The rollers are turned smooth. The support of platform is a spring-hinged affair that snaps shut, firing a 32-calibre blank cartridge, allowing the platform to drop very suddenly as soon as the candidate steps on it. Great improvements have been made in the construction of the "Onward and Downward," so that it folds up in a compact form, occupying a space 2½x3½x2 feet, and can be opened up for use in less than two minutes. Price, including 50 blank cartridges (weight, packed, 175 pounds) $52.00

THE SLIDE FOR LIFE

Another mighty good stunt—on the order of "Shoot the Chutes" but more interesting. The candidate is free to slide just as he pleases (?) consequently, there is considerable action.

The length and arrangement of slide will depend upon the space available in your hall and for that reason we can not quote price here. Tell us what length slide you can use and we shall submit prices and full particulars. But by all means get a "Slide for Life".

DO YOU WANT SOMETHING SPECIAL?

If you have in mind some piece of paraphernalia not listed in our catalog, do not fail to give us an idea of what you desire. We shall then work up the article, giving you full description and price. This will not obligate you in any way.

ELECTRIC CATCHING BLANKET

Made of strong canvas, size 5 feet by 7 feet; with reinforced hand holds; wired for electricity; may be used with any jump spark battery.

D411—Electric Catching Blanket, each $20.00

THRONE OF HONOR

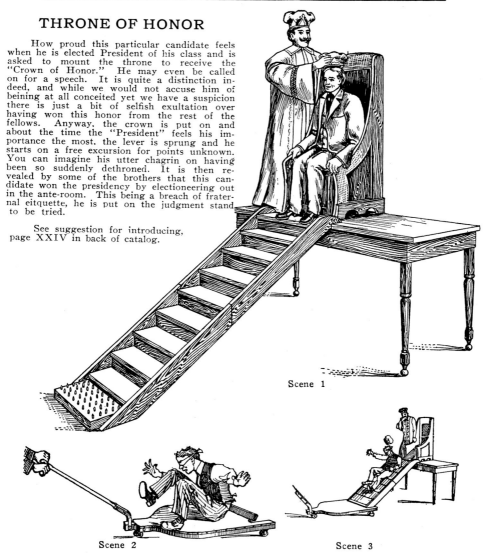

Scene 1

Scene 2

Scene 3

How proud this particular candidate feels when he is elected President of his class and is asked to mount the throne to receive the "Crown of Honor." He may even be called on for a speech. It is quite a distinction indeed, and while we would not accuse him of beining at all conceited yet we have a suspicion there is just a bit of selfish exultation over having won this honor from the rest of the fellows. Anyway, the crown is put on and about the time the "President" feels his importance the most, the lever is sprung and he starts on a free excursion for points unknown. You can imagine his utter chagrin on having been so suddenly dethroned. It is then revealed by some of the brothers that this candidate won the presidency by electioneering out in the ante-room. This being a breach of fraternal eitquette, he is put on the judgment stand to be tried.

See suggestion for introducing, page XXIV in back of catalog.

The Throne of Honor is handsomely constructed. All woodwork has a beautiful furniture finish, and the chair is nicely upholstered. By pushing a single lever the bottom of chair, suddenly drops to an inclined position, the steps adjust themselves to a smooth surface, a blank cartridge explodes with a loud report, an alarm bell rings vigorously and the candidate goes on his journey. Legs of table fold under top and stairs hinge in center, so the entire outfit occupies but little space when not in use. Weight, packed, 350 pounds.

D325—Throne of Honor, complete as described above $95.00
D326—Throne of Honor, same as D325, but without hinges on stairs, and legs of table do not fold 88.50
D327—Wagon on which to receive the candidate and give him a ride "around the world in three minutes," extra 13.00
Rubber Tires on wagon rollers, extra 3.00
D328—Spikey Block, of exact size to fit at the bottom of steps, will make the cold chills run up candidate's back to think about landing on the steel (?) spikes; extra 6.25
Some Lodges prefer both Wagon and Spikey Block, while others prefer only one. The Throne can, however, be used effectively, without either.
Extra Blank Cartridges (not mailable), loaded specially for us to give an extra loud report; per box of 50 .... .45
Electric Attachment for seat of Chair, jump spark battery and cord not included, extra... 2.00
Should either the Spikey Block or Wagon be used, we suggest the use of an Electric Carpet at the bottom of the steps; listed on page 40.

"SLIDING STAIRS OR THE SEVEN AGES"

The Sliding Stairs is one of the "smoothest" among initiation contrivances. The Throne of Honor is, however, superior to it and is recommended above all. The unsuspecting and guileless victim, usually blind-folded, is taken up the ordinary looking steps, under auspicious ceremonies, and as each step is taken he feels more and more dignified, until the top is reached, when he is asked to be seated and rest until ordered to descend. At the proper moment the attendant pulls the trigger and shuffles him off to the regions below. Just as the steps are sprung to a smooth service, a 32-calibre blank cartridge is automatically discharged with a loud report, an alarm bell is set to ringing and the candidate goes on his journey.

See suggestions for introducing under "Judgment Stand," page XXI and "Throne of Honor," page XXIV in back of catalog.

D321—Sliding Stairs, strongly made; fold up like a step-ladder, occupying but a small space; including box of 50 blank cartridges........$28.00

Extra Blank Cartridges (not mailable), loaded specially for us to give an extra loud report; per box of 50 .... .45

We suggest the use of an Electric Carpet at the foot of stairs which will keep the candidate traveling; listed on page 40.

SPIKEY BLOCK

D332

D322—Spikey Block, size 12x24 inches, set with rubber pointed spikes which are finished in aluminum, thereby exactly imitating steel. Made to fit at the bottom of either the Sliding Stairs or Throne of Honor ....$ 6.25

D322½—Spikey Block, same as D322, except set with steel spikes........$ 6.25

TUNNEL OF TROUBLE

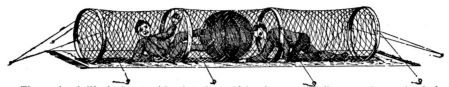

The path of life is beset with obstacles which often spell failure to those who lack the courage to tackle the hard things. It should be explained to the candidates that in going thru this tunnel they will encounter difficulties which can be overcome by perseverance. Because of the gas and smoke in the tunnel their "windows" must be closed, so they are hoodwinked. One starts in at each end and the fun begins. Each candidate thinks the other is, with malice aforethought, trying to prevent his progress. This spurs them on to do their level best to pass the ball, and in their effort to make headway, they tie themselves in a knot and perform other contortion stunts seen only in a circus.

See suggestions for introducing, page XXI in back of catalog.

D329—Tunnel of Trouble, 21 feet long, including ball, guy ropes, hooks, etc. (Weight, packed, 35 pounds) $28.50

Electric Carpet listed on page 40 may be used to advantage.

ELECTRIC SANDALS FOR TUNNEL OF TROUBLE

Two pairs of Electric Sandals will add much to the fun produced by the Tunnel of Trouble. The candidates can be "touched up" with the electric current at any time, but the best time to "turn it loose" is just after one of the candidates has succeeded in passing the ball. If neither can get that far along, just turn the current on as soon as they are about "fagged out" and see if they are too tired to get out alone. They will need no assistance, but will vacate the Tunnel like two frightened rats.

D330—Two pair of Electric Sandals with battery and two 30-foot cords..$23.25
D331—Two pair of Electric Sandals same as D330, but without battery.... 12.00

ROLLER PATHWAY

D332—Roller Pathway, 6 feet long, with plank back and stand on which to rest upper end $19.00
D333—Roller Pathway, 6 feet long, without plank back 17.25
We can make D332 to hinge in center, occupies but little space for storage; extra 1.75
Weight, packed, 95 pounds.

PILLOW FIGHT

This stunt is a reminder of the days when the kid brothers had their usual Sunday morning pillow fight in bed. It is full of fun and action, as it taxes the ability of the candidates to stay on the pole. We suggest that the "Toss-up" be held beneath the fighters. The first one to fall off is "elevated" to the next degree.

See suggestions for introducing, page XXIII in back of catalog.

D361—Pillow Fight Outfit, complete, consisting of round pole four inches in diameter and seven feet long, ropes, eye bolts and two pillows...$ 8.00

For Lodges using "Toss-up" on which to catch candidates, we suggest that "Toss-up" be covered with Electric Carpet listed on page 40.

THE TOSS-UP

When it's a "toss-up" as to which candidate has shown the most courage, this test might be used to decide the matter. It's just like the game of "head you lose, tail I win." The candidate is up in the air most of the time and never knows how he is going to light, whether head up or t'other way. This is a great stunt—perfectly harmless and full of fun.

See suggestions for introducing, page XXIII in back of catalog.

The "Toss-up" is made of extra heavy canvas, reinforced to prevent tearing. On the ends and at the sides are a sufficient number of handles for the attendants. We GUARANTEE THESE NOT TO RIP OR TEAR, provided the attendants use the handles in tossing.

D362—"Toss up," size 9½x 9½ feet $18.25
D363—"Toss up," size 11½x11½ feet 26.00

PILLORY

D438

If the candidate has never been in a tight place or in a pinch, he will appreciate (?) this stunt. To be put in a position where he is absolutely helpless is no laughing matter. 'Tis true the gang's all here, but he questions whether they are yet disposed to treat him as one of them and show him any special consideration. That his fears are well-founded is proved when the "Professor" comes forward with his large steel-bladed knives to demonstrate his ability as a knife thrower. The tension of the candidate's nerves reaches the snapping point when he is hoodwinked. He is soon convinced of the Professor's ability and the only consolation he gets is in his knowledge that a miss is good as a mile. There is no danger whatever, as the knives are not actually thrown but are struck against the pillory and at the same time a special knife in a slot is caused to vibrate. The effect produced is very realistic.

See suggestions for introducing, page XXIV in back of catalog.

The Pillory is substantial and is arranged so the head and hands are securely fastened with the least effort possible. It folds into a small space and can be prepared for use in a moment.

D438—Pillory, including 7 large steel bladed knives, boxed $26.50

D440

LYCOPODIUM FLASH TORCHES

D439—Flash Torch, of tin, with stick ......$ 2.25

D440—Lycopodium Flash Torch, so constructed that a flame six to eight feet high can be produced by blowing through the rubber tube which is attached to the torch and is ten feet long; perfectly safe. (See illustration)   5.75

D441—Lycopodium Powder, one-half pound in tin box; per box 1.25

THE BUCKING COUCH

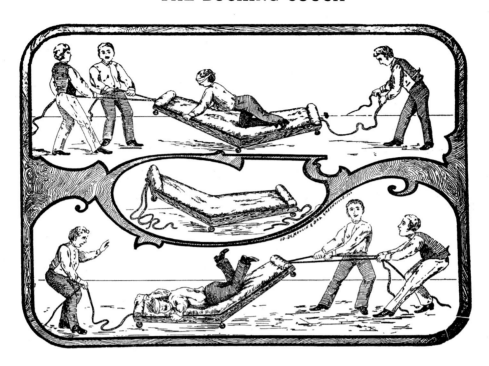

This stunt tests the candidate's ability to hold on to a good thing. He finds it about as difficult to stay on top of this couch as to keep the pledge. This is one of the funniest stunts you ever saw; in fact, it will make a lodge skeleton laugh to see the candidate struggling for a comfortable position. The attendants can give him a good sample of a railroad wreck by manipulating the ropes.

See suggestions for introducing, page XXVII in back of catalog.

D472—The Bucking Couch has a hollow back and folds up like a jack-knife; packs in a space about 16x24x48 inches; has rollers underneath so arranged that there cannot be more than three on the floor at one time; well upholstered and padded; including ropes and boxing (weight, packed, 100 pounds) $38.00
Rubber tires on rollers, extra 3.25

TESTIMONIALS

"We wish to thank you for your very prompt and excellent service which we greatly appreciate. We feel more than pleased with the blanket."—Carl A. Ramsey, Mizpah Temple, Shrine, Fort Wayne, Ind.

"Enclosed please find check covering purchase of one electric pad complete and two spanking shovels. The paraphernalia has been entirely satisfactory to date and as we have your catalog we will call on you in the future if we have need for any additional electrical supplies."—L. L. Garner, Doherty Men's Fraterity, Empire Chapter No. 17, Bartlesville, Okla.

PIE TABLE

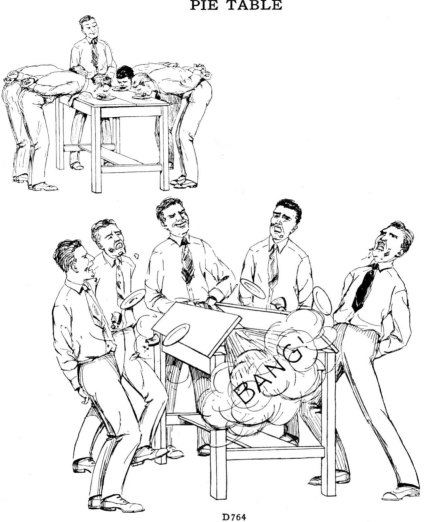

D764

Here is an exciting contest with a more exciting climax. Everybody likes pie and the opportunity to partake of his favorite kind will induce any candidate to enter into this contest with vim and a determination to win. But right in the midst of the contest the unexpected happens and the candidates get a scare that will surely make them lose their appetite for pie. There is a big explosion; the table seems to have blown up; the pies jump right up into the faces of the candidates. This stunt is a corker with the cork removed.

D764—Pie Table, with full instructions for operating $32.00

Extra Blank Cartridges (not mailable), loaded specially for us to give an
    extra loud report; per box of 50 .... .45

ICE CREAM TABLE

D420

This is a day of automatic contrivances. We press the button and machinery does the rest. In this stunt it is not a button which is pressed, but results are obtained just the same, and, after all, it is results that count. The candidates are lined up at this table for refreshments and the service they get beats that of any soft drink parlor. Imagine the surprise of each candidate when a young geyser suddenly shoots up out of his goblet, scattering the contents profusely over his face. He is convinced that the fountain is highly charged with extract of effervescence.

D420—Ice Cream Table, consisting of collapsible table, including neat containers, tubing and bulbs $32.00

HOW TO INTEREST THE CANDIDATES WHILE IN WAITING

To keep things lively and interesting among the waiting candidates and during recess we recommend the Electric Cane or Prod Pole (page 56), Wooden Shoes (page 54), Glad Hand (page 67), Cigar Box (page 74), and Hornet's Nest (page 70), all of which can be effectively used with the Portable Jump Spark Battery listed on page 47. Rubber Bells listed on page 112 also can be made very entertaining.

THE BLARNEY STONE

D466

No matter how much "blarney" the candidate has had imparted to him, he will not hesitate for a moment when commanded to kiss the Blarney Stone. He recalls that this stone is said to give to those who kiss it a cajoling tongue and he thinks he might be able to cajole the brothers into giving him a place of honor in the lodge.

It is indeed very comical and interesting to note candidate's awkward motions and peculiar method of attempting to kiss the stone, but best of all is to perceive his surprise and "take back" when an artesian well spurts forth into his mouth. He will think there is some mythological power connected with this stone.

As a climax to the candidate's touch of the stone, a touch at his other end is not out of order. Attendant should be ready with a hand spanker to deliver the "touch" just as the candidate kisses the stone.

As a closing scene of this event, a negro dame rushes up and embraces and kisses the candidate just as he arises from his dignified position. This part should be taken by one of the members dressed as a negro woman, with face blackened. She leaves some of her color on the candidate's face, much to the amusement of those present.

See suggestions for introducing, page XXVI in back of catalog.

The Blarney Stone is provided with a long rubber tubing and bulb which should be concealed under a rug or by some other similar means.

D466—Blarney Stone, an exact imitation; not heavy; size about 8x8x2½ inches .... $ 5.75

BLEEDING TEST

Here is where the candidate is the principal character in a "Merchant of Venice" scene. To him this is the very limit. He did not seriously object to a little rough treatment and some bruises, but when it comes to shedding blood —well, that's where he balks. Even though the lodge exacts a pound of flesh from each candidate, had not the presiding officer decreed that it must be taken without the shedding of a drop of blood? This stunt is a sure enough deception.

See suggestions for introducing, page XXVI in back of catalog.

The Bleeding Outfit consists of an electrical probe and magneto battery, a receptacle ingeniously arranged to produce the effect of blood trickling out of the wound, and a tin pan in which the "blood" drops. Full directions for using accompany each outfit.

D467—Bleeding Test Outfit, complete $16.25
D468—Bleeding Test Outfit, without magneto and cord 5.00

SAW MILL

While the candidate is willing to acknowledge some similarity to a tree (since he has a trunk and two limbs), yet he will set up a howl when it comes to being bound to the sliding carriage like a log and slowly drawn into the circular (imitation) saw running at full speed. Unless a person has gone through this experience, it is impossible to stretch the imagination enough to fully sympathise with the candidate. The situation looks so perilous to him that he wouldn't give two cents for his chances to survive the test. However, to his great surprise and joy, the carriage stops when the saw has run about two inches into the platform in front of his head. This machine looks real and very dangerous but it is absolutely harmless.

See suggestions for introducing, page XXVIII in back of catalog.

D476—Saw Mill is both strong and durable. It folds up into a small space, but is 15 feet long, 27 inches wide and 23 inches high when opened ready for use. Price, including curtain to seclude the operator from the view of candidate; packed in chest having hinged cover, lock and key (shipping weight 180 pounds) $52.00

ELECTRIC SAW AND BUCK

It's a safe bet that the candidate will not go to sleep on this job. He never saw such a saw before. Thinks he, it must have a very peculiar set.

There is no cord attached to saw, or anything visible that will cause the candidate to suspect any trick. He is content to believe that he will simply sweat a little over the laborious task of sawing wood. But when he attemps to finish sawing the stick in two, he will think that he has become a "live wire" in the Lodge right on the jump. The operator can inspire the candidate to quicker action with the saw by injecting more "pep" into his movements either on the installment plan or C. O. D. Two or more of these outfits can be used by putting on a wood-sawing contest. A contest with this or any of the other stunts in our catalogue always produce worlds of fun.

See suggestions for introducing, page XXVII in back of catalog.

D477—Electric Saw and Buck, including saw-buck, saw, stick of wood, magneto and cord $22.75

D478—Electric Saw and Buck, without magneto and cord 11.50

ALL BALLED UP

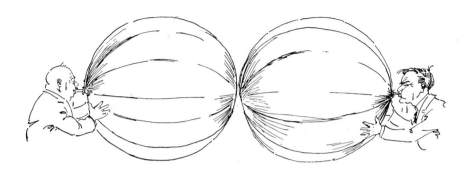

We want you to get "All Balled Up" for your next initiation, because we know this feature will take well. It results in more real honest-to-goodness sport than you can imagine.

Sometimes while the crowd is gathering and prior to beginning of the stunt work, the fellows get a little restless and anxious for the fun to start. That's a good time to spring this "All Balled Up" stunt.

To start the ball rolling, we quote:

No. 1RB—Big Rubber Ball, to be inflated (by "man power" if necessary) to 28 inches in diameter, weighs only 1¾ pounds; price, each $10.00

No. 3CRB—Big Rubber Ball, to be inflated to 28 inches in diameter, covered with soft finish duck in any color or any combination of colors; price, each 20.00

No. 3CRB can be furnished with any emblem and lettering on cover at a nominal extra charge. Price will be quoted on receipt of information as to what is wanted.

Try your local merchants on this stunt for advertisements. Any lettering can be stenciled in bright colors on the cover.

Turn one of these balls loose in the crowd and watch the fun. We promise you there will be no dull moments. Really, men, this is a mighty fine stunt.

Another good stunt is a "blowing up" contest. Give one of these rubber balls to each of two or more candidates to see who can inflate the ball first. Let the members take sides and root for their favorite "Air Station." Good chance to find out which candidate is the biggest "blow." This contest is a scream.

DECEPTIVE GLASSES

D490

See suggestions for introducing, page XXVIII in back of catalog.

D488—Deceptive Beer Glasses, filled with composition representing beer; per pair .... $ 1.15

D489—Deceptive Wine Glasses, large size and extra strong, filled with red wine-colored non-freezing solution; per pair 1.25

D490—Deceptive Outfit, consisting of one pair **D488** beer glasses, one pint bottle labeled and partially filled with composition, one corkscrew and one tray. The best and most complete Deceptive Outfit ever introduced; will deceive the keenest observer; complete outfit as described 2.50

D491—Deceptive Outfit, same as **D490**, representing wine instead of beer. 2.60

Deceptive Glasses Not Mailable

WIND MACHINE

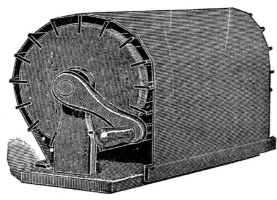

D492, D493

D492—Wind Machine, produces very realistic moaning of the wind, from a light wind to fierce gale; indispensable for producing the sound of wind .... $ 5.00

D493—Wind Machine, extra large, better effect; each. 7.50

DeMoulin Bros. & Co., Greenville, Ill.

D482

THE RICKETY RACKETY

A Cross Between a Boiler Shop and a Gatling Gun

The Rickety-Rackety is an enormous watchman's rattle; warranted to rattle the weary candidate as he is ushered into its presence. It will make him imagine that he is going to be fed right into a threshing machine or is entering the realms of purgatory especially if the pandemonium is accompanied with the savage yells of those who are conferring the degree. The din caused by this noise producer is deafening, and the shrieking hilarity that is one of its possibilities makes it exceedingly popular.

D482—The Rickety-Rackety is intended for what its name implies, viz., noise, and lots of it. It is simple to manipulate, very strongly made of best seasoned wood and neatly finished. (Weight, packed, 45 lbs.) $10.75

THE "ROOTER"

If you want noise—genuine noise—real noisy noise—get a dozen Rooters. The best noise producers made. Just the thing for initiations, picnics, parades, celebrations, etc.

D483—Rooter, size 2¼x2½ inches, made of heavy tin; each $0.15; per doz. $1.60
Special Prices on Gross Lots
Rooters may be sent by mail, but we cannot state exact amount as this depends upon the parcel post "zone." Make sufficient allowance and any surplus will be refunded with invoice.

TELEGRAPH CALL AND WHISTLE

D484—Telegraph Call, very small, to be carried in hand; makes sharp, clear click $0.15
D485—Chime Whistle, nickel plated, with chain .... .30

RATTLES

D486—Rattle, medium size $1.50
D487—Rattle, large size 1.75

NOISE MAKERS

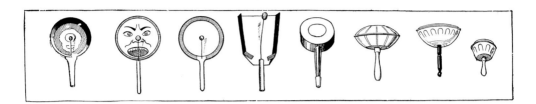

1248—**Frying Pan Rattle.** A small frying pan lithographed to simulate a fried egg, with rattle on both sides, each $0.12½

1252—**Clown Rattle.** A brightly lithographed noise maker which contains a clown's face and rattle on both sides, each .... .11

1256—**Pan Rattle.** An imitation of a small frying pan with a rattle on both sides, each.... .08½

1260—**Shovel Rattle.** A shovel which contains a rattle on both sides, each .... .11

1264—**Drum Horn.** A combination of a very loud horn and drum rattle in bright colors, each .... .11

1268—**Jumbo Metal Rattle.** A loud and attractive metal noise-maker, each .... .11

1272—**Cymbell.** A brightly lithographed metal bell, each .... .12½

1276—**Metal Rattle.** Same as Jumbo Rattle, but smaller in size, each .... .07

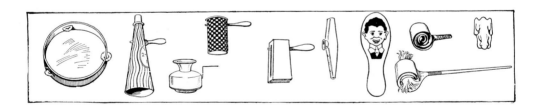

1280—**Tambourine.** A metal tambourine 6½ inches in diameter, each $0.15

1284—**Rattle Horn.** A combination of a twirling rattle and horn lithographed in attractive colors, each .... .11

1288—**Rooter.** The well-known metal noisemaker especially recommended where "real" noise is desired, each .... .15

1292—**Revolving Rattle.** An all-metal twirling rattle lithographed in attractive colors. A very loud noisemaker, each .... .11

1296—**Twirly-Click.** Another beautifully decorated revolving rattle. Very noisy, each .... .08

1300—**Kazoo.** This is the well-known Kazoo horn. It intensifies songs or music hummed into it, each .... .06

1304—**Clapper.** A clapper which contains a head on each side embossed in very attractive colors. Besides being a serviceable noisemaker it makes a very attractive table decoration, each .... .06

1308—**Blowout.** Large size snake blowout which extends about 20 inches, each .... .05

1312—**Blowout.** Small size snake blowout which extends about 11 inches, each .... .04

1316—**Frog Snapper.** A metal snapper in the shape of a frog finished in an assortment of colors. Makes a very loud noise, each .... .02

NOISE MAKERS

D41L

D57L

D41L—Genuine Chinese Tom-Tom, two pigskin heads, about 9½ inches in diameter, handsomely decorated in fancy colored dragons, etc..$ 3.80
D42L—Chinese Wood Drum or Clog Block, small size; each .... .90
D43L—Chinese Wood Drum or Clog Block, medium size; each 1.40
D44L—Chinese Wood Drum or Clog Block, large size, each 2.30
D57L—Chinese Musette, wood with spun brass bell and brass mouthpiece; length 17½ inches; very loud, fine for oriental effects 1.40
D47L—Extra Chinese Musette Reeds, each .... .05

RAIN SPRAY

D473—Rain Spray, consisting of receptacle for water, spray nozzle and rubber bulb; pressure of air in receptacle makes spray continuous; more effective han ordinary storm spray ....$ 2.75

RAIN BOX

To Produce Noise to Imitate Rain

D474—Rain Box, octagon pattern, frame well made and stayed, very satisfactory for the purpose ....$ 2.25

THUNDER SHEET

D475—Improved Thunder Sheet, size 26x34 inches; very satisfactory ......$ 2.25

LION'S ROAR

D477—Lion's Roar, a specially constructed outfit, very powerful, most realistic lion imitation ever invented; every club should have one or more; price, each ....$ 3.75

IMPROVED SONG-O-PHONES
Unequaled for Burlesque Work

These instruments are the source of much amusement. As a rule the players are termed "Little Dutch Band," and it is their duty to escort the candidate into the Lodge or to entertain the members with solos, quartettes, etc. Also very appropriate for "between-the-acts" stunts.

They can be played by anyone with only a few minutes' practice, as the tune is simply hummed (do not blow) into them.

No. 101—Cornet Song-o-Phone, 12 inches long, 4 plunger keys, made of metal, brass plated and highly polished $3.00
No. 102—Slide Trombone Song-o-Phone, 16½ inches long, 5½ inch bell; slide 33 inches open, 26 inches closed; made of metal, brass plated and polished 5.00
No. 103—Base Horn Song-o-Phone, 16 inches long, 6 inch bell; made of metal, brass plated and polished 4.00
No. 33—Clarinet, 15½ inches long, 3⅝ inch bell, made of metal, black body, nickel plated mouthpiece 2.00
No. 104—Saxophone Song-o-Phone, 23½ inches long, 5½ inch bell, 9 keys; made of metal, brass plated and highly polished 7.00
Repair package, each .... .06
D594—Wiener Wurst, good imitation; per string of seven links .... .85

BAND UNIFORMS FOR BURLESQUE BANDS

Uniforms made of heavy cotton goods, trimmed with braid in various styles, very suitable for Burlesque Bands.
D591—Coat and Cap (Cap only, $0.35) $3.70
D592—Trousers, per pair 2.10
D593—Uniform, complete 5.80
Grease Paints, Masks, Beards, Wigs, etc., see page 114.

TABLE COVER

D496—Individual Table Cloths, size 42x56 in., solid white, extra heavy crepe paper (each cover is folded and sealed in glasine envelope); per box of 24 ....$ 2.25

CREPE RIBBON

Crepe Ribbon, 2¼ inches wide, very fine strong paper, rich and elegant appearance; 480 feet to the box.
D497—Blue, per box $0.90
D498—White, per box .... .90
D499—Red, per box .... .90
(We can also furnish Crepe Ribbon in thirty other single colors and shades.)

D500—Red, White and Blue Tri-Color Crepe Ribbon, 480 feet to the box; per box ....$ 1.00
D501—Green and White Combination, 420 feet to the box; per box....... 1.00

We can also supply **D500-D501** Crepe Ribbon in the following color combinations: Purple and white, orange and black; red and green, also red, white and green.

BANQUET PLATES

D502—Banquet Plates, fluted wood, full 9 inches diameter; packed in cartons of 50 plates; per carton ....$ 0.90

MOSS PAPER FOR DECORATING

This paper is inexpensive, yet tasty and beautiful. Very desirable for decorating—presents a most brilliant and satisfactory effect. Easily made into devices, monograms, society mottoes, letters, figures, etc. Furnished in tricolors—red, white and blue or other combinations.
D503—Moss Paper, per roll of 30 feet ....$ 0.30
Per bundle of 100 rolls 24.00

WREATHS

D504—Wreaths of tissue paper, 12 inches in diameter; red, white and blue, or other combinations; per dozen ....$ 1.50

PLUMES

D505—Plumes of tissue paper, for horse's head; red, white and blue, or other combinations; per dozen ....$ 1.50

We also have Moss Paper, Wreaths and Plumes in proper colors for other Orders

CAMP FIRES

D518—Camp Fire, terra cotta, a perfect imitation of burning logs; both sides alike and finished; can be used only where gas is available; including brass connections ....$ 7.50

D519—Camp Fire, of fire-proof composition (a good imitation of burning logs), made with receptacle for alcohol; is convenient and economical and can be used in any hall; more effective than D518 on account of flames enveloping log 3.50

D520—Camp Fire, natural wood with metal receptacle for alcohol; lined with a red cloth; will answer the purpose where Lodge can not afford D519 .... 2.00

A candle or electric bulb may be used with D519 and D520 Camp Fires, but nothing except gas or wood alcohol will produce the appearance of a real camp fire.

WOOD ALCOHOL

Wood Alcohol, in tin screw-top can; per pint, $0.35; per quart ....$ 0.60

RUBBER TUBING

D494—Rubber Tubing to connect D518 Camp Fire to gas jet; per foot..$ 0.20

TRIPODS

D521—Tripod, hard wood varnished poles fastened at intersection; strong hook to hold kettle ....$ 1.75

D522—Tripod, hard wood polished and varnished poles with gilt metal tips; fastened at intersections, strong hook to hold kettle 2.25

KETTLE

D523—Kettle of iron, large size..$ 1.75

NAPKINS

D1311

Just the thing for banquets, socials, etc.; a very pleasing souvenir.

D1311—Napkins of best quality No. 1 pure white, soft absorbent crepe tissue, with emblem printed in authentic colors. The inks used are guaranteed fast colors and positively will not soil the face or clothing; per hundred, postpaid ....$ 0.75

Name, number and location of Lodge printed on Napkins, extra per hundred, $1.65; per 200, $2.35; per 500 .... 4.35

Sold only in packages of one hundred. Send for sample.

We also have other designs in stock as follows: I. O. O. F. Subordinate, Order Eastern Star, Masonic, Knights of Pythias, B. P. O. Elks, Fraternal Order of Eagles, Modern Woodmen of America, Woodmen of the World, Mystic Shrine, American Flag.

LETTER FILE

D507—Letter File, size 3x12x12 inches; wooden back, ends and front; heavy strawboard sides; the entire file neatly covered; each sheet of index is reinforced at the fastening; net weight, 25 ounces $0.85

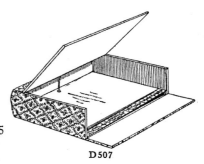

DATER

D508—U. S. Line Dater, illustration full size; postpaid $0.50

RUBBER STAMP

D509—Cushion Rubber Stamp, one line, any name; postpaid $0.60

D510—Cushion Rubber Stamp, two lines, such as name, post office and state; postpaid.... .90

Prices of special rubber stamps on request. State wording desired.

INK PAD

D511—Ink Pad, for either of above; postpaid.... $0.25

REVOLVER

D512—Revolver, 32-calibre rim-fire, double action, nickel plated $6.25

CARTRIDGES

D513—Blank Cartridges (not mailable), loaded specially for us to give an extra loud report; per box of 50 .... $0.45

D514—Blank Cartridges, 32-calibre central-fire; per box of 50 .... .90

D515—Blank Cartridges, 38-calibre central-fire; per box of 50 .... 1.25

All of our articles having cartridge attachment are made for 32-calibre rim-fire blank cartridges, except Cannon, which is made for 38-calibre central-fire.

DeMoulin Bros. & Co., Greenville, Ill.

AN EMBLEMATIC KNIFE WORTH HAVING

D526—Emblematic Knife, size of illustration; of very best material and workmanship; beneath the handles, which are almost indestructible, we place the emblem of your Order or Orders and your name; blades are razor steel, carefully forged, hardened and tempered, ground flat on the stone by hand so that when they require sharpening it is a matter of only a few strokes on an oil stone; warranted free from defect and perfect in temper, and should a blade break through a flaw or prove otherwise defective within six months, it will be replaced free of charge; price, including leather purse, postpaid $1.50

BURLESQUE RITUALS, PLAYS AND DRILLS

A MOCK TRIAL, the best play out; adapted to suit requirements of fraternal societies; illustrates a suit for breach of promise—Miss Fewclothes vs. Mr. Stringbeans—and produces one continuous round of laughter. It is so arranged that parts need not be memorized; four copies, $3.00; six copies, postpaid $4.00
KNIGHTS OF THE ZOROASTERS, a fine play, intended for public entertainments and social amusements; three degrees; six pamphlets with right of representation; postpaid 3.00
INITIATION OF A CANDIDATE, a fine play written purposely to create amusement at anniversaries of secret societies and social gatherings; six pamphlets with right of representation; postpaid 3.00
HINDU MAGIC, a book containing the most popular Hindu Tricks, with their complete exposition; postpaid .... .50
We furnish all kinds of burlesque costumes for producing these plays.
IDEAL DRILLS, an entirely new and original collection; with fullest descriptions and nearly 100 diagrams showing the different movements; arranged especially for stage use, but may be utilized for team work; paper binding, $0.50; cloth binding 1.10
Postage extra.
THE STANDARD DRILL AND MARCHING BOOK, including simple directions for training classes in Military Marching, the Military Manual of Arms, Dumb-Bell drill and exercises, Wand Drill, farm and home fancy drills, holiday drills and marches, and a new adaptation of National singing games complete with music, fully illustrated with diagrams, neat pattern binding, price postpaid .... .50

300 STUNTS

For Fraternities, Clubs, Parties, Banquets, Luncheons, Etc.
10,000 Copies Went Like Hot Cakes Last Year

Published in three volumes, each containing 100 OR MORE stunts, plans, speeches, ideas for every occasion. Guaranteed pep producers. Tested and proved. Just the books your entertainment committee needs to put on meetings and parties that the whole crowd will talk about for weeks. No paraphernalia required.

One stunt is worth the price of the book if it breaks the ice, gets a laugh, insures the success of your events, and here you get a whole fist-full of clever stunts for only $1.00. Order these books with the understanding that you may return them if not satisfactory.

ENTIRELY DIFFERENT STUNTS IN EACH BOOK

D704—Jack's Stunt Book, Vol. I; postpaid $1.00
D705—Jack's Stunt Book, Vol. II; postpaid 1.00
D706—Jack's Stunt Book, Vol. III; postpaid 1.00

PARLIAMENTARY RULES
Stiff Cover, Full Cloth Bound

No presiding officer should be without one or more of these books. The information they contain is absolutely essential for proper conducting of business meetings.
D707—Roberts' Rules of Order, revised edition, half leather bound; postpaid $1.50
D708—Cushing's Manual of Parliamentary Practice, revised edition; postpaid 1.00
D709—Smith's Diagram and Manual of Parliamentary Rules; postpaid 1.25

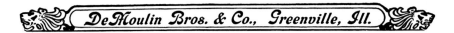

HOODWINKS
DeMOULIN'S PATENT HOODWINK

D90

D90—DeMoulin's Patent Hoodwink, superior to all others. No other hoodwink has three changes—light, darkness and tableau—produced without removing it from face; no other has such light, positive action—action so light that wearer does not feel the pressure subsequent to change of discs—so perfect that discs raise and lower with a click and never move from their desired position; no other has such simple, substantial mechanism—no springs, eyelets or buckles, and quickly put on or removed; no other has push-buttons which by their position and color, clearly indicate which discs are down. Part close to face is of kid leather, nicely lined $2.75

D91—Hoodwink, same in every respect as our **D90**, but without tableau slides. While we do not recommend this one in preference to **D90**, since it does not admit of so many changes, yet we do say that it is far superior to any single shutter hoodwink made $2.35

Postage on above Hoodwinks is five to twelve cents each, depending on the parcel post "zone." Postage must be included when Hoodwink is to be sent by mail.

CLOTH HOODWINKS

D92-D93

D94

D92—Hoodwink, stiff cloth pressed into shape of face, with tape ties......$0.12

D93—Hoodwink, stiff cloth pressed into shape of face and covered with velvet, tape ties .... .35

D94—Hoodwink of velvet, shaped to fit the eyes, tape ties .... .35

MASKS

D529

D531

D528—Mask, stiff cloth pressed into shape of face, tape tie strings, without curtain; per dozen .... $ 0.75

D529—Mask, stiff cloth pressed into shape of face, with curtain, tape tie strings; per dozen .... .90

D530—Mask, half face, made of wire, hand painted, very desirable for hot weather, tape tie strings; per dozen 4.25

D531—Mask, full face, made of wire, hand painted, with a mustache; tape tie strings; very desirable for hot weather; per dozen 4.25

RED FIRE TORCHES
(Not Mailable)

D588—Red Fire Torches, extra brilliant; burn about ten minutes; a very fine article for parade purposes; per dozen .... $ 5.75

D589—Red Fire Torches, especially made for us, and guaranteed to give entire satisfaction; per dozen 1.45

RED FIRE CONES
(Not Mailable)

D583—Red Fire Cones, small size, 24 cones in box; per box .... $ 0.60
D584—Red Fire Cones, large size, 12 cones in box, very brilliant; per box.. .60
D585—Red Fire Cones, very large size, 6 cones in box, exceptionally brilliant; per box .... .60

COLORED FIRE
(Not Mailable)

D586—Colored Fire Powder, red, white, green or blue, ¼ pound, put up in tin box; per box .... $ 0.30

RECEPTACLE FOR CONES AND COLORED FIRE

D587—Metal Receptacle in which to burn red fire cones or colored fire; a very desirable article, since carpet or floor is often ruined by intense heat where receptacle is not used .... $ 0.60

LIGHTNING TRANSPARENCY

D532—Lightning Transparency, to represent flashes of lightning, size 9x9 feet, mounted on roller and slat and arranged to roll like an opera curtain by simply pulling a cord; including screw eyes for hanging. To be used with Lycopodium Flash Torch $10.25

D533—Frame on which to hang above Transparency during the work, easily and quickly adjusted; not necessary, but very handy 5.60

BALLOT BOXES

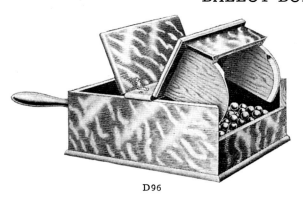

D96

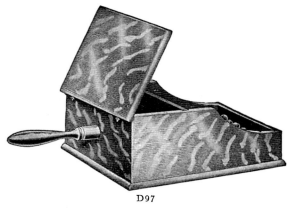

D97

D95—Secret Ballot Box, large size, to hold properly 250 ballots; genuine walnut; spring partition with lip; felt lined bottom; gilt hinges; handle has threaded shank, making fit secure and requiring less shipping space $4.50

D96—Secret Ballot Box, same as D95, but smaller, to hold properly about 175 ballots 3.35

D97—Semi-secret Ballot Box, to hold properly about 150 ballots; imitation walnut or golden oak; sliding partition with lip; handle has a threaded shank, making fit secure and requiring less shipping space 1.55

BALLOTS

D98—White Rubber Balls, per hundred $1.50
D99—Black Rubber Cubes, which sound the same as the round balls when dropped in the box; per hundred 1.50
D100—Porcelain Balls, large and fine, white or black; per hundred.... 1.50
D103—Black Composition Cubes, 7/16-inch diameter, very fine; per hundred 1.50
D105—China Balls; white or black; per hundred ... .50

THE IDEAL BALLOT BOX
Showing Interior with Drawer Open

D104—Ballot Box, absolutely secret; large size; highly polished solid walnut; frosted glass top permitting light to enter the upper ballot chamber so no error in balloting is possible; a ballot can not get into the drawer without being cast; padded upper ballot chamber, drawer and under surface of ballot box; neat, light, simple and perfect in construction $8.00

Any of our ballots can be used with this ballot box.

There is satisfaction in knowing that you have the best.

D104

SEALS

D148

D145—Seal, lion head pattern, rich oxidized copper finish; name, number and location of Lodge engraved on 2-inch die .... $ 7.75

D146—Seal, with name, number and location of Lodge engraved on die, which is 2 inches in diameter 7.25

D147—Plain Seal, with name, number and location of Lodge engraved on 1¾-inch die 5.00

D148—Aluminum Pocket Seal, improved patent latch lock; name, number, location and date of institution engraved on 1⅝-inch die; weight, 10 ounces; the lightest and most substantial pocket seal made; just the right size to carry in pocket 7.00

When ordering Seal, give name, number and location of Lodge VERY PLAINLY WRITTEN.

Seals with emblems, extra, according to design.

CASES

For Books, Papers, Etc.

D149—Case, size 13½x9¼x6 inches, very heavy tin, rich maroon enamel and gilt finish, sunken handle, combination lock ..$6.75

D150—Case, size 11⅞x7½x5½ inches, heavy tin, nicely finished in black japan and gold stripes; good strong hinges and carrying handle, lock and two keys 2.00

D150

Lettering on lid of either of above Cases—name, number and location—nicely executed by hand in oil color and high-lighted in contrasting color $1.50

GAVELS

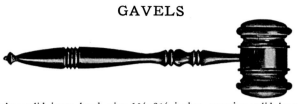

D163—Gavel, genuine solid ivory head, size 1⅝x2¾ inches, genuine solid ivory handle.... $20.25
D164—Gavel, genuine solid ivory head, size 1½x2½ inches, genuine solid ivory handle... 16.65
D165—Gavel, genuine solid ivory head, size 1⅝x2¾ inches, genuine ebony handle 14.60
D166—Gavel, genuine solid ivory head, size 1½x2½ inches, genuine ebony handle 12.15
D167—Gavel, genuine ebony, extra fine, highly polished 2.10
D168—Gavel, genuine rosewood, extra fine, highly polished 1.50
D169—Gavel, genuine walnut, varnished and polished .... .75
D170—Gavel, hardwood, varnished .... .50
    Gold plated band around head of any gavel, extra 4.40
    Silver plated band, extra 3.25
    Engraved lettering on band, extra per letter .... .10

GAVEL BLOCK AND CASE

D171—Gavel block, marble, size 5x8x2 inches; beveled edges; protected bottom .... $ 2.90
D172—Gavel Block, walnut or cherry, varnished and polished, protected bottom .... .90
D173—Gavel Case, covered with black seal grain leatherette, puffed satin lining, nickel
    trimmings; for one gavel 3.15

SPEARS

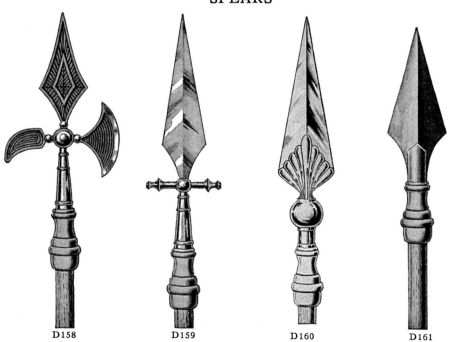

D158   D159   D160   D161

D158—Six-foot Staff, with fancy turned tip; varnished or enameled; 10-inch fancy nickel
    solid metal battle axe $3.25
D159—Six-foot Staff, with fancy turned tip; varnished or enameled; 12-inch fancy nickel
    solid metal spear head 3.25
D160—Six-foot Staff, with fancy turned tip; varnished or enameled; 12-inch fancy nickel
    metal spear head 1.15
D161—Six-foot Staff, varnished or enameled; ornamental wooden spear head; painted and
    bronzed .... .70

DeMoulin Bros. & Co., Greenville, Ill.

NOVELTIES

TRICK CIGAR BOX AND SNAKE JAR

"AH! THANK YOU."   "OH!!"??☇❋!!!
D551

The Trick Cigar Box is covered with imitation genuine black leather and when opened for the purpose of taking a cigar, a large cap is exploded. It never fails to work and always gets a laugh. We do not furnish the caps because it would necessitate unnecessary express charges. The caps, however, can be purchased from a local source.

D551—Trick Cigar Box, sent postpaid $1.00

Supposing you were to open a jar of jam and a thirty-inch snake would jump out and leap fifteen feet into the air; you'd receive the surprise of your life, wouldn't you?

This is exactly what happens when you spring our "jam" joke on your friends. The imitation of the supposed contents of the jar is so perfect and looks so real that they cannot be told from the genuine.

D14—Jam Jar (30-inch snake), each complete $0.50

D14

MASQUERADE GOODS

These may be sent by mail, but we cannot state exact amount, as this depends upon the parcel post "zone". Make sufficient allowance and any surplus will be refunded with invoice.

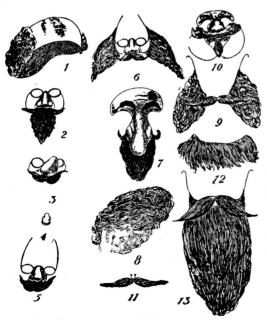

		Each
1.	Baldheaded wig	35c
2.	Nose, specs, mustache, goatee; glazed	10c
3.	Nose with specs and mustache	10c
4.	Nose, gauze, waxed	10c
5.	Nose, specs and mustache	10c
6.	Nose with specs and English beard	15c
7.	Nose, extra long with forehead	20c
8.	Men's wig	35c
9.	English beard	15c
10.	Nose, movable jaw, fancy mustache, goatee	15c
11.	Mustache	5c
12.	Irish chin whiskers	10c
13.	Large full beard	15c
14.	Ears of waxed gauze, very large, pair	50c

MASKS WITH HEADDRESSES

D527—Comic masks with papier mache or cloth headdresses. Indian, Uncle Josh, Negro, Old Woman, Uncle Sam, Irishman, Policeman, Dutchman, Clown, Witch, Alphonse Gaston, Leon, Gloomy Gus, Panhandle Pete, etc., etc., each $1.00

THEATRICAL HAIR GOODS

While not the finest theatrical grade, yet they are much superior to masquerade grade, and are made of real hair. Order these if you want something substantial and fine appearing.

(Colors: Black, brown, red or gray. Specify color when ordering.)

These may be sent by mail, but we cannot state exact amount as this depends upon the parcel post "zone." Make sufficient allowance and any surplus will be refunded with invoice.

	Each
D535—Wig, short hair	$1.50
D536—Wig, bald, hair at back	1.50
D537—Mutton Chops on gauze	1.10
D538—Chin Beard on gauze, fine hair	1.10
D539—Outlaw or Tramp Beard, Side Burns and Mustache, movable chin	1.25
D540—Goatee on gauze	.25
D541—Mustache on gauze	.25
D542—Side Burns and Mustache	1.20
D543—Irish or Dutch Whiskers	.95

BURNT CORK
D544—Burnt Cork; two-ounce box ... $0.35

SPIRIT GUM
D548—Spirit Gum, for fastening all Hair Goods on Gauze to face; half-ounce bottle ... $0.35

GRENADINE ROUGE
D549—Grenadine Rouge; per doz. sticks ... $3.00

GREASE PAINT
D550—Grease Paint, per dozen sticks ... $1.50

NOSE PUTTY
D393—Nose Putty, per jar ... $0.50

MASKS, BEARDS AND WIGS

D546

D545

D547

D545—Mask of wire, nicely painted; best quality 11-inch white hair beard and fine quality long white hair ventilated wig attached $5.00

D546—Mask of wire, nicely painted; short gray beard and best quality gray ventilated bald wig attached 5.00

D547—Mask of wire, nicely painted; short gray beard and best quality short gray ventilated wig attached 5.00

BEARDS AND WIGS
When Ordering, State Color Desired—White, Gray or Black

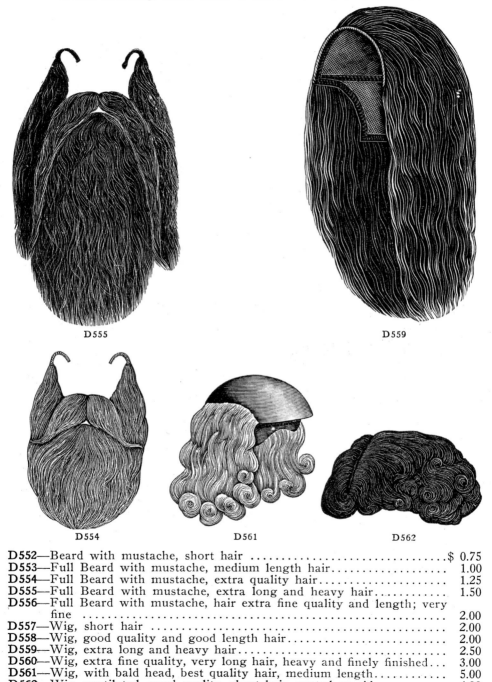

D555			D559
D554	D561		D562

D552—Beard with mustache, short hair ....$ 0.75
D553—Full Beard with mustache, medium length hair................... 1.00
D554—Full Beard with mustache, extra quality hair...................... 1.25
D555—Full Beard with mustache, extra long and heavy hair............. 1.50
D556—Full Beard with mustache, hair extra fine quality and length; very fine 2.00
D557—Wig, short hair 2.00
D558—Wig, good quality and good length hair........................ 2.00
D559—Wig, extra long and heavy hair.................................. 2.50
D560—Wig, extra fine quality, very long hair, heavy and finely finished... 3.00
D561—Wig, with bald head, best quality hair, medium length............ 5.00
D562—Wig, ventilated, good quality, short hair, parted on side 4.00

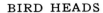
DeMoulin Bros. & Co., Greenville, Ill.

LARGE PAPIER MACHE HEADS

To be worn over head and rest on shoulders

Full size. Fine natural painted. Heads kept in stock can be shipped on short notice; those made to order require about two weeks for shipment

BIRD HEADS

Water Bird   Owl   Rooster

We carry Rooster, Owl, Water Bird, Stork, Robin, Crow, Eagle, Turkey, Hen, Parrot, etc., in stock, each .... $ 3.85
Any of the above Bird Heads made to order with movable bills and eye lids, each 6.70

HUMAN HEADS

(See illustrations on page 118)

We carry in stock Alphonse, Gaston, Happy Hooligan, Gloomy Gus, Yellow Kid, Skull, Devil, Dutchman, Englishman, Irishman, Negro, Dandy, Clown, Indian, Jew, Old Lady with Hat, Old Lady with Night Cap, Santa Claus, Bridget, Tramp, Turk, Wench, Chinese, Soldier, Billiken, etc., each .... $ 3.85
Policeman with Helmet, extra large 6.00
Any of the above Human Heads, except Policeman with Helmet, made to order with movable mouths and eyelids; each 6.70
Policeman with Helmet, extra large; movable mouth and eyelids; each... 9.50

SPECIAL ANIMAL HEADS

(See illustrations on page 119)

We carry in stock Goat, Hog, Ram, Babboon, Frog, Sheep, Rabbit, Alligator, Horse, Cat, Bear, Wolf, Camel, Giraffe, Mouse, etc., each....$ 3.85
Any of above Animal Heads made to order with movable mouth and eyelids, each 6.70
Elk Head, no movable parts 5.75
Buffalo Head, in stock, no movable parts 4.25
Elk Head, large size; movable mouth and eyelids 8.50
Buffalo Head, large size; movable mouth and eyelids 7.10
Moose Head, large size; no movable parts 5.75

DeMoulin Bros. & Co., Greenville, Ill.

LARGE PAPIER MACHE HUMAN HEADS

(See description and prices on page 117)

Old Lady
with Night Cap
Devil
Alphonse

Yellow Kid
Englishman
Gloomy Gus

Irishman
Skull
Gaston

LARGE PAPIER MACHE ANIMAL HEADS

(See description and prices on page 117)

Dog	Donkey	Tiger
Elephant	Lion	Goat
Hog	Ram	Babboon
Cow	Ice Bear	Cat

DeMoulin Bros. & Co., Greenville, Ill.

MASKS OF NATIONS

Assortment D580

D579—Masks, waxed gauze, assorted, representing twelve characters of nations: 1, French; 2, Dutch; 3, Turk; 4, English; 5, Japanese; 6, Indian; 7, Italian; 8, Yankee or Uncle Sam; 9, Bedouin; 10, Irish; 11, Negro; 12, Jew. Each, $0.20; per dozen .... $ 1.50

D580—Masks, style **D579**, but all have artificial hair and beards, and of better quality; each, $0.30; per dozen 2.75

These masks may be sent by mail, but we cannot state exact amount as this depends upon the parcel post "zone." Make sufficient allowance and any surplus will be refunded with invoice.

MASKS OF CELEBRITIES

Assortment D582

D582—Masks, waxed gauze, assorted, representing newspaper celebrities: 1, Foxy Grandpa; 2, Gloomy Gus; 3, Mrs. Katzenjammer; 4, Leon 5, Yellow Kid; 6, Montmorency; 7, Gaston; 8, Happy Hooligan's Father; 9, Alphonse; 10, The Captain; 11, Panhandle Pete; 12, Happy Hooligan; each, $0.40; per dozen .... $ 3.00

These masks may be sent by mail, but we cannot state exact amount as this depends upon the parcel post "zone." Make sufficient allowance and any surplus will be refunded with invoice.

DeMoulin Bros. & Co., Greenville, Ill.

SKELETONS, SKULLS, ETC.

D569—Skeleton of papier mache, one-half length, with arms and hands...$12.50

D569½—Skeleton of papier mache, one-half length, no arms 3.50

D570—Corpse of composition, one-half length, an exact representation of a dead man, including shroud 5.00

D571—Skeleton of papier mache, full length, carefully made, well set up.. 23.00
Skeleton, genuine, deodorized, from $110.00 to $200.00, according to quality and fluctuation of market. Prices and full particulars on application.

D572—Skull, natural size, of papier mache 2.25

D573—Cross Bones, papier mache 1.35

D574—Cross Bones, genuine and deodorized 4.50

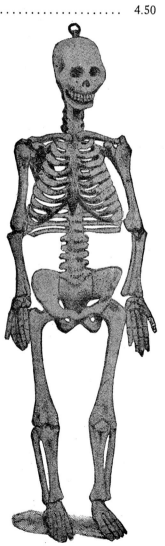

SCENE CASES

Our Scene Cases are made with hinged top—can be instantly turned back to expose the scene. When a full length scene is used, we make the Scene Case so the entire top may be quickly removed. If Scene Case is ordered without a scene, and the entire top is wanted removable, please make mention to that effect.

We do not list a plain wooden Scene Case. It does not give satisfaction and is an obsolete style.

D575—Scene Case, full size, octagon ends, paneled top, moulding around bottom, outside covered with heavy black cloth, nicely lined, four fine silver plated handles $25.00

D576—Scene Case, full size, octagon ends, elaborate paneled top and bottom mouldings, outside covered with heavy black casket cloth, nicely lined, six fine silver plated handles 27.50
Trestles, folding pattern, on any of above Scene Cases, extra 1.70

PALLS

Our Palls will adjust to any size Sxxxx Cxxx and are arranged so they can be instantly attached and as quickly removed. Palls are ruined more by storing away, when permanently fastened to Sxxxx Cxxx or Trestles, than by actual use.

D577—Pall of heavy black cloth, fancy scalloped edge ....$ 3.00

D578—Pall of black mercerized cashmere, neatly draped, trimmed with worsted fringe 4.90

SMOKING CAMEL

D413

Smoking Camel—put him at the head of the parade, then follow his smoke.

This Camel is substantially built, can carry a rider if desired and is comfortably padded for carrying the load; made for two men inside; the men stand upright, one in each hump, which allows perfect freedom for operating the several parts, also provided with breathing screens. Tail and lower jaw movable. Long cigar in camel's mouth which produces a dense smoke; cigar connects to an arrangement by which smoke is drawn in, then forced out through the nostrils.

D413—Smoking Camel, including large cigar..........................$75.00

D414

COW BELLS

Cow Bells—they were never used in the chimes of Normandy; they are all sizes and all out of tune; scatter them among the crowd to be used for applause.

D414—Cow Bells, per set of 7, assorted sizes, $2.50

ANIMALS

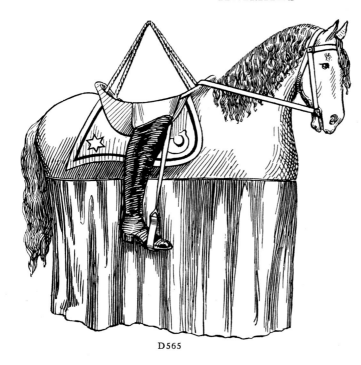

D565

D565—Horse, finely painted; curtain conceals legs of man, who, though standing through saddle, appears to be riding ...$25.00

D566—Donkey, same as **D565**, but has moving mouth and tail $36.00

No extra charge for crating.

Movable ears and eyes, extra...$5.00

D567—Camel or donkey, life size, well stayed and framed; legs for two men inside; jaw and tail can be moved at will of the men inside $50.00

Tiger, lion horse, elk, moose, elephant, etc., as above $60.00

Movable ears and eyes, extra ..$5.00

No extra charge for crating.

D567

BURLESQUE COSTUMES

This is a subject to which considerable attention has been given of late, by some of the best known secret society organizations in the country. In fact, few of those who use burlesque paraphernalia perform the work without grotesque costumes. These should be worn by the attendants and all those taking part in the initiation. It will also be found effective to have the candidates attired in burlesque costumes during some of the tests. This feature will create much amusement for the members and will also add to the confusion of the candidates.

While we illustrate only a few of these special costumes, we make others; in fact, we can furnish an appropriate outfit for any character.

D596—Der Captain. Coat, trousers, pad, wooden leg, cane, cap, bald wig, mask ....$ 9.80
D597—Schniddlefritz. Coat, trousers, gaiters, tie, hat, wig and mask 7.40

D600—Indian. Complete costume, with mask and headdress ....$ 5.40
D601—Uncle Josh. Coat, vest, trousers and mask with headdress 6.35

DeMoulin Bros. & Co., Greenville, Ill.

D602

D603

D602—Panhandle Pete. Coat, trousers, stomach pad, mask and suitable headdress ....$ 6.85

D603—Cecil. Coat, trousers, mask and bald wig 6.10

D604

D605

D604—Smoky. Coat, trousers, stomach and back pad, mask, bald wig and pipe ....$ 9.20

D605—Yens Yensen. Sweater, trousers, cap and mask 7.30

D780—Hawkshaw. Coat, trousers, hat, mask and pipe ....$ 6.40
D781—Colonel. Coat, trousers, hat and mask 6.20

D410—Bolshevik costume, consisting of coat, trousers, hat, wig and beard with mustache ....$ 6.90

D387—Convict's costume, of good quality striped material; the trousers without fly front but with drawstring at waist, one patch hip pocket, including cap, blouse and trousers; complete 6.35

D786—Andy Gump. Coat, trousers, mask, wig, hat, collar and tie ....$ 7.80

D787—Pa. Vest, trousers, nose, specs, mustache and bald wig 5.90

D788—Barney Google. Coat, trousers, hat and mask ....$ 6.10

D633—Spark Plug, with substantial horse head and tail, arranged for two men to walk under 30.00

D634—Spark Plug, blanket only 8.00
Grease Paints—See page 114.

DeMoulin Bros. & Co., Greenville, Ill.

D782—Jiggs. Coat, vest, trousers, pad, hat and mask .... $ 7.65
D783—Maggie. Dress, mask and headdress 6.50

D784—Jerry. Coat, vest, trousers, hat, mask and collar .... $ 6.70
D785—Dinty Moore. Coat, vest, trousers, hat, mask and collar 6.70

DeMoulin Bros. & Co., Greenville, Ill.

D606—Mutt.   Coat, vest, trousers, hat and mask ....$ 6.45
D607—Jeff.   Coat, vest, trousers, hat and mask 6.60

PAPIER MACHE HEADS

With Water Attachment

What would you think if some dumb brute would walk up to you and spit in your face? The act seems preposterous, yet you can imagine how it would make you feel.

NOTE—Any of our papier mache heads listed at $3.85 on page 117 can be furnished with water attachment. The water may be squirted from any part of the head desired. When ordering advise definitely.

D608—Papier Mache Head with water attachment.$ 5.75

D609—Papier Mache Head (any one listed at $3.85, on page 117), made to order with movable mouth and also arranged with water attachment 8.50

D610—Donkey Costume and Papier Mache Head with water attachment 10.00

D611—Donkey Costume and Papier Mache head with movable ears and jaws, and also arranged with water attachment 13.40

DeMoulin Bros. & Co., Greenville, Ill.

D613

D614

D613—Minstrel Costume. Coat, vest, trousers, fine hat, cane $10.90
D614—Uncle Sam. Coat, vest, trousers, tie and mask with headdress 6.60

D615

D616

D615—Negro. Hat, mask, coat and trousers ....$ 5.60
D616—Knight. Helmet, armor coat, belt with thong, sword, shield, hose
and sandals 13.85

D617   D618

D617—Alphonse. Coat, trousers, tie, hat, gloves and mask ....$ 6.20

D618—Gaston. Coat, trousers, tie, hat, gloves and mask 6.20

D619   D620

D619—Leon. Coat, trousers, front and back pads, hat, bald wig, mask....$ 8.60

D620—Happy Hooligan. Coat, vest, trousers, can, bald wig, mask 6.90

D621—Irishman. Coat, vest, trousers and mask with headdress $6.40

D622—Clarence the Cop. Coat, trousers, belt, club, star and mask with headdress 6.90

D623—Ballet Girl. Complete costume, with blonde wig ....$ 6.50
D624—Dutchman. Coat, vest, trousers and mask with headdress 6.20
D303—Wooden Shoes for Dutchman, made in extra large sizes 2.75

D625—Clown. Complete suit, including slippers and mask with headdress.$ 5.85
D758—Mexican Costume. Hat, sleeveless jacket, shirt, sash and trousers.. 10.35

D627—Cowboy. Hat, coat, belt, dagger, trousers and leggings ....$ 9.40
D512—Revolver, 32-calibre 6.25
D628—Jew. Hat, mask, coat, vest and trousers 6.40

DeMoulin Bros. & Co., Greenville, Ill.

D629

D630

D629—Santa Claus. Cap, coat, trousers (hairgoods, pages 129, 131 and 132) .... $ 7.90
D630—Gloomy Gus. Duster, handkerchief, hat and mask 4.80

D631

D632

D631—Ghost. White robe with black crossbones, candle and large papier mache skull head .... $ 5.60
D632—Montmorency. Coat, vest, trousers, hat rim, bald wig, mask and cane 7.20

—135—

DeMoulin Bros. & Co., Greenville, Ill.

D636—Yellow Kid. Robe and large naturalistic papier mache head ......$ 6.30
D637—Witch. Dress, apron and mask with headdress 5.90

D638—Monkey. Complete costume, including head ....$ 9.25
D655—Monkey. Complete costume, including head, very fine imitation.. 25.00
D229—Devil. Complete costume, including head 9.25
D639—Trident for Devil (pitchfork), very desirable 1.25
D640—Skull for Devil, to hold in hand, arranged with holder on top for
    red fire torches, very fine for tableaux 3.00

D754 Liberty

D755 Geo. Washington

D756 Cow Boy

D757 Colonial

Prices are not quoted on above costumes, as same can be furnished in a wide range of prices depending upon what materials are used in their construction. If interested in any of these costumes, give us an idea as to what quality is desired.

DeMoulin Bros. & Co., Greenville, Ill.

D790-D792

D626

D790—Yama Yama Costume, of good quality figured cloth, including cap. $ 7.20

D791—Yama Yama Costume, of army duck, including cap 6.40

D792—Yama Yama Costume of near silk, including cap 4.35
(Write for samples of materials)

D626—Donkey. Union Suit of fuzzy goods with tail, and large papier mache head 7.60

D767—Frog Costume. Green worsted union suit, painted to look like a frog; leather soles; head with movable mouth and eyes included.... 40.00

D768—Alligator Costume. Made up in same manner as **D767** Frog Costume except with long tail added 55.00

D769—Giraffe Costume. Union Suit of cotton flannel with a very long neck supported by a spiral spring, the suit striped with paint, including attachment for manipulating head and neck 60.00

We can make up costumes similar to **D626** Donkey Costume for most any of our papier mache heads listed on page 117. Price would be same as for Donkey Costume.

RACE COSTUMES

| D643 | D647 | D650 | D654 |

D641—Black Race—North African Negro. Coat, trousers, sash, hose, slippers, and headdress ....$ 8.20
D642—Mask, extra quality waxed gauze, with mustache and beard 1.50

D643—Complete Costume ....$ 9.70

D644—Mohammedan—Young Turk. Shirt, trousers, jacket, sash, hose, slippers and fez ....$ 8.85
D645—Mask, extra quality waxed gauze, with mustache 1.50
D646—Sword of wood, blade covered with smooth bright tin to look like polished steel 1.75

D647—Complete Costume $12.10

D648—Yellow Race—Chinese. Tunic, trousers and slippers ....$ 6.35
D649—Mask, extra quality waxed gauze with queue 1.50

D650—Complete Costume ....$ 7.85

D651—Red Race—American Indian. Coat and leggings ....$ 9.10
D652—Mask, headdress and wig 1.25
D653—Bow and Arrow 2.00

D654—Complete Costume $12.35

RACE COSTUMES

D658　　　　D661　　　　D664　　　　D667　　　　D670

D656—Mohammedan—Old Turk. Tunic, trousers, sash and headdress....$ 7.70
D657—Mask, extra quality waxed gauze with mustache and long beard... 1.50

D658—Complete Costume ....$ 9.20

D659—Black Race—Nubian. Long tunic, sash, hose and headdress .....$ 6.80
D660—Mask, extra quality waxed gauze with beard 1.50

D661—Complete Costume ....$ 8.30

D662—Yellow Race—Japanese. Tunic and trousers ....$ 6.10
D663—Mask, extra quality waxed gauze with mustache and queue 1.50

D664—Complete Costume ....$ 7.60

D665—Brown Race—Parsee. Robe, sash, slippers and headdress ....$ 7.10
D666—Mask, extra quality waxed gauze, mustache and short beard 1.50

D667—Complete Costume ....$ 8.60

D668—Pagan—Fire Worshipper. Robe, sash and headdress ....$ 7.20
D669—Mask, extra quality waxed gauze, with mustache and long beard... 1.50

D670—Complete Costume ....$ 8.70

RACE COSTUMES

EGYPTIAN

D686-D689

YELLOW

D690-D693

Robe, belt with pendants, and headdress; silk embroidery and metal ornaments.

D686—Fine satin and fine figured goods $18.60

D687—Moire and fine figured goods 12.00

D688—Mercerized sateen and figured goods 10.95

D689—Near silk and figured goods 9.80

Tunic, pantaloons and headdress: figure of goods may vary somewhat.

D690—Very fine quality Chinese goods and fine satin ....$ 6.65

D691—Good quality Chinese goods and moire 5.65

D692—Good quality Chinese goods and mercerized sateen 5.40

D693—Fair quality Chinese goods and near silk 5.20

RACE COSTUMES

BLACK BROWN

D694-D697

D698-D702

Skirt, sash-throw and black knit shirt; silk embroidery.

D694—Fine satin and fine figured goods; black silkoline knit shirt $11.40

D695—Moire and fine figured goods; black knit shirt.. 7.95

D696—Mercerized sateen and figured goods; black knit shirt 7.00

D697—Near silk and figured goods; black knit shirt... 6.15

Robe, sash-throw and turban; silk embroidery.

D698—Fine satin and fine figured goods $13.25

D699—Moire and fine figured goods 9.25

D700—Mercerized sateen and figured goods 8.00

D702—Near silk and figured goods 7.20

COSTUMES

D818-D829

D830-D841

ROBES

Full lined; elaborately silk embroidered; girdle with tassels.

D818—Fine silk plush	$33.80
D819—Fine silk-finished velvet	20.75
D820—Fine satin	18.10
D821—Moire	12.35
D822—Mercerized sateen	11.60
D823—Banner sateen	10.75

TURBANS

Silk embroidered; with tassel.

D824—Fine silk plush	$ 4.05
D825—Fine silk-finished velvet	2.55
D826—Fine satin	2.20
D827—Moire	2.00
D828—Mercerized sateen	1.55
D829—Banner sateen	1.40

ROBES

Full lined; front panel, yoke and cuffs of contrasting color, elaborately silk embroidered.

D830—Fine silk plush	$33.60
D831—Fine silk-finished velvet	19.15
D832—Fine satin	15.95
D833—Moire	10.60
D834—Mercerized sateen	9.90
D835—Banner sateen	8.90

CROWNS

Silk embroidered; adjustable.

D836—Fine silk plush	$ 2.85
D837—Fine silk-finished velvet	1.95
D838—Fine satin	1.60
D839—Moire	1.30
D840—Mercerized sateen	1.05
D841—Banner sateen	1.00

Write for Illustrations and Prices on Other Styles

COSTUMES

D870-D882

D883-D895

ROBES

Trimmed with bands of contrasting color; fly front with concealed buttons; girdle with tassels.

D870—Fine satin, full lined	$17.05
D871—Moire, yoke lined	6.55
D872—Banner sateen, full lined	7.90
D873—Mercerized sateen, yoke lined	6.15
D874—Banner sateen, yoke lined	4.70
D875—Near silk, yoke lined	4.70
D876—Cambric, yoke lined	4.20

TURBANS

In two colors, with ornament.

D877—Fine satin	$ 1.80
D878—Moire	1.50
D879—Mercerized sateen	1.10
D880—Banner sateen	1.05
D881—Near silk	1.00
D882—Cambric	.95

ROBES

Silk embroidered on front and sleeves; girdle with tassels.

D883—Fine silk plush, full lined	$29.10
D884—Fine silk-finished velvet, full lined	18.45
D885—Fine satin, full lined	15.10
D886—Moire	6.85
D887—Banner sateen, full lined	6.55
D888—Mercerized sateen	5.80
D889—Banner sateen	5.50

CROWNS

Silk embroidered; adjustable.

D890—Fine silk plush	$ 2.55
D891—Fine silk-finished velvet	1.85
D892—Fine satin	1.65
D893—Moire	1.40
D894—Mercerized sateen	1.15
D895—Banner sateen	1.10

Write for Illustrations and Prices on Other Styles

DeMoulin Bros. & Co., Greenville, Ill.

COSTUMES

D900-D909

D910-D919

ROBES
Buttons down front; girdle.

D900—Moire	$	4.15
D901—Mercerized sateen		3.35
D902—Banner sateen		2.75
D903—Near silk		2.75
D904—Cambric		2.45

TURBANS
Plain, with sweat band.

D905—Moire	$	1.15
D906—Mercerized sateen		.95
D907—Banner sateen		.90
D908—Near silk		.85
D909—Cambric		.80

ROBES
Buttons down front; girdle with tassels.

D910—Moire	$	4.50
D911—Mercerized sateen		3.85
D912—Banner sateen		3.15
D913—Near silk		3.15
D914—Cambric		2.80

COWLS
Including mask with curtain and pressed into shape of face.

D915—Moire	$	.75
D916—Mercerized sateen		.60
D917—Banner sateen		.50
D918—Near silk		.45
D919—Cambric		.40

Write for Illustrations and Prices on Other Styles

DeMoulin Bros. & Co., Greenville, Ill.

COSTUMES

D951-D958

D963-D978

COATS
Front body interlined; trimmed with metal ornaments and embroidery; belt and collar of contrasting color.
D951—Fine satin, full length ....$ 9.85
D952—Moire, body half lined 5.75
D953—Mercerized sateen, body half lined 5.25
D954—Banner sateen, full lined 5.75

HELMETS
Flexible body; front shield with fancy metal ornament; spike and base; leather sweat band.
D955—Fine satin ....$ 3.25
D956—Moire 3.00
D957—Mercerized sateen 2.95
D958—Banner sateen 2.90

HOSE AND SANDALS
D959—Hose, thigh length, fine quality silkoline; colors, black, blue, red, yellow, white or flesh; pair .....$ 2.60
D960—Hose, thigh length, fine quality cotton; various colors; pair 1.60
D961—Sandals, oak-tanned leather, cross straps over feet, substantial and full value for the money; pair... 1.60
Other style Sandals quoted on request.

COATS
Front body interlined; trimmed with metal ornaments and gold lace; belt and collar of contrasting color.
D963—Fine silk finished velvet, full lined.$11.00
D964—Moire, body half lined 6.50
D965—Mercerized sateen, body half lined 6.00
D966—Banner sateen, full lined 6.60
D967—Near silk, body half lined 5.45
D968—Cambric, body half lined 5.20

HELMETS
Flexible body; top, front and side ornaments and strap.
D969—Fine silk finished velvet ....$ 2.50
D970—Moire 2.40
D971—Mercerized sateen 2.35
D972—Banner sateen 2.30

LEGGINGS
Thigh length; full lined; adjustable straps.
D973—Fine silk finished velvet ....$ 3.60
D974—Moire 2.05
D975—Mercerized sateen 1.90
D976—Banner sateen 1.70
D977—Near silk 1.70
D978—Cambric 1.60

Catalog of Costumes on Request.

DeMoulin Bros. & Co., Greenville, Ill.

WE MANUFACTURE UNIFORMS

For Lodges, Bands, Firemen, Colleges, Military Academies, Boys' Brigades, Drill Teams, Uniform Ranks, Etc.

A HANDSOME UNIFORM
Is Our Style D, Made as Follows:

Style D—Cap, full bell top, gilt or silver front strap, side buttons, wide braid band, metal wreath and lyre on front. Coat with standing collar, fly front, trimmed around collar, down front, around bottom, up side vents and back seams and on sleeves with 1¼-inch mohair braid, traced with narrow soutache braid, as shown in illustration. Trousers trimmed down outside seams with braid; regular hip, watch and side pockets. Trimming white, black, scarlet, yellow, brown, purple, green, blue or gray.

THE PRICES

Style D—Made of our Quality 10 all-wool fast-color uniform cloth in any standard color. Cap $2.90; Coat, $16.70; Trousers, $9.55. COMPLETE UNIFORM..$29.15

Style D—Made of our Quality 5 all-wool fast-color uniform cloth in blue, olive drab or gray. Cap, $2.70; Coat, $15.10; Trousers, $8.15; COMPLETE UNIFORM $25.95

Style D—Made of extra fine quality shrunk U. S. Army Duck. Colors: Khaki, olive drab, new army shade of brown; also shrunk white standard. Cap, $1.80; Coat, $5.70; Trousers, $3.85. COMPLETE UNIFORM ..$11.35

Style D—Made of good quality shrunk U. S. Army Duck. Colors: Red, yellow, green, purple, blue, black or gray. Cap, $1.85; Coat, $6.00; Trousers, $4.10. COMPLETE UNIFORM ..$11.95

See Our Catalog for Prices on Other Grades of Cloth

IMPORTANT

Style D duck caps have only a partial hair-cloth body. At an extra charge of 20 cents each, we furnish these caps with full hair-cloth flexible body. We highly recommend this, as it gives the cap permanent shape and the exact appearance of a wool cap.

CATALOG AND SAMPLES

Our catalog shows the very finest and most up-to-date styles of uniforms. Our samples afford a wide range of choice as to quality and shade of cloth. No other uniform house in existence offers such an opportunity for you to get axactly what you want. Catalog and sample will be mailed free upon request. It will be to your interest to send for them before purchasing uniforms elsewhere.

ZOUAVE UNIFORM NO. D980

Jacket, lined, trimmed with ¾-inch silk braid and silk soutache, inside pocket.

Vest, to fasten down front with gilt or silver buttons, standing collar.

Bloomers, fly front like regular trousers, belt loops and suspender buttons, adjustable strap and buckle fasteners at bottom, one watch and two side pockets, ¾-inch silk braid and silk soutache design at sides.

	Jacket	Vest	Bloomers
R-13 superfine silk plush	$17.85	....	....
R-9 silk plush	13.25	....	....
Silk velvet	13.05	$5.35	....
Guaranteed Skinner's satin	11.40	4.65	$11.80
Silk poplin	8.10	3.95	8.70
Quality 5 cloth	9.65	4.15	9.25
Quality 10 cloth	11.00	4.50	10.95
Quality 20 cloth	12.10	4.85	12.40
Quality 40 cloth	13.60	5.00	13.15
Quality 50 cloth	14.05	5.40	14.90

Mohair trimming instead of silk, deduct: Jacket, $0.25; Bloomers, $0.10.

Jacket, army duck, cotton trimming, not lined, $3.80; vest, army duck, $1.85; bloomers, army duck, cotton trimming, $4.25.

D981—Sash, guaranteed Skinner's satin, cut 18x114 inches and double tubular style with seam along one edge, 9-inch silk tassels $6.25

D982—Sash, silk poplin, otherwise as above satin sash 4.15

D983—Sash, silk poplin, cut 12x114 inches and edges hemmed, not tubular, 9-inch silk tassel 3.10

D984—Sash, moire, cut 9x114 inches, otherwise as silk poplin sash last listed above 2.10

D985—Sash, mercerized sateen, otherwise as silk poplin sash last listed above 1.80

D986—Sash, mercerized sateen, cut 12x114 inches and edges hemmed, 7½-inch mercerized tassels 1.20

D987—Athletic Hose, heavy ribbed worsted; pair 1.60

D988—Athletic Hose, heavy ribbed worsted, footless style with strap for under instep; to be worn over the shoetops like leggings; pair 1.60

D989—Athletic Hose, heavy ribbed cotton, with or without feet; pair .... .80

D990—Leggings, white heavy canvas, to lace at sides; pair 1.80

D991—Leggings, black canvas, to lace at sides; pair 1.70

D992—Leggings, army duck; red, yellow, green, maroon, purple or gray; lined with canvas; to lace at sides; pair 1.95

D980

Complete Catalog of Uniforms Will Be Sent on Request.

PARADE UNIFORMS

Samples of material and measure book mailed on request. The cheaper uniforms are usually made assorted sizes, although we make any part to individual measures if desired.

ULSTERS

D1032—Ulster, army duck, not lined, all seams doubly stitched, collar and lapels same color or contrasting color, large gold or silver buttons, patch pockets $6.55

Ulster, wool cloth, choice of a great variety of colors, skeleton lined, black grosgrain collar and lapels; large gold, silver, ivory or cloth covered buttons; two side inserted or patch pockets with or withopt flaps.

D1034—Quality 5 cloth $24.55
D1035—Quality 10 cloth 28.10
D1037—Quality 17 cloth 29.20
D1039—Quality 20 cloth 30.85
D1040—Quality 40 cloth 32.25
Left breast pocket on any of the above wool ulsters, extra .... .35

CAPS

D1042—Cap, army duck ....$ 1.35
D1043—Cap, army duck, better quality, spring front, gilt or silver buttons, braid band and cord of any color 1.70

Cap to match Ulsters D1034-D1040, spring front, gilt or silver cord and buttons, braid band of any color.

D1044—Quality 5 cloth ....$ 2.55
D1045—Quality 10 cloth 2.75
D1047—Quality 17 cloth 2.85
D1049—Quality 20 cloth 2.95
D1050—Quality 40 cloth 3.00

TROUSERS

Trousers, one patch hip pocket, without fly front but a slit opening at left hip with draw-string at waist for adjusting and fastening. The slit is concealed by the coat and the draw-string makes the waist adjustable. These are the cheapest trousers we can make.

D1089—White shrunk standard duck ....$ 2.55
D1090—Army duck, red, blue, khaki, gray, black, olive, drab, brown 2.80
D1092—White shrunk army duck 3.05

Trousers, fly front, belt loops and suspender buttons, regular inserted pockets—one hip, one watch and two side. We recommend these in preference to those listed above.

D1096—White shrunk standard duck ....$ 3.35
D1097—Army duck, red, blue, khaki, gray, black, Olive drab, brown 3.60
D1099—White shrunk army duck 3.60

D1032-D1050

CANES

D1052—Cane, very light weight, with crook, varnished mahogany finish.
Less than 100, each ....$ .06   200 or more, each ....$ .04
100 or more, each .... .05   300 or more, each .... .03½

D1053—Cane, light weight, with crook; bamboo; finely finished; a first-class cane.
Less than 100, each ....$ .50   200 or more, each ....$ .40
100 or more, each .... .45   300 or more, each .... .35

Sketches and Samples Will Be Submitted on Request.

DeMoulin Bros. & Co., Greenville, Ill.

AMATEUR MINSTREL COSTUME SET AND CHAIR COVERS

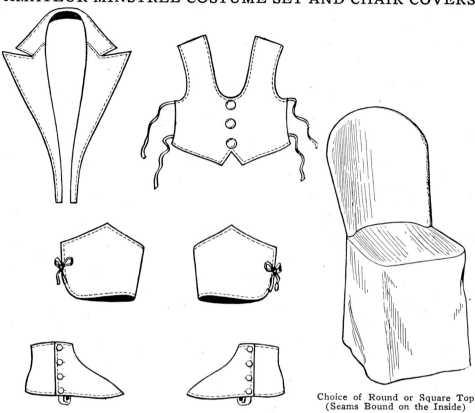

Choice of Round or Square Top
(Seams Bound on the Inside)

AMATEUR MINSTREL COSTUME SET

D741—Set consisting of collar and lapels, pair of cuffs and over-gaiters (spats); mercerized sateen of any color .... $ 2.85

D742—Minstrel Vest Front, mercerized sateen of any color or fancy cotton goods; three large gold buttons; tie tapes; two safety pins for the shoulders .... .85

With this Set you can transform any business or dress suit into an up-to-date Minstrel Costume.

CHAIR COVERS

D744—Chair Cover, front and sides of silk-finished velvet, back of near silk ....$ 4.00
D746—Chair Cover, front of silk poplin, back of near silk 3.90
D747—Chair Cover, front of moire, back of near silk 2.75
D748—Chair Cover, front of galatea, back of near silk 1.90
D749—Chair Cover, front of mercerized sateen, back of near silk 1.60
D750—Chair Cover, to cover back of folding chair, not the seat and legs; galatea 16 inches wide and 20½ inches long; tape tie strings ...... .65

LETTERING OR EMBLEM

We can place most any lettering or emblem on the covers, either above or below the seat. If you state about what lettering or emblem you have in mind, we shall submit full information and sketch embodying our ideas. Please mention also how many covers you want and about what quality.

SASHES FOR MARSHAL

D1009-D1016

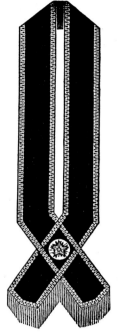

D1017-D1024

SILVER OR GOLD TRIMMED

Sashes, lined and interlined; silver or gold laces, 2¼-inch silver or gold bullion fringe, 2½-inch silver or gold bullion tassels and two raised silver or gold bullion stars, one star having a ribbon rosette background.

D1009—Fine silk velvet ....$ 5.20
D1010—Fine silk finished velvet. 4.20
D1011—Moire 4.15
D1012—Banner Sateen 3.75

SILK TRIMMED—SILVER OR GOLD STAR

Sashes, lined and interlined; silk laces, 2-inch silk fringe, 2½-inch silk tassels and two raised bullion stars, one star having a ribbon rosette background.

D1013—Fine silk velvet ....$ 3.80
D1014—Fine silk finished velvet. 2.85
D1015—Moire 2.50
D1016—Banner Sateen 2.35

SILVER OR GOLD TRIMMED

Sashes, lined and interlined; ½-inch silver or gold lace, 2¼-inch silver or gold bullion fringe and one raised silver or gold bullion star-and-ribbon rosette.

D1017—Fine silk velvet ....$ 4.40
D1018—Fine silk finished velvet. 3.25
D1019—Moire 2.80
D1020—Banner sateen 2.70

Above sashes with 3-inch silver or gold bullion fringe instead of 2¼-inch, extra each .... .20

SILK TRIMMED—SILVER OR GOLD STAR

Sashes, lined and interlined; silk lace, 1½-inch silk fringe and one raised bullion star-and-ribbon rosette.

D1021—Fine silk velvet ....$ 3.35
D1022—Fine silk finished velvet 2.35
D1023—Moire 1.85
D1024—Banner Sateen 1.70

Above sashes with 2-inch silk fringe instead of 1½-inch extra, each .... .20

Catalog of Other Styles Supplied on Request

SWORDS

(Designed and Made to Order)

D1159—Long Sword, etched oval blade; gold plated and burnished mounts, embossed nickel plated steel scabbard with rings; black leather twist grip bound with fancy plated wire $12.65

D1160—Long Sword, same as **D1159**, but all mountings nickel plated instead of gold 11.60

D1161—Long Sword, same length as **D1159**; steel blade; nickel plated steel scabbard with two rings; white corrugated bone grip; nickel plated mountings 7.50

D1162—Long Sword, same as **D1161**, but scabbard has button instead of two rings 7.50

D1163—Sword, blue enameled metal scabbard with button, corrugated aluminum grip, nickel plated mounts 7.00

D1164—Sword, same as **D1163**, but brass mounts 6.25

D1165—Short Sword, full size; steel blade; polished nickel plated scabbard with button; polished nickel plated mountings 6.50

D1165

D1163-D1164

CONTINENTAL UNIFORMS

D1168—Continental Uniform, consists of three-cornered wool hat, with cockade on left side, blue broadcloth coat with proper trimmings, white duck vest, blue broadcloth knee trousers with buckles at knees, and leggings of black artificial leather with spring fastenings; complete $27.10

D1159—Continental Uniform, consists of three-cornered wool hat, blue duck coat with proper trimmings, white duck vest, blue duck knee trousers with buckles at knees, and black leggings; complete 15.40

SWORD WAIST BELTS

(Designed and Made to Order)

D1173

D1170—Belt, fine quality red, black or russet leather, gilt plain or eagle military clasp having leather fly to prevent wear on garment; two detachable slings with gilt trimmings; for sword with two rings and gold plated mountings ....$ 3.80

D1171—Belt, same as **D1170**, but all metal parts nickel plated; for sword with two rings and nickel plated mountings 3.80

D1173—Belt, red or black enameled leather, doubled and with turned edges, fancy white silk stitched; nickel plated plain or eagle military clasp having leather fly to prevent wear on garment; improved thong having swivel links; for sword with button ....$ 2.40

D1174—Belt, fine quality red, black or russet leather, nickel plated plain or eagle military clasp having leather fly to prevent wear on garment; improved thong having swivel links; for sword with button. 1.85

Any of above belts with solid metal clasp having any raised letters desired; extra, per letter .... .12

SHOULDER BELTS

D1175-D1176

D1175—Shoulder Belt of any color fine silk plush, lined and interlined, edged with gold or silver lace and embellished with metal ornaments; for sword with button ....$ 2 60

D1176—Shoulder Belt of any color fine silk finished velvet, otherwise same as D1175 .... 2.20

D1177—Shoulder Belt of any color fine silk plush, lined and interlined, edged with gold or silver lace; for sword with button 1.90

D1178—Shoulder Belt of any color fine silk finished velvet, lined and interlined, edged with gold or silver lace; for sword with button 1.55

D1179—Shoulder Belt of red leather, for sword with button 1.70

D1180—Shoulder Belt of webbing, for sword with button .... .60

Any of above Shoulder Belts with swivel snaps for sword with rings; extra .... .65

PICNIC AND PARADE UMBRELLAS
About 38-inch Spread

D1110

D1110—Picnic and Parade Umbrella, having regular parasol frame—steel ribs and handle with crook; alternating sections of red, white and blue cotton goods, or any other combination of colors; far superior to the usual parade umbrella—no clumsy unfinished wooden handle and ribs; 25 or more, each ....$ 1.15

50 or more, each 1.09

100 or more, each 1.00

250 or more, each .... .98

500 or more, each .... .95

Straight wood handle, deduct for any quantity, each .... .07

BATONS FOR MARSHALS

D1113

D1112—Baton, enameled in white, fancy gilt metal ends; wrapped with red, white and blue ribbons ....$ 1.75

D1113—Baton, same as D1112, but without ribbons 1.40

D1114—Baton, rosewood finish, gilt metal ends .... .90

U. S. FLAGS
U. S. SILK FLAGS
Finer Flags Made to Order

D1181—U. S. Flag, heavy silk with interlined pole hem and full number of stars embroidered in white silk on both sides; fast color; yellow silk fringe as mentioned below and heavy yellow silk cord and having gilt joint and large gilt eagle tip; including patent leather carrying belt and rain and dust proof cover.

Size	2½-inch hand knotted pure silk fringe	2-inch bullion silk fringe
6 x10 feet	$114.70	$94.20
6 x 9 feet	106.15	87.25
5 x 8 feet	87.60	71.05
4 x 7 feet	65.70	50.00
4 x 6 feet	59.00	46.40
4⅓x 5½ feet	57.05	44.95
3 x 5 feet	46.25	35.10

D1182—U. S. Flag, unmounted, 4x6 feet; light weight silk; sewed stripes, printed stars; fine for indoor decorations $9.00

U. S. WOOL BUNTING FLAGS

These U. S. Flags are made of the best grade all-wool bunting, with full number of stars sewed on both sides. All seams double stitched. All flags have canvas heading and grommets.

Size	Each	Size	Each	Size	Each
10x15 feet	$24.10	6x10 feet	$9.60	4x7 feet	$5.45
8x12 feet	14.70	6x 9 feet	8.95	4x6 feet	4.80
6x12 feet	11.50	5x 8 feet	7.50	3x5 feet	3.40

Larger or small sizes made to order.

D1184—U. S. Flag, size 4x6 feet, all-wool bunting with full number stars sewed on both sides; 2-inch yellow silk fringe and heavy silk cord and tassels; mounted on fine wax-polished hardwood staff having gilt socket joint and gilt eagle on tip; including leather carrying belt and rain and dust proof cover $16.00

D1186—U. S. Flag, size 4x6 feet, all wool bunting; mounted on wax-polished hardwood staff having gilt socket joint and 12-inch nickel plated spear; including belt 9.65

U. S. COTTON BUNTING FLAGS

These flags are made of fine quality, fast color bunting, full number of stars showing on both sides alike; sewed stripes. Edges bound and all seams double stitched. Canvas headings with grommets. We guarantee these flags to be satisfactory in every way, and will refund your money if you are not pleased.

Size	Each	Size	Each	Size	Each
8x15 feet	$4.50	6x10 feet	$2.35	4x7 feet	$1.30
8x12 feet	3.70	6x 9 feet	2.10	4x6 feet	1.15
6x12 feet	3.05	5x 8 feet	1.80	3x5 feet	.80

D1187—U. S. Flag, size 4x6 feet, fine quality cotton bunting, mounted on wax-polished hard-maple staff having gilt socket joint and 12-inch nickel plated spear .... $ 5.00

STAND FOR FLAGS

D1189—Stand for Flags, 16-inch base; or iron, enameled, solid and very substantial ...... $ 6.90

D1190—Stand of iron, finished in high-grade gold bronze or black enamel; satisfactory for flags not larger than 4x6 feet 1.80

FLAG CARRYING BELTS

D1191—Flag belt, double style, passing over both shoulders and hips and crossing at back, distributing weight over different parts of body; fancy silk-stitched black patent enamel leather, doubled and interlined; buckles at front permitting adjustment; socket thong; specially desirable for large flags and very neat in appearance ..... $ 4.45

D1192—Flag Belt, same as D1191, but single style, passing over shoulders only 3.10

D1193—Flag Belt, fancy creased leather with socket thong 1.60

FLAG STAFFS

D1194—Flag Staff, 15 feet long over all, of fine wax-polished hard-maple, having improved gilt socket joint and large gilt eagle on tip $14.60

D1195—Flag Staff, 11½ feet long over all, otherwise as D1194 .... 11.05

D1196—Flag Staff, 10 feet long over all, of fine wax-polished hard-maple, having improved gilt socket joint and gilt eagle on tip 5.70

D1197—Flag Staff, same as D1196, but with nickel plated spear instead of eagle 4.10

BANNERS

D1200-D1202

D1200—Banner, size 40x62 inches; all parts of extra quality satin; lettering artistically executed in gold leaf, finely shaded and high lighted in oil colors; scene and emblems in oil colors; trimmed with fine gold laces, extra heavy brilliant gold bullion fringe and jeweled tassels; cross-bar and tips, chain, balance and eagle plated in bright gilt; fine wax-polished hard-maple staff with improved gilt socket joint $147.80

D1201—Banner; size 36x56 inches, otherwise same as D1200 .... 143.60

D1202—Banner, size 32x50 inches; lambrequin, front and puffing of satin; back of sateen; lettering executed in gold leaf, nicely shaded in oil colors; scene and emblems in oil colors; trimmed with gold laces, heavy gold bullion fringe and gold bullion tassels; cross-bar and tips, chains, balance and eagle plated in bright gilt; fine wax-polished hard-maple staff with improved gilt socket joint 113.00

We manufacture Banners of any style and for any organization, ranging in price from $5 to $300. Send for catalog, or give us idea of what is wanted and we shall submit sketch and prices.

DeMoulin Bros. & Co., Greenville, Ill.

BADGES

D1203-D1204

D1205-D1206

Badges may be trimmed and embossed either in gold or silver. Unless otherwise specified, trimmings will be gold; front and back silver embossed.

Any Emblem and Ribbon of Any Color

D1203—Reversible Badge, 2½x9 inches; front of red, white and blue satin ribbon, back black satin ribbon, with embossed lettering; metal bar with celluloid medallion having very fancy rim and conteaining emblem of Order in colors, suspended by a satin ribbon on which are flags of silk; double bullion fringe; per dozen.$12.00

D1204—Non-Reversible Badge, same as front of D1203; per dozen 10.35

Medallion with plain rim instead of fancy rim, 70c less per dozen badges.

D1205—Reversible Badge, 2½x9 inches; front of red, small curtain white, and frayed curtain of blue satin ribbon; back black satin ribbon; embossed lettering; metal bar; fancy shield celluloid medallion containing emblem; double bullion fringe; tassels extra, see note below; per doben $12.60

D1206—Non-Reversible Badge, same as front of D1205; per doben.... 11.95

Bullion Tassels on any of above badges, extra per dozen badges ....$ 2.50
Braid on edges of ribbon, extra per dozen badges 1.25

These Badges may be sent by mail, but we cannot state exact amount, as this depends upon the parcel post "zone." Make sufficient allowance and any surplus will be refunded with invoice.

If less than one dozen Badges of one kind are ordered, add 35c to defray expense of setting up form for lettering.

We manufacture Badges of any style and for any organization. Send for Catalog, or give us an idea of what is wanted and we shall submit sketches and prices.

We manufacture a complete line of furniture for Lodge room or Church. WE MAIL EITHER OF THESE TWO FINE CATALOGS FREE ON REQUEST.

D1216   D1219   D1217   D1218

Plain solid oak; top of altar and pedestal also all panels of built-up veneered quartered oak; rich golden oak carried in stock, other finishes to order; varnished and rubbed.

CHAIRS

D1216—Large Chair, 54 inches high, 26½ inches wide; cushioned seat and back upholstered in leatherette $28.15
    Entirely of select quartered solid oak; extra 2.25
    Walnut or cherry; extra 7.00
    Varnished, highly polished piano finish; extra 2.40
    Upholstered in leather; extra, $3.70. Spring seat, extra 1.90

D1217—Small Chair, 50 inches high, 26½ inches wide; cushioned seat and back upholstered in leatherette $27.25
    Entirely of select quartered oak; extra 2.00
    Walnut or cherry; extra 6.45
    Varnished, highly polished piano finish; extra 1.80
    Upholstered in leather; extra, $1.85. Spring seat; extra 1.90

We recommend the spring seat. The value is enhanced much more than the slight extra cost.

ALTAR AND PEDESTAL

D1218—Altar, 33 inches high, top 23x27 inches $34.65
    Entirely of select quartered solid oak; extra 3.35
    Walnut or cherry; extra 12.50
    Varnished, highly polished piano finish; extra 3.00
    Leather cushioned top; extra 3.50

D1219—Pedestal, 33 inches high, top 11x16 inches $18.45
    Entirely of select quartered solid oak; extra 1.65
    Walnut or cherry; extra 5.90
    Varnished, highly polished piano finish; extra 2.50

Any of the Altars may have leatherette cushioned top without extra charge.

DeMoulin Bros. & Co., Greenville, Ill.

DeMOULIN'S PORTABLE LODGE STEREOPTICON

D1220 With Color Wheel Attached

The **No. D1220** DeMoulin Portable Stereopticon is the favorite Lodge room equipment today, for it combines compactness, light weight and ease of operation with perfect projection efficiency. This model is capable of projecting a big, clear, brilliantly illuminated image at any distance up to 100 feet from the screen, while interchangeable lamps and lenses take care of all distances of "throw" and types of electric current.

Price complete, including one special concentrated filament 500 watt, 110-volt Mazda nitrogen lamp, condensing lenses, projection lens, 8-foot wire connection and slide carrier $61.00
D1221—Metal Carrying Case for above 5.00
D1222—Color Wheel which quickly converts stereopticon into either an efficient spot or flood light 5.00
For Lodges wishing to secure the dissolving effect upon the screen, a special double unit equipment, the DeMoulin Dissolving Stereopticon, is recommended. The cost of this outfit, complete with 500-watt lamps, perfectly matched precision lenses and dissolving rheostat, is $146 00

EASY TO ORDER
When ordering, merely state: 1. Model desired and voltage of current. 2. Distance of "throw" (number of feet between machine and screen). 3. Size of image required. We'll do all the rest.

SCREENS FOR USE WITH STEREOPTICON
The surface of screen should be parallel with the front of the objective, and the four corners of screen should be equidistant from it. A convenient method of ascertaining the correct position is to tie a long cord to the objective and measure the distance to each corner of the screen.

Screens of good quality heavy bleached cotton, with edges seamed. We include 75 feet of heavy cord and four strong screw-eyes with each screen.

D1227—Screen, 9 feet square .... $ 6.90
D1226—Screen, 12 feet square 10.65
D1225—Screen, 18 feet square 14.40

Those desiring a very fine screen, and one which will cause the least trouble in getting ready for use, should order the following, which are made of best victor hand-made oil opaque and mounted on genuine Hartshorn rollers. We include brackets for mounting

D1229—Screen, 8½x9 feet, no seams $17.50
D1224—Screen, 9 feet square, no seams 34.65
D1228—Screen, 12 feet square, no seams 79.80

RITUALISTIC SLIDES
Improved—Modernized—Extra Fine

The slides we now furnish are far superior to any offered heretofore. Every improvement possible has been made. The figures are better, the coloring more elaborate and artistic. In fact, if you have never seen our new slides, there is a pleasant surprise in store for you.

D1309—Stereopticon Slides, standard size 3¼x4 inches; beautifully colored, sealed with special varnish; very brilliant and transparent, set in frame; each .... $ 1.00
D1310—Stereopticon Slides, same as **D1309**, but not framed; bound with dark colored paper; each .... .75

Slides can be furnished for all fraternal organizations, or to illustrate any lecture you may wish to put on. Also slides to illustrate religious and patriotic songs. Write us about your requirements.

GONGS

D1207-D1208

We list only eight and ten-inch Gongs. Smaller ones are not satisfactory as they have a very sharp, high tone and do not sufficiently prolong sound. Then, too, our Gongs are listed at such a low price that you can secure a large one from us just as cheap as a small one elsewhere. We invite comparison.

D1207—Ten-inch Gong, nickel plated; mounted on metal stand having fancy solid nickel plated base; finest tone obtainable; automatic striker $12.35

D1208—Eight-inch Gong, otherwise as **D1207** 11.85

D1209—Ten-inch Gong, nickel plated; mounted on metal stand having fancy solid nickel plated base; finest tone obtainable; including padded hand striker 8.40

D1210—Eight-inch Gong, otherwise as **D1209** 6.95

D1212-D1213

D1212—Ten-inch Bell, nickel plated, with padded striker, rich deep tone..$ 7.50

D1213—Eight-inch Bell, nickel plated, with padded striker, rich tone..... 5.25

D1214—Ten-inch Flat Japanese Gong, nickel plated, with padded striker, good tone 4.75

FINIS

APPENDIX I

"FUN IN THE LODGE ROOM" SUPPLEMENT

DeMoulin Bros. & Co., Greenville, Ill.

Let Us Develop Your Ideas on Any Novel or Distinctive Stunts. Write Us About Them. That's a Part of Our Service as Well as to Manufacture and Supply Them Economically.

SUGGESTIONS AND DIRECTIONS
For Introducing and Using Our
Burlesque and Side Degree
PARAPHERNALIA

Before conferring any initiation, it will be well for those taking part to memorize the plans in this book and rehearse at least once, so that everything will run smoothly.

The principal work is done by the Chief Officer. For this Officer, the Society should select a man who has had experience as a presiding officer, or one who is a good talker. The success of the work depends much on the ability to this Officer to properly render his part.

The initiation will be much more impressive if each one taking part is disguised with a burlesque costume, and all in the room are masked so candidate will recognize none. Candidate is also often dressed in a burlesque costume, to make him look ridiculous. One special advantage of members wearing masks is that they may smile and enjoy the work unknown to candidate. All persons should be careful not to laugh aloud.

There should be two or three selected as floor managers or attendants. It should be their duty to familiarize themselves with the paraphernalia used, as much of the success of the work rests with them, and in their ability to properly handle candidate.

Initiatory work should be performed like a drama; each person to master his part and the attendants to prepare the paraphernalia and settings.

IMPORTANT

Before bringing candidate in the Lodge room, he must be warningly instructed by attendant that it is necessary to step very high while traveling the paths upon which he is about to venture. Make it emphatic by telling him that there has been barbed wire stretched and obstructions placed in various places whereby he might be tripped. Impart this to him in an earnest manner and see what an amusing effect it will have.

DeMoulin Bros. & Co., Greenville, Ill.

GOAT (Any Kind)

The goat is usually the first "stunt" introduced. Candidate is hoodwinked in ante-room and when he enters the lodge room he is placed on the goat and given a ride several times around the room, then dismounted in front of Chief Officer's station, where he is presented for instructions.

A NOVEL WAY TO INTRODUCE THE GOAT

Candidate is hoodwinked in ante-room and conducted to Chief Officer's station.

Conductor: "Chief Officer, I present you Mr. —————————, who is a candidate seeking the mysteries of our Order. He awaits your instructions."

Officer: "My friend, before advancing you into this grand and noble Order, it is my duty to examine you. Your answers will be considered by the Lodge and your advancement will depend upon the answers."

"What is your name in full?"
"How old are you?"
"Are you single or married?"
(If married) "How many children have you?"
"What is your occupation?"
"Have you always been able to earn a good livelihood?"
"Do you consider yourself to be sound and in good health?"
"Have you a good appetite?"
"Do you eat meat?"
"Do you like butter?"
"Which do you prefer; genuine butter or oleomargarine?"

(If the candidate says butter:)

"Very well, we will try to satisfy your appetite. We have the best butter in this section of the country. This butter has been tried by every candidate, and they all testify that it is genuine butter. Attendants, bring forth Billie, our butter, and administer some of his good qualities to our candidate."

(If the candidate says olemargarine:)

"Very well, we shall try to satisfy your appetite. We have the best manufactured butter in this section of the country. This butter has been tried by every candidate, and altho it is not the genuine article, yet all of them testify that it is a good, hard butter. Attendants, bring forth Oleomargarine, our manufactured butter, and administer some of its good qualities to our candidate."

(Goat is brought in. Candidate is mounted and given a ride around room, and finally dismounted in front of officer's station, when the following is introduced, if desired:)

Officer: "Well, sir, how do you like our butter?"
(Candidate is liable to say it's all right.)

Officer: "Now, my friend, you said, I believe, that you liked meat any old way. I am glad to know that you do, because we have an obligation in the way of a meat test which I will have to administer to you."

(Introduce courage or meat test described on page IV.)

TRICK OR SURPRISE CHAIR

(The chair can be introduced to candidate without suspicion of any catch.)
(One of the best methods is to have chair set either to right or in front of Presiding Officer during entire initiation, and after candidate has been put through various tests, the Officer will congratulate him for his courage, etc., and after giving him the secret work will say:)

Officer: "Now, sir, you have withstood all the tests and proved yourself worthy of becoming a member of our Lodge and as you have the secret work,

I will ask you to take a seat at my right (or on the chair in front of my station) while we proceed to close the Lodge in regular form."

(Candidate congratulates himself that it is all over and is glad to take the seat offered. The electric attachment adds much to the merriment. If this is used, turn current on just as trap is sprung.)

TRICK OR SURPRISE CHAIR (Another Way)

A member may be seated on the trick chair and officer will ask him to kindly let the newly adopted member be seated on the chair while the brothers arise and give him the grand honors. (Officer will give three raps and all will rise and he will then ask candidate to take the seat of honor.)

SURPRISE CHAIR (Another Way)

When candidate is seated on the chair, confront him suddenly with a gun, telling him you have reason to believe he has papers in his possession belonging to the Lodge. Command him to throw up his hands that he may be searched. Meanwhile an officer comes up ready to search him. As soon as both hands are well up, spring the trap. Having his hands up will cause him to turn a complete somersault. The electric attachment adds much to the merriment. If attachment is used, turn current on just as trap is sprung.

DE STINK OR BAD EGG TEST

Prepare atomizer, just before using, by dropping a small quantity of de-stink liquid inside of receptacle. Then lay it out of sight of candidate. Having also in readiness one egg with the contents blown out and the shell filled with water; also one perfect egg.

Candidate is now presented to Officer, who will enter into following dialogue:

Officer: "There are three essentials you must possess in order that your name be enrolled on our record. First, a positive vision—second, a sensitive touch—third, an acute sense of smell. We cannot accept parties who are liable to get killed by a train just because they couldn't see it coming. We absolutely refuse to act on the application of any fellow who really cannot detect any difference between an egg and a 'sock darner.' Yet the most important of all is the sense of smell. This we must test thoroughly. I, therefore, ask you to give me both brief and precise answers to the following questions:

(Showing candidate the egg.)

"What is this I hold in my hand?"

Candidate: "An egg."

Officer: "Correct. Your vision is good. I will now test your sense of touch. (Hookwinks candidate and places egg in his hand.) What is it you hold in your hand?"

Candidate:—"An egg."

Officer: "Very good, you are doing nicely. Now for the hardest test—is it a good or bad egg?"

Candidate: "I don't know, or I think so."

Officer: "I will now ascertain if your judgment is correct."

(Strike candidate on top of head with the shell that has been filled with water. This will break and cause water to trickle down his face. At this moment, an attendant standing a few feet in front of candidate presses the rubber bulb of atomizer, directing nozzle toward candidate's nose.)

"Now, sir, is the egg good or bad?"

Candidate: "Bad."

Officer: "I am sorry to say that you were compelled to pronounce it as such, and I pronounce your sense of smell perfect. I regret very much, that the egg with which I made the test happened to be a bad one, as I had instructed our janitor to select a good fresh one. The attendant will please get a towel and remove as much as possible the horrible contents of the bad egg, which has been scattered over your head and clothing. I will also advice you to air yourself well before going to your place of abode as it would be very embarrassing for you to try and make explanation to anyone who might ask what makes you stink so. If you cannot get all the bad taste out of your mouth, I would recommend that you eat a few limburger cheese sandwiches or suck a piece of asafoetida."

COURAGE TEST, OR MEAT TEST

(Candidate is hoodwinked and presented to officer.)

Officer: "My friend, every Lodge of this organization has in its possession a portion of the embalmed body of one of the patriots of our country. Each person becoming a member of this Order must partake of this body, so that the blood which flowed through the veins of those grand men, who gave up their lives for their country, may be instilled into your veins, giving you that courage and patriotism which every good loyal citizen should have, if called upon to shoulder a gun and defend our country. If you eat of this body, you will have that courage. Every member of this Order has partaken of it. Now, sir, are you ready to take this test?"

(Candidate consents.)

(Have some fresh raw meat or an oyster and a de-stink atomizer containing a few drops of de-stink liquid. An attendant will blow the fumes of this chemical towards candidate's nose and at the same time Officer will have him open his mouth, so he can place the meat or oyster into it for him to eat. The scent from the atomizer, which smells like spoiled meat, will gag him.)

(If candidate eats the meat, applaud him and tell him that his courage certainly makes him worthy of becoming a member of the Order, that you want him to step upon the throne of honor to receive the grand honors that he deserves. Here have candidate ascend the stairs to throne of honor or step upon judgment stand. Then announce to the lodge that Mr. ———— has shown his faith in the Order by taking a test which had been refused by hundreds of men, that you will crown him with the crown of honor that he has so nobly won. At this moment squash the crown having wet sponge down on his head, and at the same time, spring the trap, letting him slide down the stairs.)

(If candidate refuses to eat, call him a coward and request him to ascend the throne of judgment (throne of honor) or the judgment stand while the lodge disposes of his case. When in proper place, members may discuss his case and make threats of different kinds, suggesting punishments to be administered for his cowardly conduct, then allow or request him to explain to the Lodge why he refused to eat the body of our hero. If he is on the throne of honor, accept his excuse and announce to the Lodge that you are going to crown him for his good judgment in refusing this horrible test, which should be refused by any sane man. Then spring the trap when crown is applied.)

(If candidate is placed on the judgment stand, spring it just as he finishes telling the Lodge why he refused.)

THE TRICK CAMERA

(Used With Surprise Chair)

The trick camera is a good article to introduce after candidate has been put through several "stunts". Conductor will present him to Presiding Officer's station as follows:

Conductor: "Chief Officer, Mr. ————————, who has been tried by our various tests, has proved himself worthy of being adopted into our Order. I present him to you for final obligation."

Officer: "My friend, I am pleased to adopt you as one of us. However, before imparting to you the secret work, such as the signs, grip and pass-word, you will please advance to the Secretary's desk and register your name. While you do this our Official Photographer will prepare his camera to photograph you. We have adopted the custom of photographing each of our members as they are taken into this Order. Their photos are kept in our Lodge album for identification."

("Photographer" prepares trick camera and his candidate seated on surprise chair. When all is ready, he says to candidate:)

Photographer: "Now, then, look perfectly natural, and remain very quiet for just a moment."

(Just then attendant pulls off the chair and photographer presses bulb, and down goes candidate, who receives a free shower bath from camera.)

THE DEVIL'S SLIDE

(Conduct candidate to ante-room and while the Diving Elk is being prepared, blindfold him and tie apron snugly around his neck. Then conduct him to Chief Officer's station.)

Conductor: "You are now in front of the Chief Officer, who will address you."

Chief Officer: "Mr. ——————, while we are assured that you are a man of courage, yet assurances are of little value, as they have often proven untrue. We trust they are true in your case, however. You are undoubtedly familiar with the daring of the high diver. The attendants will soon place you in an easy chair and will elevate you thru a large trap door in the ceiling to a height of about 25 feet, when you will demonstrate your right to associate with men of courage by diving off into a shallow pool of water." (In a commanding tone of voice, "Attendants, prepare to elevate the candidate.")

(Attendants then seat candidate and buckle the straps, binding him to the chair. He is then slowly elevated by means of the windlass and at the same time the clattering crank is turned about three times as fast as the windlass. An attendant nearby calls instructions to manipulators and gives words of encouragement to candidate, finally speaking through a pasteboard mailing tube or roll of paper which is pointed downward. This makes the speaker seem many feet below candidate. The manipulator should draw him up a little distance and then let him back part way again, thus taking longer to reach the top and causing him to lose all idea of distance. There should be a large galvanized iron tub near by with water in it, and two men should alternately dip up a bucket of water and pour it back, making a sound of abundant water. As soon as top is reached, the trigger is set, the rope is unhooked and candidate is ready for his plunge. As he starts down, give exclamations, shouts and cries. Attendant standing near foot of incline receives him with a strong blast of water from the squirt gun. As soon as chair stops, attendant will wipe candidate's face, unstrap him and lead him to ante-room, where he will remove the apron and hoodwink while the lodge room is being cleared. At a signal from lodge room he is conducted to Chief Officer's station, where he is commended for his courage.)

Chief Officer: "My friend, while you did not make the dive in quite the proper way, yet you have shown that you are a man of courage and we are pleased to admit you to intimate association with us. (To Conductor), Conductor, conduct our friend to the looking glass and aid him to take away all traces of the results of the dive, after which you will conduct him to a seat among us."

(Conduct him to trick mirror, see page XXVI, and then to surprise chair, see page II.)

THE CANNON

(The Cannon may be introduced at close of initiation, just before the obligation is taken. Conductor is asked to retire with candidate so the Lodge may consider his eligibility. In a few minutes they are called and Conductor presents candidate at Chief Officer's station, who addresses him thus:)

Chief Officer: "Mr. ——————, I am very sorry to say that you have not proven yourself eligible to become a member of this Lodge. You have failed to lift the required number of pounds on our lifting machine. You also did not register very high on our Lung Tester. However, as you have gone so far, it would not be advisable to turn you out to expose what you have passed through. The Lodge has therefore decided that you must be shot. You will therefore prepare yourself to be shot, and in case you have any papers or word which you desire delivered to your family or friends, I will be glad to grant a dying man's last request."

(Cannon is then prepared as per instructions.)

TRICK GUNS

(William Tell Method)

By using both Guns, the William Tell act can be performed very effectively. Candidate is told that his confidence in the Order is to be tested by having a member act as William Tell and shoot the apple off his head. Apple is placed on head of candidate. Member doing the shooting uses front action rifle, and the result is that candidate gets a free bath. He is then given the privilege of acting the part of William Tell and is to shoot the apple from the head of another supposed candidate.

(Let someone whom candidates will not recognize as being a member act the part of the other candidate.)

The back-action rifle is then substituted for the front action, but this must be done without candidate's knowledge. He will of course expect the rifle to shoot water out of the end of barrel as it did before, but instead it will shoot backward and he himself will again be the victim.

If desired, the act described above can be reversed, letting candidate use back-action rifle first. Apple is then placed on his head and front-action rifle is used by person doing the shooting. The result is that candidate unexpectedly gets another free bath.

TRICK GUNS

(Duel)

Another amusing and positive method of introducing both rifles is the so-called "duel." Hand candidates back-action rifle and give a member acting as supposed candidate, the front-action rifle. Instruct both participating parties of the reward to be given for the better shot and also name a severe penalty which will be preferred against the fellow who makes a bad aim. Insist upon the necessity of each aiming at the face and not the heart.

Prior to duel, advise the member with front-action rifle that he must shoot first and instruct him to be particular in getting his face behind the rifle so candidate will do likewise. This part must be done quickly. We discourage prolonged aim since candidate will have a tendency to question the manipulation of rifle and may hold it in a position which would not produce the desired results. If member succeeds in hitting him squarely in the face, particular care will be taken upon the part of candidate to see that he gets revenge in like manner. However, he finds himself foiled again.

HOW TO USE ONE GUN ONLY

(One Method)

If Lodge does not want to invest in both guns, the one shooting backward can be used to good advantage. Have a target placed at one end of room and tell candidate that you wish to test his ability as a marksman before he is admitted to the Order, that members of this Order must be able to defend themselves and even their country if called upon. Candidate will receive the full charge of water in his face whether he gets good aim on the target or not.

BACK-ACTION GUN

(Another Method)

Have a member adorned with the Donkey Costume and specify that the head be made with water attachment. Tell candidate that he must prove his ability as a marksman by hitting the Donkey in the eye. Make it understood that no individual is admitted to the Order unless he is able to defend himself, after being provided with a gun properly loaded, against a common old donkey. Warn him that if he does not hit the animal in the weak spot mentioned, he is liable to receive a warm reception from its heels, which are always ready for action.

Let candidate also receive a full charge of water from "donkey" just as he discharges gun. He will then be satisfied that "everything is coming his way."

ELECTRIC BRANDING

(Form One)

(In order to perform this "feat" with good effect it is necessary to have a fake candidate and pretend to initiate two at once.)

Conductor: (Enters Lodge room with both candidates and halts in front of officer's station.) "Chief Officer, I present two candidates who desire to be initiated into the mysteries of this Society."

Officer: "My friends, before giving you any of the secret work, you must be branded with the insignia of our Order. It is the custom of this Society to brand each candidate so he can be identified if found dead. Are you both willing to undergo this ordeal?"

(Both give their consent.)

"Conductor, you will retire to ante-room with both candidates, and you will return with one at a time when notified."

(Conductor escorts candidates to ante-room.)

(The brand will then be prepared. When ready, the Door Keeper opens ante-room door and announces that Officer is ready for the branding. Conductor then enters with fake candidate, who will scream as if hurt shortly after entering the Lodge room. He will then take a seat on a chair at side of Officer's station and powder his face so as to look pale, and a physician with one or two brothers may be fanning him and pretending to be waiting on him when the real candidate is brought in and presented to Officer.)

Conductor: "Chief Officer, I present to you the other candidate to be branded with the insignia of this Order."

Officer: "My friend, the candidate just branded did not have courage enough to withstand the branding without fainting. I hope that you will be able to endure it better. It is true that the branding is painful, but it is of short duration and had to be endured by all members of this Order."

(Fake candidate keps groaning all the while as if suffering.)

"Attendants, you will prepare candidate for the branding. It might be well to hoodwink him so he cannot see the operation performed. I believe he can better endure it if not permitted to see."

(Conductor will have candidate sit astride a common chair facing its back, and then hoodwink him while attendants pull his shirt out of his trousers, exposing his back. When all is in readiness, Officer will say:)

Officer: "Chief Brander, is the iron good and hot?"

Chief Brander: "It is, your honor."

Officer: "Then advance and perform your duty by branding the candidate."

ELECTRIC BRANDING
(Form Two)

Introduced same as Form One, except that Conductor enters with candidate and halts near the door just after fake candidate screams. Fake candidate then pretends to faint and attendants lay him down and fan him and put cold water on his brow. They may also ask if there is a physician in the room, and the officers gather around and look worried, etc., making the scene as realistic and impresesive as possible. After a moment, fictitious candidate "comes to," is assisted to arise and is led to a chair, where someone continues to fan him. The Lodge is then called to order again.

ELECTRIC BRANDING
(Form Three)
Deceptive Brand and Ink Pad Required

Introduced same as Form One, except that candidate remains in the room throughout the proceedings. Proceed as follows:

While preparing brand, conductor retires near door with candidate and requests him to be seated, at the same time locking the door. He then returns to fake candidate and has him set astride a common chair facing its back. Attendants pull shirt out of his trousers, exposing his back. Fake candidate should be in such a position that real candidate can see the deceptive brand applied to back. When fake candidate is branded with deceptive brand he should squirm and writhe as if in great agony, adding emphasis to his action first by a scream and then by continued groaning. He may then pretend to faint, etc., as suggested in Form Two.

A More Severe Way of Using the Branding Outfit With Operating and Whirling Table

Officer: "My friend, you have so far proved yourself worthy of becoming a member of our Order. Some of the tests were to teach you valuable lessons which you will no doubt not soon forget. Others were to amuse our brothers, but you will now have to undergo a painful ordeal before registering your name on our records. This organization is probably the only one which brands each of its members."

(The attendants will prepare for the branding.)

"Now, my friend, let me assure you, while the branding is painful, it is not dangerous. We have had but one die from the results of blood poison and one of heart failure, but your blood is in good condition, and judging from your nerve in withstanding all former tests, I do not think there is any danger of blood poison or heart failure."

Officer: "Attendants, prepare the candidate to be branded; fasten him securely to the operating table and have the brand heated red hot so it will burn our mark well into his flesh."

(Attendants hoodwink candidate and strap him securely to whirling board prepared especially for the purpose. Unbutton candidate's shirt so as to brand him on the breast.)

Officer: "Chief Brander, is the iron good and hot, and are you ready to perform your duty?"

Chief Brander: "Officer, the iron is hot and I am ready to perform my duty."

Officer: "Then apply the brand."

(Chief Brander advances and applies the Electric brand.)

"Great horrors! He is dead! He has been unable to withstand so severe a test, and he lies dead upon the table!"

(Much confusion and many suggestions as to better way to dispose of body, it being finally decided to bear it away and deposit it in an old well near the hall. After marching several times around room and through doors, carrying candidate with whirling board on their shoulders, a halt is called at the place where framework for "whirling board" is placed, and the hooks are quietly attached to the rings at ends. Attendants whisper to each other to drop body head first into well, when, at a given sign, candidate is given a whirl which sends him spinning "end over end." The board is then stopped and attendants quietly walk a little distance away, discussing in a low tone, so that candidate can hear, whether or not he was really dead. One will say that he thinks he saw him move, etc., etc. Finally they decide to draw him up out of well and return him to Lodge room for careful examination. They quietly step up to candidate, give him another whirl and then take him on their shoulders again, walking around Lodge hall a few times, when they come to a halt and lay him down. One then addresses Officer:)

"We took his body to the old well and after letting it down, some of the brothers had good reasons to believe that the candidate was not dead, so we drew him up again and brought him back for a careful examination."

Officer: "You did well under such circumstances to return with him, as in the event that he might have life, he could have called assistance by loud cries, and the discovery of our deed would end in serious results."

(Officer advances, feels candidte's pulse and places his ear over candidate's heart and exclaims:)

"The heart still beats, and he is now breathing!" "Attendants, unbind him."

(Attendants unbind, remove hoodwink and stand him on his feet.)

Officer: (Shaking hands with candidate, says): "My friend, I congratulate you on your nerve through this test. We are always glad to have men of iron nerve to become members of our grand Order."

THE PLEDGE ALTAR

The Pledge Altar may be introduced after candidate has been through most of the other various stunts. The very fact that the word "pledge" is connected with the name of the Altar assures him that all trials are over and he is soon to be admitted into full ranks.

Officer: "Now, sir, we have tried your faith and sincerity in the presence of the members of this Lodge and it is fully agreed that you possess all the necessary qualities to make a good member. All that remains is taking the pledge. This will not bind you to any particular sect or creed but is done simply to preserve the secrets of our fraternity. By taking the pledge now, you will have the pleasure of seeing the other poor victims initiated. Are you willing to proceed with the obligation?"

(Candidate answers, "I am.")

Officer: "I am glad for your affirmative reply." "Attendant, escort our friend to the altar."

(Officer precedes attendant who is assisting candidate and approaches the front side of Pledge Altar, where an electric carpet is placed upon which candidate is asked to stand. After candidate is properly stationed, officer passes around to opposite side.)

Officer: (Gives three raps; members rise.) "Brothers, we have assembled here tonight to teach this applicant the good things to be derived from a fraternal society, founded on principles of true love and friendship and may I beseech you, one and all, to give your very best attention and respect while we now participate in the obligation." "Applicant, you will please kneel where you are and fold your hands resting them on the altar. Remember, you are not to change this position until I command you to rise. By this act, you publicly signify soundness of mind in pledging your sacred honor to this solemn vow, which I now ask you to repeat after me."

"I (your name)—in the presence of these members assembled—pledge my hearty approval of all the methods adopted tonight—to teach me the lessons so requisite for a plain understanding of the requirements of this fraternity—and I will forever, faithfully and conscientiously—perform all duties connected with my membership—necessary to maintain the high standing of this fraternity in our community. If I flinch in this obligation—or show signs of deceit—may I be chastised severely at this altar for ever asking admittance into your ranks—but if I am worthy—pray receive me."

DeMoulin Bros. & Co., Greenville, Ill.

(Right at this point give him a quick electric shock. When he flinches, attendants will say:)

Attendant: "Officer, our friend has changed his position, thus violating the pledge even while taking it. Trust him no further."

Officer: (Gives one rap; members all sit.) "Brothers, I must confess my disappointment in this applicant, but you have probably noticed like myself that with this exception, he has conducted himself very nobly and I hardly think we should censure him for this apparent nervousness. I, therefore, take the privilege of continuing with the pledge." "My friend, I have expressed confidence in you to all members present, so if you fall below their expectations again, I am powerless as far as rendering any assistance is concerned, to get you in this Lodge. We will now continue with the pledge, but do not forget my remarks."

"I further promise—that under no circumstances or conditions—will I—even though threatened with dire calamity—or tempted with great reward—ever forget to put in practice—the lessons that have been imparted to me. May the ghost of Satan forever haunt me—if I falter in my promise."

(As officer repeats last sentence, he should raise his right hand, as if taking an oath and, whether or not the candidate does likewise, should spring the lever just the moment the sentence is uttered. At same time attendant should give him anoher shock. A most startling effect can be produced by introducing this Altar as suggested.)

THE MOLTEN LEAD TEST

Officer: "My friend, it was a Datto who suggested dropping a prisoner in boiling oil, but we, as civilized men, do not resort to such barbarism. We do, however, have certain tests which, while not necessarily fatal, are dangerous if performed carelessly. The test which I am now going to introduce is one which will prove your faith in this Order. It will require iron nerve, but I believe that you have the necessary courage. You will be asked to plunge your hands into a pot of molten lead."

(To masked attendants, who have been pretending to be heating and melting the lead where candidate can see them;

"Attendants, is the lead good and hot?"

Attendant: "It is, your honor We have it red hot."

(The officer then leads candidate to the molten lead.)

Officer: "Now, sir, I demand you, if you are not a coward, to plunge your hands down deep into this molten lead."

(If he refuses, attendants take hold of him and force his hands into it. When the electric attachment is used, candidate should be requested to remove his shoes and sox before the test is introduced. The officer should see that candidate stands on the mat.)

(Optional)

If candidate refuses to plunge his hands into the molten lead, officer may proceed as follows:)

Officer: "Coward! Coward! I am surprised at you, and I regret that some of our brothers used such poor judgment in presenting you for membership. We have no use for cowards here." "Attendant, I will ask you as one of our brave brothers, to plunge your hand deep into this molten lead to prove to this cowardly candidate the courage he lacks."

(To candidate:)

"Now, sir, since you have proved yourself unworthy of proceeding further toward becoming a member of this Lodge, I ask you to take a seat at my left while the Lodge decides how to dispose of your case."

(Seats candidate on trick or surprise chair and touches it off. Or candidate may be asked to step upon the judgment stand or throne of honor while the Lodge disposes of his case, and when he tries to explain why he refused the orders given him by the officer, trap is sprung.)

THE SPIKEY STOOL

Officer: "Now, sir, since you have demonstrated to us that you are too much of a coward to plunge your hands into molten lead, I will test your courage on something easier. You will seat yourself on that spikey stool. If you are not a coward, you will obey my orders and sit squarely on the points of those steel spikes."

(Use either the spikey stool with or without water attachment; the one with water attachment is preferable. If candidate refuses to obey orders, attendants should be requested to force him to sit on stool. The spikey stool with real steel spikes may be used to advantage by having the candidate examine it and then slyly substitute stool with rubber spikes.)

SPIKEY STOOL
(Another Way)

Officer: (To Candidate). "Now, sir, to prove your faith in this Order, I command you to sit on that stool, set with steel spikes. If you have the required faith and courage you will obey my orders."

(Members may call him a coward, others will ask him not to be so foolish as to try it etc. If he refuses, officer will say:)

"Attendants, do your duty."

(Attendants will then force him to sit on the rubber spikes, or one of them may sit on them himself and all hiss candidate and call him a coward.)

Then presiding officer may prefer charges against candidate for being a coward and not having sufficient courage to obey his commands, etc., and then lead him onto judgment stand, throne of honor, or any other catch or test, or punish him by branding him as a coward, or making him undergo the iron test.

If candidate is on to "rubber spiked affairs," the spikey stool with water should be introduced and the water will remind him that he is not "on" to all spikey things, after all.

THE MUTOSCOPE
(Form One)

When introducing the mutoscope in connection with other articles, such as Lung Tester, Lifting and Spanking Machine or Invisible Paddle Machine, Iron Test, Trick Camera, Trick Telephone, Judgment Stand, etc., see that the sign-board is turned so words "The Mutoscope" are in front.

(Attendant brings candidate hoodwinked to the officer's station.)

Officer: "My dear applicant, you can indeed consider yourself very fortunate that this Lodge decided, prior to your initiation, to be unusually lenient with you. We have omitted over half of our regular work so you can guess what would have been left of your poor anatomy if the full course had been pursued. We shall now put all fun aside and reveal the mysteries of this Order. See that you heed my admonition and be ever mindful of your obligations." "Attendant, remove the hoodwink."

(Hoodwink is removed.)

Officer: "The secrets of this Order are communicated different from any other fraternity. Instead of speaking the password and showing how the grip is given, etc., we demonstrate by illustrations through a mutoscope. In this way all danger of outsiders becoming familiar with our secret work is eliminated. It shows just how to give all the signs and participate in all the tests. You will now follow the attendant to the mutoscope and he will show you how to work it. In the meantime, I shall prepare your membership papers and after the mysteries of this Order have been revealed, it will only take your signature to entitle you to the full rights and privileges of this Lodge."

(Attendant escorts candidate to machine and sees that it is ready for operation. By the attendant looking in it several times and pressing the button, candidate will not hesitate to "follow suit.")

THE MUTOSCOPE
(Form Two)

When Mutoscope is used in club rooms or in Lodge room prior to opening of regular session of Lodge, it should have the sign-board turned so picture of a ballet girl and words 'For Men Only" are in front. The machine should be placed next to wall where it may be readily seen and most conveniently reached.

TRICK COFFEE URN

The Coffee Urn may be introduced after candidate has passed through several good hard stunts. Attendant should see that top of urn is filled with ridiculous, unappetizing things. The more absurd, the better. Have bottom receptacle filled with coffee before inroducing candidate.

Attendant: "Most Worthy Officer, I notice that the candidate displays signs of weakness. This may either be the result of not having had enough to eat before coming here, or of some physical ailment. However, I would suggest that he be given a cup of coffee."

Officer: "I have also noticed somewhat of a weakness in our candidate. Our Lodge is composed of strong, healthy men, and we cannot permit an invalid to become one of us and absorb all our treasury as sick benefits, neither do we want any among us who are not able to furnish their families with the necessaries of life. However, if it is just a matter of not being able to get enough to eat, some of us might give, or find him a job, whereby he would be able to support himself and family. You will therefore give him a cup of coffee, and we will judge from that, what action is best in the matter."

(The coffee must be of a drinking temperature. As soon as candidate commences to drink, attendant will pull out an old dish rag, some limburger cheese, feathers, a piece of soap, etc. If candidate refuses to drink after seeing these things, officer will make him mount the Judgment Stand and pledge before leaving the Lodge room that he will not reveal any of the proceedings he has witnessed. If the Lodge has the Shoot the Chutes, it would be preferable to use it because candidate will think he has been put out by lightning express.)

TREAD MILL

(Conductor escorts candidate hoodwinked to presiding officer's station and addresses officer as follows:)

Conductor: "This candidate still shows obstinate characteristics and you know our noble Order will never receive a man of such qualities. I am rather inclined to think he did not ride the goat long enough to get these 'butted' out of him. A penitentiary 'work-out' is the thing he needs. Let's commence at his feet first."

Officer: "My friend, you are not unlike other candidates in this respect so you must pass through an ordeal that we all have had some experience with. The lesson you will learn from this 'work-out' may seem the hardest task you ever undertook, but it will be a sweet remembrance. The principles will be so vividly imparted that you can not help but grasp them. Fraternalism teaches that when you are called upon to do certain things, or render assistance to a brother, your response must be prompt. Standing still and expressing regrets, etc., will not accomplish anything. A responsive, unselfish and kind-hearted man is the kind of material we want. Are you willing to prove that you are such a man?"

(Candidate answers, "I am.")

Officer: "Then, go with the conductor and do as he bids."

(Conductor takes candidate to tread mill and "trys out" his pedal extremities until he acknowledges that he has traveled far enough to have been around the globe, had he been on a straight road.)

THE GUILLOTINE

Introduced as a punishment by giving candidate a sentence to be beheaded for any fictitious charge such as refusing to plunge his hands into the molten lead, to wash his hands in the electric lavatory, to drink at the electric fountain, etc.

Alto introduced by ordering candidate expelled from Lodge room for some fictitious reason, and then someone says that if he be allowed to go out into the world he will give away all the secrets of the Order. Then another argues that it would be better to do away with him, which prevails. He is then introduced to the guillotine.

May also be introduced the same as the saw mill. See page XXVIII.

TRIP THROUGH A STORMY DESERT

(In Ante-Room)

Escort: "Before you take the journey through our Lodge, I must require of you certain pledges. First, will you promise to obey all commands?"

Candidate: "I will."

Escort: "Are you willing to submit to severe and humiliating tests of your good intentions and will you absolve all members from any blame or censure should they in any manner displease or offend you in the obligation?"

Candidate: "Yes."

Escort: "Then submit to this hoodwink until I please to remove it."

(Candidate and Escort then enter Lodge room which has in the meantime been properly arranged.)

Officer: "How dare a stranger enter this desolate place, and pray, what do you seek?"

Escort: "We are on a journey and have come this way to avoid the dense woods whose inhabitants are more deceitful and dangerous than all the snares and evils ever planned by human mind. I beg you to be our guide, so while we traverse your domain no harm can befall us."

Officer: "I will do so, but before starting, let us make proper preparations and take sufficient provisions. I see the stranger is provided with a hoodwink to shade his eyes from the glaring hot sun but has no sandals. He will please remove his shoes and sox, and my attendants will buckle on sandals."

Candidate sits down and takes off his shoes and sox and attendant steps up with pair of electric sandals which are substituted instead. Large baskets filled with heavy articles should be brought forth and set at his feet.

Officer: "We will now proceed. Stranger, take hold those baskets at your side and bring them along."

(Escort will conduct candidate around Lodge room several times until his burden gets the best of him. All lights can be turned off in the meantime and escort will remove the hoodwink when they stop to rest. Presently the rumbling of thunder is heard in the distance, followed at intervals by a dull flash of lightning. Escort commences to groan and members to make strange sounds. The storm will continue to get worse and worse, until the vivid flashes of lightning and loud peals of thunder change into the sound of rain and wind.)

Escort: "Worthy Guide, let us get away from this approaching storm. The air and ground seem filled with electricity."

(Attendant must be ready to turn on electricity in candidate's sandals when escort says above.)

Officer: "The storm has changed its course, so we are safe in resuming our journey. Gather up your provisions and follow me."

(Escort will hoodwink candidate again and hand him the baskets to carry. The lights in the room can then be turned on. If the Lodge will buy our patent hoodwink, it will be much more convenient because the light, darkness and tableau effect can be produced without removing hoodwink.)

Officer: "We are now in the center of the desert. Yonder remains the only well within fifty miles of us. Shall we not refresh ourselves?"

Escort: "Yes. The stranger is completely fatigued, and must be revived in order to finish this journey."

Officer: "I warn you, however, to be careful when approaching this well and see that you keep straight in the path that I point out, or else you will encounter numberless reptiles of all descriptions, ready to thrust their poisonous fangs into you."

(After marching around the Lodge room another time, they will approach the well. If candidate complains of his burden, touch him up occasionally with an electric shock in his feet. Imitation reptiles should be placed along the pathway to the well.)

Officer: "I have been to the well and satisfied myself with its pure, sparkling water. You will perceive my footprints leading to it and if you step in them, no danger will befall you. Let the stranger's eyes be uncovered and burdens removed so he can safely approach and partake of the reviving elements."

(Candidate is then brought to well and the moment he attempts to drink from the bucket, a blank cartridge is exploded, the water upset on him and an electric shock received.)

IRON TEST

When candidate is conducted into Lodge room, or after he has been put through some "stunt" and acts a little nervous, a member addresses the presiding officer and states that candidate seems to be nervous; that he judges from his actons that he lacks confidence in the Order; he then moves that candidate be put to a severe test to judge whether he possesses the courage required to become a member. Candidate may be asked to lie on a cot or on the floor just below the pulley which has been previously attached to ceiling; the iron ball is then attached to hook and handed to him that he may satisfy himself that it is solid iron; just at that moment a member moves that candidate be blindfolded so he cannot see the torture. As soon as blindfolded the hollow rubber ball is hung on hook in place of iron one and drawn to the ceiling. Motion is then made and carried that candidate be allowed to see and that he himself be compelled to pull the string and cause the ball to drop. The blindfold is then removed. The result can better be imagined than described.

If candidate refuses to pull the string, the officer will order conductor to do it, and if candidate attempts to arise to prevent the ball from falling on him, the officer will command attendants to hold him down.

The iron test may also be introduced as a punishment for refusing to obey some order or upon some fictitious charge.

MORAL ATHLETICS, OR DEFENDING YOURSELF IN THE DARK

Two candidates or one candidate with one impersonating a candidate are required for this "stunt" unless our "Dummy Man" is used as a fake candidate for the real candide to box.

The candidates are brought from ante-room without being hoodwinked and are halted near the center of hall. Two pairs of boxing gloves are thrown at their feet by the officer, who addresses them as follows:

Officer: "Gentlemen, our members are all required to be able to defend themselves in the dark and we have here a test which will enable us to judge if you are made of the proper material for adoption in this Order. These gloves are soft, so that there will be no danger of hurting each other. While putting on the gloves, the conductor will place on each of you a hoodwink and a prize fighter's belt. I will act as referee."

(After candidates are hoodwinked, let attendants buckle the belts with ropes attached around their waists. Fasten them together in front by the small rope so that they will stand about four feet apart. See that the large rope on the back of each candidate's belt is securely fastened to strong screw eyes in floor or held by attendants. A middle-man wearing a pair of gloves quietly steps between, and this man is to start the boxing and to use his own judgment as to how hard or how lightly to box. When all is ready, the officer will call time.)

Officer: "Time."

(Middle man puts in his work.)

(The boxing can sometimes be made more interesting by some of members gathering around before the boxing commences and betting on each man as the winner, or officer may offer a prize to winner.)

(Prize may consist of something ridiculous, not shown until after it has been won.)

We would highly recommend the use of the Electric Carpet in addition to Moral Athletics. Have candidates remove their shoes and stand on the mat. Whenever there is a lull just renew their spirits with a little "strength-giving sensation." They would prefer a dozen hits in the face revealing the "solar regions" rather than endure such a feeling. Revenge is sweet—so watch them try for another harder swipe at that other fellows block.

THE ELECTRIC WHEELBARROW

After candidate has passed through some very trying experiences, such as a "Trip Thru a Stormy Desert," "Electric Branding Irons," etc., and seems to be somewhat exhausted, the attendant may suggest a rest. A member may then suggest that while resting the candidate be given a ride. When he is seated (after the manner shown in the illustration) the attendant may proceed to give him a ride.

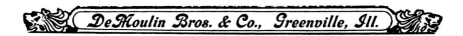

(Another Way)

If there are two candidates (or one of the members may act as a fake candidate), they may be presented to chief officer's station, by conductor, as follows:

Conductor: "Chief Officer, I present two friends who are desirous of becoming members of this Lodge."

Officer: "My friends, I am pleased to see you take a step in the right direction, and trust this Order may be of great benefit to you. However, owing to the many dangerous experiences through which you are about to pass, and as we only have one Physician present this evening, it is impossible to initiate more than one candidate at a time. Then, too, our ceremonies are very trying and we sometimes have more than we can do to care for one man, and we do not think it best to take any unnecessary risk by doubling the responsibility. This being the case, one of you will be excused from initiation. We do not want to show any partiality, therefore we will give each one a ride in our wheelbarrow, and the one that stays in the longest will be excused from further initiation."

(Candidates are then taken out and brought in one at a time and given a ride in Electric Wheelbarrow.)

ELECTRIC CARPET

Officer: (To candidate)—"My friend, I presume that it is your desire to become a member of this Order, or (to proceed further into the mysteries of this Order). It will be necessary for you to travel over a rugged road, and perhaps you may be asked to cross the hot sands of the desert. Are you willing to proceed?"

(The candidate will answer in the affirmative.)

Officer: "Very well. Conductor, you will escort candidate to the anteroom and prepare him to travel the road that leads to the place where he can obtain the secret work of this Order."

(Conductor escorts candidate to ante-room, has him remove shoes and stockings, and then hoodwinks him. During this time attendants prepare electric carpet.)

(Conductor gives three raps.)

Door Keeper: "Who comes here?"

Conductor: "A brother, leading one who is unable to see or understand the mysteries of this Order, but being prepared, desires to be conducted over the hot sands of the desert to reach the throne where our king will impart to him the knowledge he seeks."

Door Keeper: "Give me the pass word and you may enter."

(Conductor pretends to whisper pass word.)

Door Keeper: "Correct. You may enter and proceed on your journey."

(Conductor leads candidate over electric carpet. Candidate may be led around the room and over carpet several times if desired. Then carpet is quietly removed and candidate is conducted to officer's station. Just before reaching the station conductor may say:)

Conductor: "We are now approaching the king, who will impart the knowledge sought."

(Arriving at station, hoodwink is raised and conductor bows and says:)

"Most Noble King, I present to you this candidate who has traveled over the hot sands, that he might receive the secret work of this Order."

(Officer advances, gives candidate "glad hand" (electric hand shake), saying:)

Officer: "My friend, I congratulate you. By joining this Lodge you derive benefits which could not otherwise be obtained."

(Any of following tests may then be introduced: "Throne of Honor, Trick Chair or Lung Tester.)

THE TACK TEST

(Introduction to Electric Carpet)

(Conductor will present candidate to chief officer, and say.)

Conductor: "Chief Officer, I present to you this candidate, who desires to be admitted into this Order."

Officer: "My friend, we have here a test that will try your courage. If you have read the history of our country, you have seen that thousands of sons have shed their blood for it. Now, sir, to see if you possess the necessary courage, in case you were called upon to shed your blood for this noble Order, I will ask you to walk with your bare feet upon those tacks made from steel bayonets used in the Revolution of 1776. Every man that becomes a member of this Order must undergo this test. Are you willing to proceed?"

(Candidate will consent.)

"Guard, conduct candidate to the ante-room and prepare him."

(Conductor will have candidate remove his shoes and sox while in ante-room, and hoodwink him. While this is being done, the electric carpet will be substituted for the one with tacks.)

(Conductor gives three raps on door. The door is then opened by watchman.)

Watchman: "Who comes there?"

Conductor: "A candidate who is prepared to undergo the tests of this Lodge."

Watchman: "Then enter and advance to yonder test, and let him prove his courage."

(Conductor escorts candidate to electric carpet.)

Officer: "My friend, you are now standing before the steel tacks. You have agreed to undergo this test of courage. I therefore command you to walk with your bare feet upon those tacks made from steel bayonets. Prove your courage."

(Conductor escorts candidate over electric carpet, and after he has finished, officer greets him with glad hand—electric hand shake.)

"My friend, I congratulate you for having proved yourself worthy of membership in this Order. You will now advance and ascend the throne of honor, preparatory to receiving the obligations."

(Candidate may now be led onto the judgment stand or throne of honor. If Lodge has neither of above articles, he may be asked to take a seat on the surprise chair.)

ELECTRIC CARPET

(Another Way)

This is especially recommended when a large sized electric carpet is used.

(Conductor escorts candidate to ante-room, and has him remove his shoes and sox. During this time attendants prepare the electric carpet and members form in a circle around it. We would suggest that several members be equipped with some of our burlesque papier mache heads having water attachment and the balance with false faces. A few hand spankers will add much merriment to the initiation. While candidate with wooden shoes on his feet is being conducted to the officer, members should purposely make audible remarks about what will happen to that poor fellow, etc.)

Officer: "My friend, it appears from reports that have reached my ears, you are not to be recommended tonight as eligible for membership. I, myself thought you possessed the qualities which would make a good member. However, it seems that a majority of the members present disagree with me and they claim that your good traits which I have heretofore praised are only assumed attributes. At any rate, we have a test which will readily determine the truth in this matter. Are you willing to undergo the ordeal?"

(Candidate will answer in the affirmative.)

Officer: "Very well. Conductor, you will allow those gentlemen who have raised objections to make the test, but see that they do not seriously injure him."

(Remove wooden shoes from candidate's feet and escort him inside the "ring" on electric carpet. After using plenty of electric "spurting" try a little water "squirting" and use the spankers quite frequently. Tantalizing remarks will also have much effect.)

THE ELECTRIC SPIKED PATHWAY

(Attendant enters Lodge room with candidate hoodwinked, when officer addresses him as follows:)

Officer: (To attendant)—"Halt! I fear you are entering our threshold unprepared, as the proper signs were not given when entering. Are you sure the candidate was properly instructed by our chief advisor prior to his admittance? If not, a sad fate awaits him. However, all will be well if the proper answers known only to the advisor and myself are given in response to these questions. Should he fail to answer correctly then the Lodge must have a reason for this negligence." (Officer now walks up to candidate and, putting his hand on his shoulder, says:) "My friend, please either repeat verbatim the answers that the advisor instructed, or forever hold your peace. What is the motto of the Lodge?"

(Candidate will no doubt say, "I don't know.")

Officer: "Brothers, this candidate gives a random answer, thus betraying our advisor. I believe he is a deceitful man, but before affirming this statement it would be better to give him another trial. While the attendants prepare the barricade that protects the entrance into our Lodge, the escort will take him into the ante-room and have his shoes and sox removed."

Candidate retires and attendants place electric spiked pathway near ante-room door. When escort reappears with him, officer says:)

Officer: "Stranger, in the times of Chaucer, it was customary to cast all deceitful men into a cistern whose sides and bottom were covered with sharp-edged swords. Prior to this merciless punishment, a trench was dug and needle-pointed spears set vertically about three inches apart. Dirt was then filled in until the points only remained about an inch above the ground. If the accused victim could walk farefooted on the steel points without showing any signs of distress in his countenance, he was acquitted. We have a similar test whereby we will prove by your countenance whether you are deceiving us. Escort, you will proceed to find out whether his trilbies are easily punctured or not."

(Plenty of attendants should be on hand to see that he is kept on pathway while electric current is turned on. Every time he touches a spike and gets a shock simultaneously, he will think his feet are being terribly lacerated.)

A CURRENT AFFAIR

(Electric Wooden Shoes)

Conductor: (To candidate in ante-room)—"My friend, before placing your feet on the sacred grounds of this Order, I must hoodwink you and you will have to remove your shoes and sox and enter the room wearing these wooden shoes. The path that leads to the threshold of this noble Order is sometimes strewn with sharp-pointed tacks by some of our enemies; you may also step upon poisonous reptiles, and for your protection we place these shoes upon your feet. As you walk, you will, for your own safety, lift your feet high, as there are often wires stretched across our path. I caution you to beware, for if you should stumble, it might be a fatal fall. With this warning and with my assistance in escorting you, there is but little danger."

(When candidate has been prepared, the electric cords are quietly fastened back of shoe heels, and he is escorted into lodge room. Attendant follows behind with battery, and as soon as candidate has made a few high steps, attendant reminds him of the tacks by turning on the electric current. If he protests, presiding officer may prefer charges against him for being stubborn. He may then be placed on the judgment stand or surprise chair. If he is game, conductor will halt in front of officer's station and address the officer:)

Conductor: "Chief Officer, I present to you Mr. ——————, who seeks the mysteries of this Order."

(Officer, extending hand, graps candidate's hand and gives him "glad hand" (Electric hand shake), and says:)

Officer: "My friend, I congratulate you for your wise judgment, etc."

(If candidate jerks his hand loose, officer may prefer charges, then introducing the throne of judgment, guillotine, pillory or stocks, etc. If he is game, then he may be conducted to the mutoscope to receive the secret work, etc.)

CROSSING THE SWINGING BRIDGE

(Electric Bridge)

Conductor enters Lodge room with candidate and stops in front of officer's station.

Conductor: "Worthy Chief Officer, I present to you Mr. ———————, who has expressed a desire of being initiated into the mysteries of this Order. He is willing to do what others have, in order to receive the secret work."

Officer: "My friend, this is one of the most noble and honorable orders the world has known. However, before introducing you into our sublime mysteries, I, as grand officer of this Lodge, deem it my duty to inform you that trials and dangers beset your pathway. Dangers most terrible in their nature will be encountered. You may be called upon to endure untold tortures more terrible than that of being burned at the stake, or you may be hurled into a yawning chasm or bottomless pit. It is the inexorable law of our noble Order to press forward and never turn back until the goal is reached. You are now standing upon the blood-stained spot where many a brave man has sacrificed his precious life by becoming weak-kneed and showing the white feather before completing his journey through our significant ceremonies. With this knowledge, are you willing to proceed?"

(Candidate answers, "I am.")

Officer: "Very well. Conductor, you will return with candidate to anteroom and remove his shoes and sox so that his footing may be more secure. Then return with him hoodwinked."

(Conductor prepares candidate, then returns to officer's station.)

Conductor: "Grand Officer, the candidate now awaits your orders."

Officer: "My friend, you will now have to cross the river on the swinging bridge. This bridge is strongly built, but its swinging makes it hard for a weak-kneed coward to cross. For this reason and also to prove if you have that courage of which you boast, you will be compelled to cross it blindfolded. You will find an iron railing on either side for support in case you lose your balance. You will now proceed and remember our motto: 'Always press forward and never turn back'."

(Conductor leads candidate to bridge and as soon as he gets started, causes it to swing while attendant turns electric battery. Candidate will be compelled to take hold of railings to keep from falling, but he will not hold them long, as every time he touches one or both he gets an electric shock.)

The battery we furnish with this bridge and all our electrical appliances cannot injure any one, though, to some who are very sensitive to electricity, it may prove a little painful if turned on too strong. We therefore suggest that the crank be turned slowly at first and increase the speed if necessary, but not enough to make it too uncomfortable to candidate.

ROCKY ROAD TO DUBLIN

This may be introduced and used same as electric carpet. See page XV.

ELECTRIC RAZOR

(This may be introduced nicely, especially on a candidate who has not been smoothly shaven.)

Officer: "My friend, I note that you owe the barber for a shave which you neglected before entering this Lodge. We accept only nice smooth-faced fellows here for membership, and I will ask our barber to perform the duty that you have neglected."

("Barber" steps forward and has candidate placed in chair in proper position for shaving. He should use our large mug of questionable character and a large brush. While he is applying the lather, he may ask candidate if he wants 'em shaved close. He should appear to handle the brush carelessly (not getting lather in his eyes), and when candidate attempts to answer apply the lather over his mouth.)

Barber: "I have here a special razor that does the work without lathering the face. I am what is called a dry shaver. This razor has such a keen edge that it takes them off smooth. If it strikes a snag, it simply pulls it right out. Now keep perfectly cool, and I will soon put you in proper shape to be adopted into this Lodge."

After candidate has been shaved the barber may use the trick comb and brush.

THE JAG PRODUCER

The "jag producer" can be used nicely by walking candidate over it a time or two before leading him on the "electric carpet" or "rough roads".

It may also be used nicely just inside of Lodge room door, to make hoodwinked candidate walk over it upon entering. Conductor may tell him he will have to travel over rough and uneven roads in order to reach the threshold of the Lodge; that he will have to travel over the same road that all had to travel to seek the mysteries of this Order, etc.

INVISIBLE PADDLE MACHINE

The same introduction may be used for this machine as for the lifting and spanking machine. The results are very similar as far as the spanking effect is concerned, but the principles of accomplishing these results are altogether different. Candidate need not be hoodwinked.

IMPROVED LIFTING AND SPANKING MACHINE
(Form One)

(Candidate is hoodwinked and presented at officer's station.)

Officer: (To candidate)—"My friend, before advancing further into the secret work of this Order, it will be necessary for you to prove that you are an able-bodied man, as none but the strong and healthy can become members of the Order. We have an automatic lifting machine which registers your weight and also the number of pounds you can lift. Your weight and strength are to be recorded on our Lodge records for future reference, and in order that you may not have the opportunity of 'faking,' you will have to be hoodwinked while you make this test. We have a record of each of our members. You will now be conducted to the lifting machine, and the conductor will instruct you how to proceed."

(Conductor places candidate on lifting machine, and instructs him to stoop and take hold of handles and lift all he possibly can.)

LIFTING AND SPANKING MACHINE
(Form Two)

(Conductor enters Lodge room with candidate hoodwinked, and stops in front of presiding officer's station. The lifting and spanking machine is in readiness, and conductor addresses officer.)

Conductor: "Chief Officer, I present to you Mr. ——————, who desires to be initiated into the mysteries of our noble Order."

Officer: "My friend, I congratulate you, and I am glad to have the opportunity of adopting you as one of our brothers. However, before permitting you to see and divulging to you any of the secret work, you will have to satisfy the Lodge that you are of sound health, as it is not our intention to accept for membership any who will have to be supported by this Lodge. I will first test your strength. We have, for that purpose, an automatic scale and lifting machine. You will please state your weight."

(Candidate states weight.)

"Now, sir, I will set the scale at just twice your weight, and if you have the necessary strength to pass, you will lift twice your weight. If you lift the required amount, the bell will ring and our recorder will make a record in his book which will entitle you to proceed with the initiation. You will step upon the platform, stoop to take hold of the two handles, and proceed to lift."

(The candidate pulls and the machine does the rest.)

LIFTING MACHINE

(With Water Attachment)

Officer: (To candidate)—"My friend, before advancing you further into this Order, there is one requirement. I would be wasting time to consider your application if you cannot successfully pass the examination connected with a test we are about to make. The head officials of our Order have wisely passed a law prohibiting men of weak physical conditions from joining our ranks. There is no better method of determining the real facts than by an exhibition of your strength. In order to qualify and meet the requirements of this test, it is necessary that you lift the requisite number of pounds scheduled according to your weight. We have for this purpose an automatic self-registering machine. If you do not make good, we shall be obliged to dismiss you and refund the initiation fee. Please take your position at the machine as instructed by the attendant while I note the results of your strength."

(Candidate takes hold of handles and as soon as he pulls, the machine shoots a blank cartridge, and at the same time delivers a free bath.)

THE MUSCULAR TEST

(Conductor presents candidate to officer.)

Officer: "My friend, before imparting any of the secret work to you, I will have to test your strength. None but strong, able-bodied men can become members of this Order. You will please display your strength to the members of this Lodge by lifting this two hundred pound weight. If you can lift this weight and hold it up one minute without letting it rest against your knees, you will be permitted to proceed. (Officer takes out his watch.) Now, sir, you will show us what you can do."

(Candidate will, of course, drop it when he feels the electric current.)

Officer: "My friend, I am sorry to discover that you are not an able-bodied man, and that you cannot be admitted except by a two-thirds vote of the Lodge. You may be seated while the Lodge votes on the question."

(Seats candidate on trick chair, or places him on judgment stand or throne of judgment (throne of honor) and disposes of him as described on pages II, XXI and XXIV.

DeMOULIN'S PATENT LUNG TESTER

The lung tester can be introduced nicely after candidate has been put through other trials. It is such an innocent looking instrument and is introduced so nicely, that candidate will not suspect a joke.

Officer: (To Candidate)—"My friend, you have thus far proved yourself worthy of becoming a member of this Order. You have undergone various tests, some of which were intended for the amusement of the Lodge, while others were to impart or illustrate valuable lessons to you, showing how easy it is for one to be deceived unless he is constantly on the lookout. You have been taught that even among friends, you may be deceived. This proves how important it is to always use care and good judgment in all your actions. We who have been benefited by these lessons, have also been taught the importance of having all of our candidates rigidly examined by a prominent physician before accepting them as members, and now that the attendants have finished with you, it becomes my duty to have you receive the final examination for adoption. According to statistics, a greater per cent of insured men die of tuberculosis than from any other disease and our head physician has compelled us to adopt an instrument for making this test when there is any reason to doubt the ordinary examination as being sufficient evidence of perfect lungs. I have in my possession a letter from a member of our Lodge in which he cautions me to have you examined carefully; he says that his acquaintance with your relatives justifies him in making this request, hence I will turn you over to our physician for examination. Physician, please advance and make careful examination of this candidate's lungs."

(A physician, or one impersonating a physician, advances with lung tester, or he may be stationed at a desk on which the lung tester is placed, and he will invite candidate to step over to his desk. He will then examine candidate as per regular blank forms furnished with lung tester, which will lead him on without fail.)

(After candidate has blown in the lung tester the physician may say:)

Physician: "Grand Officer, I recommend this candidate as having a good pair of lungs; in fact, they were too much for my instrument. He blew so hard that he caused it to explode."

(In making this report, physician will conduct candidate to officer's station, and officer may congratulate him, grasping his hand with the "glad hand" (electric hand shake). This never fails to work at this moment, as candidate is not suspecting anything just then. The "warm" hand shake will make him wonder if he'll ever be on his lookout enough to not get the worst of it.)

TRAITOR'S JUDGMENT STAND

One of the easiest and most honest-looking pieces of Lodge furniture to introduce.

Candidate, after having met with various experiences, such as the molten lead test, the branding test, iron test, spikey stool, electric lavatory, or any test where a fictitious charge can be originated, is asked to take a position on judgment stand while Lodge disposes of his case. After members have discussed his case, pro and con, one makes a motion that they let the "subject" drop. The presiding officer announces that the motion has carried, ending with a loud rap of the gavel, and just at that moment the attendant presses the lever, allowing the "subject" to drop.

Or the candidate might be given an opportunity to plead his own case. Just when he gets very earnest in explaining the reasons for his conduct, the attendant does his duty.

If the candidate is found guilty and sentenced to be shot, bring out the cannon. Just as it is fired, let the candidate drop.

If electric lights are used in Lodge room, this scene can be made more impressive by throwing the switch, leaving the room in total darkness, just as the cartridge explodes. Everybody should keep perfectly quiet for a moment. Then turn the lights on again and candidate will be looking up for the hole in the ceiling though which he thinks he has fallen.

TUNNEL OF TROUBLE

Two candidates are required for this "stunt." Conductor escorts them to officer's station, and officer addresses them.

Officer: "My friends, you know that this world is full of obstacles, often preventing one from achieving success, on account of lacking courage and perseverance. It is not our desire to accept members into this Order who lack the proper amount of courage and push, as we do not want members who will be altogether dependent on the good will and benefits of this Order. We have prepared a test which will enable us to judge your merits before accepting you. You will be blindfolded and divested of shoes and then be required to enter, one at each end of that tunnel (pointing to tunnel), and the one out at the opposite end first will receive a reward of merit."

(Candidates are hoodwinked. The large ball is then quietly rolled into the center of tunnel, and candidates are started in, one at each end.)

Officer: "Now, gentlemen, remember not to allow anything to block your way or to interfere with your passage if you want to be eligible to membership."

(When candidates reach ball the fun begins.)

The electric carpet sold with tunnel is a splendid addition for bushels of fun, as candidates can be "touched up" occasionally if they get tired or if they are not inclined to work lively.

BABY DOLL

After initiation has been completed (?) and candidate is seated in Lodge, have some member appearing excited, enter with a spoiled baby, the baby screaming and calling "Ma! Ma!" etc. After everything has become quiet have member with baby make the following announcement:

Member: "This baby was left on the steps outside ante-room door, and will have to be cared for until Lodge has adjourned, at which time it can be placed in proper hands. Who will care for the child until that time?"

All members will look at each other questioningly, each member being certain that he never was very successful in quieting infants; especially any with such a bad disposition as this one. After this has gone on for a short time some member get up and make the following remark:

"Sovereigns, since our newly elected member has quite a number of these of his own at home, and knowing that he has had a great deal of experience in this line, I think he is the best qualified member to look after the wants of the baby until Lodge has adjourned."

Hand baby to candidate and watch developments. When the child has given evidence that it is "wet", hand candidate the diaper and request that he "change" the kid.

STRIKING MAUL

(Candidate is hoodwinked and presented to chief officer's station.)

Conductor (to candidate): "My friend, you now stand before our grand officer. You will get down upon your knees in Oriental fashion and prostrate yourself in obeisance to him."

When candidate gets in proper position and trousers are nicely stretched at the seat, the maul may be applied with telling results.

(May also be introduced with Blarney stone. (See page XXVI.)

UPWARD, ONWARD, DOWNWARD

(This may be introduced in same manner as roller pathway, but with much better effect and results. It is an excellent means whereby charges may be disposed of and can be appropriately used in connection with almost any of our initiatory devices. When candidate refuses to obey instructions and he is commanded to account for his actions, let him tread his way in pursuit of some place where he might rest and ask the pardon of the Order. Just at that moment the platform for which he is so thankful drops, and he is precipitated down the inclined shoot in a very accelerated motion. Simultaneously a cartridge will be exploded with a loud report.)

THE WIRELESS TRICK TELEPHONE

This trick 'phone should be erected at some convenient place in the Lodge room. It may be placed on wall back of presiding officer's station, with call or push button concealed under top of stand so officer may cause bell to ring when ready to spring the surprise on candidate.

(The 'phone rings.)

Officer: (Answers the call.) "Hello, yes this is the Lodge hall. Who did you say? Mr.————. Ah, yes, he is here. Do you want to talk to him? All right, just hold the 'phone a minute and I'll have him talk to you."

Officer: (Addressing candidate)—"Mr. ————, you are wanted at the telephone."

(Candidate will advance and say "Hello" a time or two, but receive no reply.)

Officer: "Perhaps your party has hung up his 'phone; you better ring him up."

(Candidate rings, and then cartridge explodes with a loud report, blowing white powder all over his face.)

Use in Club Rooms

The trick telephone is also conveniently used in Club room. It may be introduced the same as in Lodge work. It may also be kept loaded and a city telephone directory hung by its side. This will cause many to be caught without the assistance or suggestion of any one. It is often worked in Club rooms by several persons entering into an argument about something, and they tell the person to call up some one to prove who is right in the matter.

Or, it may be worked by having an engagement at Club rooms with party you wish to catch. Tell him to meet you at the Club at a given hour, and if you are not there when he arrives, to call you up by 'phone and you will come at once, etc., etc.

PILLOW FIGHT

(This can be introduced nicely when there are two or more candidates.)

Officer: "Brothers, having more than one candidate to initiate this evening, I would request that two of them participate in a pillow fight, and the champion be excused from further initiation. I will then permit him to take a seat among the brothers and enjoy the work. Attendants, prepare the candidates and also have plenty of strong brothers to hold the canvas tightly underneath the pole, so that in case one of the candidates should fall he will not be hurt."

(Here the proper number of men come forward with "Toss-up Blanket," and as soon as one of the candidates falls into it, carry him in blanket from underneath pole and give him the "toss-up performance." Care should be exercised not to be too rough and not let the blanket slack enough to allow him to strike the floor. With a little practice, this can be performed with perfect safety, and will create much merriment.)

THE TOSS UP

Tossing blanket is spread smoothly on floor a short distance in front of presiding officer. Conductor enters the room with candidate who is hoodwinked, and escorts him to a position in center of blanket, then halts.

Officer: (Gives three raps with gavel and announces): "All will be seated."

Conductor: "Chief Officer, there are no chairs for the candidates and myself."

Officer: "Our good attendance this evening makes us short of chairs. You may seat yourselves on the floor for the present."

(Conductor and candidate sit on blanket, but as soon as seated, conductor quietly steps off blanket and attendants quietly take hold of the straps round edges of blanket.)

Officer (to candidate): "My friend, before conferring any of the secret work on you, you will have to favor the brothers with a song. You will proceed to sing, 'Nearer, My God, to Thee'."

(If candidate refuses to sing, the brothers will cry out. "Throw him out, he's no good," etc., etc. Then attendants at a given signal start candidate up and put him through the "toss-up" as they see fit.)

(If candidate sings or attempts to sing, then the brothers will say "That's bum!" "It's horrible!" "He's no good!" "Throw him out!" etc., and attendants will then toss him up.)

Some care and judgment should be exercised not to let the blanket slack enough to allow candidate to strike the floor.

PILLORY

To introduce the pillory, a fictitious charge is made against candidate, and, as a penalty, or to test his courage, officer will proceed as follows:

Officer: "Brothers, before satisfying ourselves as to the qualities of this candidate it will be necessary to test his courage. I note that we have with us this evening Professor Jackson, who is an expert at knife throwing. With the consent of this Lodge, attendants may place candidate in the pillory, and I will ask Professor Jackson to display his ability at knife throwing, by showing us how close he can stick them to the candidate's head without injuring him. Attendants, bring forth the pillory and prepare candidate."

(Attendants place candidate captive in pillory and "Prof. Jackson" comes forward and places a table or stand about 20 feet in front of pillory. He then brings the twelve large steel knives and drops them hard upon the table, and with one knife in hand looks toward candidate and says:)

Prof. Jackson: "Brothers, I am going to show you how expert one becomes in knife throwing by continued practice. I am going to show you that I can imbed the points of these knives within half an inch or less of the candidate's head, but before beginning, I want to request the candidate not to move his head or try to dodge any of the knives, as the slightest move on his part might prove fatal."

Officer: "I would deem it safest to hoodwink him, as I fear it will be impossible for him to refrain from dodging. Attendant, hoodwink the candidate."

(Attendant hoodwinks him.)

Prof. Jackson: "Now, sir, hold perfectly quiet. I will not attempt to throw the first two or three knives very close."

(Instead of throwing the knives, they are quietly brought near pillory, and when the special large knife has been placed in slot on pillory, Prof. Jackson says:)

Prof. Jackson: "Now ready."

(Attendant strikes the handle of one of the knives hard against the pillory and lets it drop to floor.)

Prof. Jackson: "That was a wild throw. I must be out of practice. I will try again."

(Another knife is struck against the pillory and the large one in slot is caused to vibrate by springing the blade and let it go suddenly.)

Prof. Jackson: "That is a little better."

(The test may be continued on this line for some time. After throwing a few, "Jackson" may say:)

Prof. Jackson: "Gee, that was close! The knife slipped just as I threw it, etc., etc."

(With a little practice and judgment, this test can be made very realistic.)

THRONE OF HONOR

The throne may be introduced as the last part of any initiation by telling candidate that he has now finished his work, and may ascend to the Throne of Honor, where he will be crowned with the crown he has won. To assure him he will not be molested during the remainder of the evening, a slab of steel (rubber) spikes is placed at bottom of stairs. After taking his seat, and he seems to think that all is well, the officer says, "Crown him," and he is crowned with a crown which has a wet sponge in the top. At the same time, attendant touches a trigger and he starts his downward course from a celestial Arcadia to a lamentable Abyss. On arriving at the bottom (if Lodge has one of our wagons) he is surprised to find a cab (?) in readiness, and as soon as he secures his equilibrium two attendants proceed to give him a ride around the world in three minutes. Our spikey block can also be arranged on the wagon so he will have a most comfortable (?) seat. Candidate must be blindfolded when wagon is used.

THE LIQUID AIR TANK

Tank will produce much amusement if kept loaded in Club or Lodge room.

It may also be introduced to candidate while being initiated, as follows:

After candidate has been put through several "stunts", conductor in a very natural way suggests that a nice cool drink would be very refreshing to himself as well as to candidate, or, it would probably be preferable to introduce it in this manner:

Have the tank on a stand near officer's station and after candidate has gone through several "stunts" and appears to be rather warm and thirsty, he is taken to officer's station for further instructions:

Officer: "My friend, you appear to be warm and you are no doubt thirsty. Before proceeding further, you may refresh yourself with ice water from the tank and I will also ask you to fill a cup for me before I recite the obligation to you."

(Candidate will attempt to draw water from the faucet, but he will change his mind when the "durned thing goes off.")

ZIG ZAG ROAD

Here are the following things a candidate imagines when he gets on this road: Looping the loop; meandering through a lumber camp strewn with logs; dodging a tin can and club in a game of "shinney on your own side"; running a footrace on a pile of rock, etc.,, etc. It is a mighty fine thing to introduce when candidate is first brought into Lodge room. Have it right at the door, and the moment he steps on it let attendants get busy. Two escorts--one on each side of candidate--are really necessary at times to enable him to keep his equilibrium while attendants manipulate the ropes. This is a real live "stunt" and will cause mysteries to revolutionize in the mind of candidate that would never have materialized otherwise.

CLEANLINESS IS NEXT TO GODLINESS

(The Electric Lavatory)

Officer: (To candidate, who has previously been requested to remove his shoes and sox)—"Now, sir, before proceeding further toward becoming a member of this Order, you will have to wash your hands as a token of the purity of your intentions. You will then be permitted to advance further." "Conductor, you will escort the candidate to the lavatory."

(Conductor escorts candidate to lavatory and has him stand on mat. When he gets his hands well into the water, attendant turns crank of electric battery and candidate will suddenly make up his mind not to wash. He may be requested to proceed, but will not be able to do so. Conductor then says:)

Conductor: "Most noble King, the candidate refuses to obey your orders."

(Officer may then prefer charges against him and order him placed on judgment stand, throne of judgment (throne of honor) or any other test that the Lodge may have to introduce.)

THE COIN TEST

(The Electric Lavatory)

Drop a coin in the basin and order candidate to take it out and deliver it to chief officer, telling him that this coin will permit him to advance to a place of high honor in the Lodge. If he delivers the coin, conduct him to throne of honor, where he is crowned with a wet sponge. If he fails to deliver the coin he may be introduced to the guillotin, the judgment stand or the spikey stool, etc.

THE ELECTRIC FOUNTAIN

(After candidate has been put through several "stunts" officer suggests that he looks warm and asks that all officers advance with candidate to fountain and drink to his health and honor in becoming a member. The presiding officer will take candidate, who is in his bare feet, and lead him to fountain, and have him stand on the mat. All other officers will congregate around, each dipping a cup of water and asking candidate to help himself when they will drink with him. As he attempts to dip up the water, electric current will do the rest. Ask him to try again, and tell him if he refuses to drink, it will be an insult to the Lodge.)

(Upon candidate's refusal to drink, with officers of Lodge, the officer may prefer charges against him, leading him on to the judgment stand, throne of honor, trick chair, branding, etc., etc.

SPANKER

A splendid article to use on candidate when a startling effect is desired. If you happen to have one who imagines that he knows it all, just let someone tap him from behind and remind him that there are other things just as explosive as his mouth. It is surprisingly how meek he will become.

There are many places where it can be introduced during the initiation.

TRICK MIRROR

The trick mirror should be the last stunt introduced. Have it hung in a very conspicuous place, so candidate cannot help but notice it among the other Lodge fixtures when he first comes in from ante-room. At various times during initiation when candidate is not hoodwinked, different members should step up to mirror and, in a natural way, comb their hair. Of course, candidate will observe, but nevertheless, he will think nothing of the trick to follow. Therefore he can easily be brought before mirror by attendant, who states that as soon as he combs his hair and appears like a gentleman the Lodge will permit him to take a seat with the rest of the members. Or, he may be instructed to prepare for the banquet, which will follow very soon.

THE BLARNEY STONE

(Every Lodge should have this device for it is easily introduced. Place the stone about 5 feet from officer's station but be careful that connection is concealed by a rug.)

Officer: "My friend, ever since the creation of the world, there has been superstition in the minds of all people. I shall venture to assert that you never were more superstitious in all your life than just before you came into this Lodge room tonight. Just what you have expected to happen, I can't say, but nevertheless, I know you are considerably interested as to the condition of your physical anatomy when we are through demonstrating the mysteries of this great Order to you. However, we have not failed to make provisions whereby you will be greatly benefited if you only do as we bid. Now, listen very carefully to what I have to say, and promise me before proceeding that you will do as instructed. (Candidate promises.) Just a slip of the tongue or an unthoughtful action will be the cause of you suffering many severe penalties. Therefore, to protect you against any mistakes very liable to occur, we have secured—at a great expense—a piece of the stone taken from the Blarney Castle in Ireland. It is the peculiar and singular property of this stone to give wonderful skill in speech, thought and action to every individual who kisses it, and you should consider yourself very lucky that we afford you such an opportunity. You now have the privilege of kissing the Blarney Stone, but, understand, you must be sincere in this matter and obediently do as I have bidden." "Conductor, show the candidate the Blarney Stone, for I have promised him protection if he complies with my request."

(Candidate's hands must be handcuffed or tied behind him and also insist that he get down upon his knees to kiss the stone. When opportune, officer will squeeze the bulb and a small geyser will immediately be prevented from pursuing its upward course by coming in contact with candidate's face.)

BLEEDING TEST

This test can be introduced to candidate who wants act "smart" or "frisky" while he is put through some test.

Conductor: "Chief Officer, this candidate seems to be a little too 'frisky.' I think something should be done to tame him a little before proceeding further."

Officer: "Worthy Conductor, I have also noticed that the candidate seems to make light of this initiation. I think he needs cooling down a little. Suppose we bleed him." "Attendants, take charge of candidate, and draw a quart or more of blood from him, and see if that will tame him."

(Attendants advance, take candidate and lay him on a table or across a few chairs, and hoodwink him. They then pretend to bleed him, using the electric probe according to directions sent with bleeding test. While the bleeding is performed, a doctor, or one pretending to be a doctor, will feel of candidate's pulse and make remarks about bleeding reducing the pulse, and he will advise when enough "Blood" has been drawn.)

ELECTRIC SAW AND BUCK

Officer: (To candidate)—"My friend, you are no doubt aware that this Society accepts only strong, able-bodied persons as members; men who are able to earn a livelihood by the sweat of their brow; therefore, we always permit all members present to judge for themselves if a candidate is worthy of adoption. For this purpose, we have a test of wood sawing. The last candidate who tried, was to saw a stick of wood in two in one minute, but he only sawed it about half in two, so was rejected. Now, sir, if you are of the right kind of material you will finish sawing the same stick of wood in one minute. You may remove your coat, if you desire, and then show us what you can do. I shall appoint as judges to keep time on this task, Brothers .... and ...."

(Two brothers are named. They advance, each one taking a watch from his pocket, and when candidate is ready, one of them calls time. As soon as he starts sawing, the man at battery starts turning the crank, gradually increasing the speed until candidate lets go of the saw. Timekeepers then say:)

"Time is up. Officer, the candidate failed to accomplish the task in the given time."

Officer: "Conductor, you will present the candidate to my station."

(Conductor performs the orders.)

Officer: "My friend, I am astonished at the result. I regret very much that you failed in this test, because I cannot permit you to advance any further now without the consent of two-thirds of the members present. You will please take a seat at my right."

(Have him sit on trick chair, or officer may direct him to go on judgment stand or throne of judgment (throne of honor), while the Lodge disposes of his case. Members then prefer charges against him for trying to force himself upon them, knowing that he was not an able-bodied man, etc., etc., and finally allow or request him to offer to the Lodge any excuse he desires. When he does so, the trap is sprung and he realizes that he has been "worked" again.)

THE BUCKING COUCH

After candidate has been put through several "stunts", conductor will present him hoodwinked to officer's station, and will address officer as follows:

Conductor: "Most Worthy Officer, I again present this candidate to you for further instructions. It is not my desire to dictate to you, but with your approval, I would suggest that we let him rest while the other candidate who is waiting receives part of his initiation."

Officer: "Worthy Conductor, your suggestion is indeed a good one. We can advance the other candidate to where this one has left off, and then administer the secret work to both at once. You will therefore conduct this candidate to the lounge, where he may rest while we confer the degree on the other candidate. I would suggest that you keep him hoodwinked, as he is not yet eligible to membership, and is not entitled to see the work performed." (To candidate.) "My friend, while you recline on the lounge, you may find it a little 'buggy,' and if you should have a nightmare, do not permit it to disturb you. You may dream that you are in a railroad wreck, or that you are riding a goat, but when we awaken you, you will then realize that it was only a dream. I hope, however, that you will have pleasant dreams and feel rested when we call on you to finish the work."

(Conductor leads candidate to bucking couch, attendants having hold of the ropes. As soon as candidate gets a comfortable position, they start the "dream" a little slow at first to give candidate a chance to brace himself, and then let him have it pretty lively, but be careful not to be so rough as to throw him off on the floor. After he has had enough "nightmare", officer will go to lounge, grab candidate by the shoulder, shake him and say:)

Officer: "Here! Here! Wake up! Wake up! You must be having a nightmare. You have been raising such a disturbance that we could not proceed with our work. Conductor, you had better return the candidate to my station, and we will finish giving him the work before bringing in the other fellow."

(The candidate may then be led to some other test if desired.)

THE SAW MILL

This may be introduced nicely after candidate has received some of the secret work. He is then returned to ante-room with instructions to gain admission by proper raps and password. As he enters, he is seized by four or more persons who are masked to impersonate outlaws. They throw him down and demand password or secret work. He refuses, of course, to give it, as he has pledged himself never to reveal it. They then threaten to take his life or put him in some torture to compel him to reveal the secrets of the Order. One suggests to cut off his fingers or toes, another suggests some other torture, until finally they decide to bind him to the platform of a saw mill and saw him in two. When they have him bound to platform they start the mill running, and as he is drawn closer and closer to saw, they ask him if he will give the secret yet. Just before he is drawn into saw, several members come running and shouting:

"See the outlaws! Capture them! They are trying to make our candidate reveal the secrets of our Order." (Outlaws run away and candidate is unbound.)

Captain of the Rescuers: "What means this? Have you proved yourself worthy of our protection by refusing to give these outlaws our secret work?"

(Candidate will answer "Yes".)

"We congratulate you on your honor and courage, and we are glad to recommend you to this Order."

(Leading candidate to officer.)

"Grand Officer, we present you this candidate, whom we found a captive of outlaws, and he was going to permit them to take his life rather than reveal to them the secrets of this Order. We recommend him to you as a worthy person for adoption into our Order."

(From this test, candidate may be introduced to any of the following tests: Lung Tester; Lifting Machine; Electric Fountain; Trick Chair, or officer may give the "glad hand" (electric hand shake), while congratulating him.)

DECEPTIVE BEER OR WINE GLASS

After candidate has gone through several "stunts", he is conducted to officer's station for further instructions. Officer having deceptive glasses and bottle with platter on his stand, will say:

Officer: "My friend, I am now glad to greet you as a brother of our Order and invite you to drink with me to your good health."
(Hands candidate glass.)

"May you prosper in wealth and remain in good health to a good old age."

(Officer raises glass to his lips as if to drink and candidate will do likewise. This should all be done rather quickly so candidate will not give it much thought. The wine glass deception may be made more perfect by putting about a teaspoonful of water in the top. When candidate has made attempt to drink, officer will say:)

Officer: "The intention of this test was not to trifle with your feelings, but to teach you how easy it is to be deceived, even among those whom you may take to be your friends. Let me impress upon your mind the one important thing in this world. Be ever watchful and cautious in all that you do. This will often save you trouble and money."

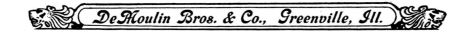

INDEX
TO FUN IN THE LODGE ROOM

BURLESQUE RITUAL

Containing Directions and Suggestions for
Introducing and Using Our

BURLESQUE AND SIDE DEGREE PARAPHERNALIA

ARTICLE	Page	ARTICLE	Page
A current Affair (Electric Shoes)	XVII	Lifting Machine	XX
A Few Suggestions	I	Lifting and Spanking machine	XIX
A Pointed Affair	XI	Liquid Air Tank	XXV
Altar, the Pledge	IX	Lodge Guns	VI
		Lung Tester	XX
Baby Doll	XXII		
Back Action Gun	VII	Meat Test	IV
Bad Egg Test	III	Molten Lead Test	X
Blarney Stone	XXVI	Moral Athletics	XIV
Bleeding Test	XXVI	Muscular Test	XX
Boxing Outfit (See Moral Athletics)	XIV	Mutoscope	XI
Branding and Whirling Table	VIII		
Bucking Couch	XXVII	Patent Lung Tester	XX
		Pledge Altar	IX
Cannon	V	Pillow Fight	XXIII
Cleanliness Is Next to Godliness	XXV	Pillory Test	XXIV
Courage Test	IV		
Coffee Urn	XII	Rocky Road to Dublin	XVIII
Coin Test	XXV		
		Saw Mill	XXVIII
Deceptive Glasses	XXVIII	Spanker	XXVI
Defending Yourself in the Dark	XIV	Spikey Stool	XI
DeMoulin's Lung Tester	XX	Striking Maul	XXII
De Stink Test	III	Surprise Chair	II
Devil's Slide	V	Swinging Bridge	XVIII
Electric Branding	VII	Tack Test	XV
Electric Bridge	XVIII	Telephone Trick	XXII
Electric Carpet	XV	Throne of Honor	XXIV
Electric Fountain	XXV	Tossing Blanket	XXIII
Electric Razor	XVIII	Toss Up	XXIII
Electric Saw and Buck	XXVII	Traitor's Judgment Stand	XXI
Electric Spiked Pathway	XVII	Treadmill	XII
Electric Wheel Barrow	XIV	Trick Bottom Chair	II
		Trick Camera	IV
Fountain, Electric	XXV	Trick Coffee Urn	XII
		Trick Chair	II
Goats	II	Trick Mirror	XXVI
Guillotine	XII	Trick Lodge Guns	VI
Guns, Lodge, Trick	VI	Tunnel of Trouble	XXI
		Upward, Onward, Downward	XXII
Invisible Paddle Machine	XIX		
Iron Test	XIV	Wireless Telephone	XXII
		Whirling Table	VIII
Jag Producer	XIX	Wooden Shoes	XVII
Judgment Stand	XXI		
		Zig Zag Road	XXV

APPENDIX II

PATENT APPLICATIONS FROM DEMOULIN BROS.

May 15, 1923. U. S. DE MOULIN 1,455,113
INITIATION DEVICE
Filed Oct. 30, 1922

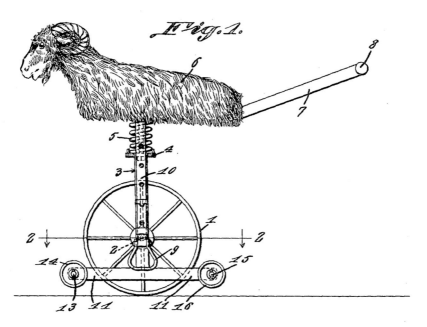

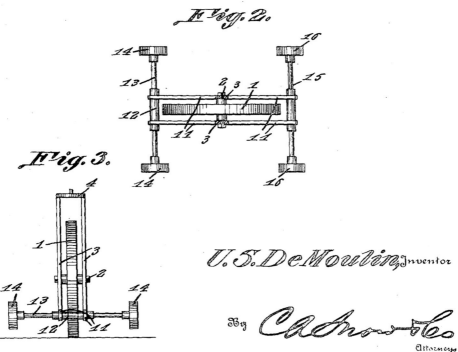

U. S. De Moulin, Inventor

Patented May 15, 1923.

1,455,113

UNITED STATES PATENT OFFICE.

ULYSSES S. DE MOULIN, OF GREENVILLE, ILLINOIS.

INITIATION DEVICE.

Application filed October 30, 1922. Serial No. 597,889.

To all whom it may concern:

Be it known that I, ULYSSES S. DE MOULIN, a citizen of the United States, residing at Greenville, in the county of Bond and State of Illinois, have invented a new and useful Initiation Device, of which the following is a specification.

This invention relates to initiation devices and more particularly to vehicles the bodies of which simulate animals.

One of the objects of the invention is to provide the body or saddle portion of the vehicle with a movable support of novel construction whereby the said saddle portion or body can be given a tilting motion in any direction so as to render it exceedingly difficult for the rider to maintain his position on the saddle portion or body.

A further object is to so construct the supporting or running gear that the operator is relieved of much of the strain to which he would otherwise be subjected.

With the foregoing and other objects in view which will appear as the description proceeds, the invention resides in the combination and arrangemeont of parts and in the details of construction hereinafter described and claimed, it being understood that, within the scope of what is claimed, changes in the precise embodiment of the invention shown can be made without departing from the spirit of the invention.

In the accompanying drawings the preferred form of the invention has been shown.

In said drawings—

Figure 1 is a side elevation of the device.

Figure 2 is a section on line 2—2, Figure 1.

Figure 3 is an end eelvation of the running gear of the device.

Referring to the figures by characters of reference 1 designates a supporting wheel the axle 2 of which is journaled in standards 3 suitably connected at their upper ends as shown at 4 in Figure 3. A spring 5 is suitably secured upon the connection 4 and constitutes a yielding support for a saddle or body portion 6 which, in the structure shown in Figure 1 simulates the body of a goat. A handle bar 7 is extended from one end of this body and has a grip 8 thereon so that the person pushing the device can obtain a strong grasp thereon. Stirrups 9 may be connected to the sides of the saddle or body 6 by means of straps 10 so that the rider can place his feet readily within the stirrups.

The standards 3 extend below the axle 2 and are provided, at their lower ends, with arms 11 extending forwardly and rearwardly therefrom. The front arms are connected by a sleeve 12 in which is mounted the axle 13 of rollers 14 and the rear arms 11 are similarly connected and carry an axle 15 having rollers 16 at its ends. The rollers 14 and 16 are supported considerable distances beyond the outer sides of the arms and serve to limit the forward, backward and lateral tilting of the structure about the point of contact between the supporting wheel 1 and the surface on which it is mounted.

In using this device a candidate is placed on the body or saddle portion 6 while the same is held balanced on the wheel 1 by the operator grasping the grip 8. As the device is moved forwardly it can be caused to tilt in any direction, thus making it difficult for the rider to maintain his position. The tilting movement will be limited by the rollers 14 and 16 coming into contact with the floor, these rollers serving to prevent the device from turning over. By providing the spring support 5 a bouncing action will be produced during the tilting of the body portion 6, thus rendering it even more difficult to ride the device.

Although only one wheel 1 has been illustrated it is to be understood that under some conditions more than one wheel might be desirable. The spring 5 could be dispensed with and instead of the rollers 14 the ends of the axles 11 or some similar structures could be used for limiting the tilting of the device. While the device described is designed primarily for initiation purposes it can also be used as a children's toy or vehicle.

What is claimed is:—

1. An initiation device including a supporting wheel, a structure carried thereby, a body or saddle portion mounted on the structure, a handle bar connected to said body, and means carried by the structure for limiting the tilting movement of the structure in any direction.

2. An initiation device including a supporting wheel, a structure carried thereby, a body or saddle portion mounted on the structure, spaced means carried by the structure for contacting with the surface on

which the wheel is mounted to limit the tilting of the structure on said surface in any direction, and a handle bar connected to the body.

3. An initiation device including a supporting wheel, standards at the sides thereof and supported thereby, a body or saddle portion supported by the standards, and means connected to the structure and spaced apart laterally and longitudinally for limiting the tilting movement of the structure in any direction by coming into contact with the surface on which the wheel is mounted.

4. An initiation device including a supporting wheel, connected standards supported by the wheel, a body or saddle portion, a resilient connection between said body and the standard and constituting a support for the body, forwardly and rearwardly extending arms at the lower ends of the standards and below the axis of the wheel, means on the arms for limiting the tilting of the structure in any direction by coming into contact with the surface on which the structure is mounted, and a handle bar for manipulating the structure.

In testimony that I claim the foregoing as my own, I have hereto affixed my signature in the presence of two witnesses.

ULYSSES S. DE MOULIN.

Witnesses:
H. C. DIEHL,
J. McGOWAN.

(No Model.) 2 Sheets—Sheet 1.

E. & U. S. DE MOULIN.
INITIATION APPARATUS FOR SECRET SOCIETIES.

No. 555,499. Patented Mar. 3, 1896.

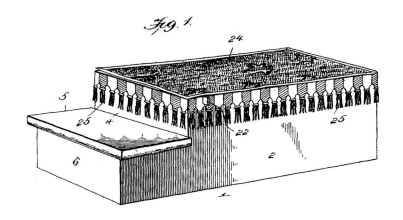

Fig. 1.

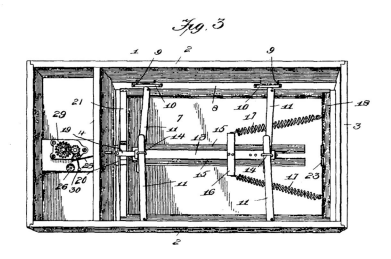

Fig. 3.

Witnesses
John C. Shaw
H. F. Riley

Inventors
Edmund DeMoulin
Ulysses S. DeMoulin,
By their Attorneys,
C. A. Snow & Co.

UNITED STATES PATENT OFFICE.

EDMUND DE MOULIN AND ULYSSES S. DE MOULIN, OF GREENVILLE, ILLINOIS.

INITIATION APPARATUS FOR SECRET SOCIETIES.

SPECIFICATION forming part of Letters Patent No. 555,499, dated March 3, 1896.
Application filed June 12, 1895. Serial No. 552,581. (No model.)

To all whom it may concern:

Be it known that we, EDMUND DE MOULIN and ULYSSES S. DE MOULIN, citizens of the United States, residing at Greenville, in the county of Bond and State of Illinois, have invented a new and useful Initiation Apparatus for Secret Societies, of which the following is a specification.

The invention relates to improvements in initiation apparatus for secret societies.

The object of the present invention is to provide for secret societies an initiation apparatus which will be simple and inexpensive in construction, and which will be capable of surprising a candidate without the least danger of injuring him in any wise, and which will present an appearance that will not arouse his suspicion or in any wise warn him of its operation.

The invention consists in the construction and novel combination and arrangement of parts, hereinafter fully described, illustrated in the accompanying drawings, and pointed out in the claims hereto appended.

In the drawings, Figure 1 is a perspective view of an apparatus constructed in accordance with this invention. Fig. 2 is a similar view, the platform being raised to show the operating mechanism. Fig. 3 is a perspective view looking at the bottom of the stand. Fig. 4 is a vertical longitudinal sectional view. Fig. 5 is a transverse sectional view.

Like numerals of reference indicate corresponding parts in all the figures of the drawings.

1 designates a substantially rectangular stand constructed in the form of an open box and composed of similar sides 2 and ends 3 and 4 and provided at its front end with a step 5, which is supported by longitudinal extensions of the sides 2 and a connecting end piece 6.

The stand is provided with a rectangular platform 7 at its top, and has longitudinal cleats 8, secured to the inner faces of the sides 2 and located at the upper edges thereof and forming a support for the platform, which is adapted to fit within the upper edges of the stand and to have its upper face flush with the same. The longitudinal cleats 8 are provided with recesses 9, and have metal plates 10 secured at the bottoms thereof to strengthen the cleats, and the platform is supported by pivoted locking-bars 11 arranged in pairs at each side of the platform and pivoted at their outer ends on the lower faces of longitudinal strips or battens 12. The outer ends of the pivoted bars 11 are cut at an angle and project beyond the side edges of the platform when the bars are disposed transversely of the platform, as illustrated in Fig. 3 of the accompanying drawings, and rest upon the cleats 8, or rather the strengthening-plates thereof, to support the platform in an elevated position.

The inner ends of the pivoted supporting-bars 11 are loosely connected with a longitudinal slide 13 by being arranged in loops or keepers 14 thereof, and the slide is spring-actuated, and when the apparatus is tripped is adapted to swing the pivoted supporting-bar out of alignment to the position illustrated in Fig. 2 of the accompanying drawings, whereby the outer ends of the bars 11 will be drawn inward, leaving the platform unsupported and causing it to drop to the floor or other support. The longitudinal slide 13 is arranged in ways 15 formed by grooved or other strips, and it is provided with a transverse piece forming laterally-projecting arms 16, to which are connected spiral springs 17, which have their outer ends secured to a transverse strip or batten 18 at the rear end of the platform. The pivoted supporting-bars 11 are held in substantial alignment to cause their outer ends to project from the platform to support the same by a resilient catch 19, mounted on the front end of the slide 13 and adapted to engage a metal plate 20, secured to a front transverse strip 21 of the platform.

The apparatus is tripped by an operating-lever 22, located at the front of the stand and fulcrumed at one side thereof and projecting through an opening of the other side of the stand a short distance, as illustrated in Fig. 1 of the accompanying drawings; and this operating-lever is arranged to engage the spring-catch 19, to withdraw its lug from engagement with the plate 20, to cause the spiral spring 17 to reciprocate the slide and release the platform.

The surprise and astonishment of a candidate are intensified by the explosion of a blank

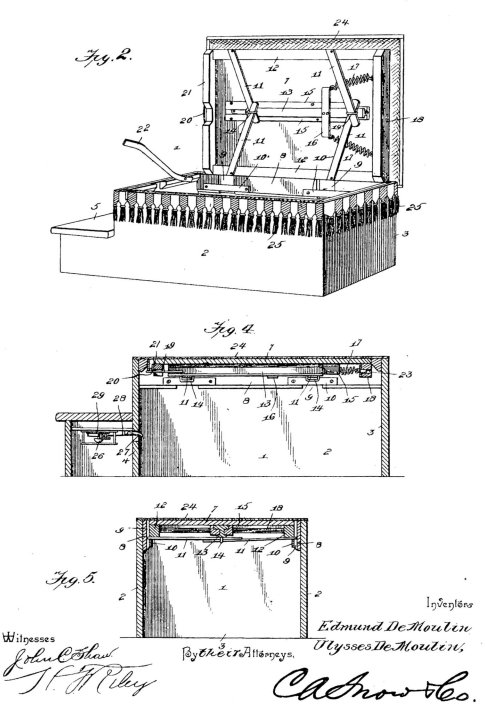

cartridge, which is placed in a chamber 23, located at the rear end of the platform in the transverse batten or strip 18 and arranged to be engaged by the rear end of the slide 13, which is provided with a suitable firing pin or projection for exploding the cartridge.

The falling of the platform starts an alarm-bell 26 ringing. A lever 27 is fulcrumed on a support and is located at the inner side of the step and projects through an opening of the front side or wall 4 and is adapted to be engaged and depressed by the platform, as clearly illustrated in Fig. 4 of the accompanying drawings; and the lever is connected by a rod 28 with bell-actuating mechanism 29. The inner end of the rod 28 is provided with a pawl or arm, which, when the lever is set, as illustrated in Fig. 4 of the accompanying drawings, interlocks with the gearing of the actuating mechanism and prevents a bell-hammer 30 from striking the bell; but as soon as the lever is thrown downward or inward by the platform the actuating mechanism oscillates the bell-hammer and rings the bell.

The platform is provided with a suitable carpet or flexible covering 24, projecting beyond the sides and ends of the platform, and completely concealing the fact that the platform is arranged within the sides and ends of the stand, and forms a trap-door. The stand is also designed to be ornamented by a border of fringe 25, which may be made to conceal partially the projecting end of the tripping or operating lever.

A candidate is placed on the platform, and at the desired time the apparatus is tripped, causing the platform to drop and a cartridge or cap to explode, and it will be seen that the alarm mechanism is automatically operated when the platform falls, and is adapted to surprise and startle a candidate without liability of injuring him in any manner, and that the purpose of the apparatus is entirely concealed from the candidate.

Other objects and advantages of the invention will be readily understood by those skilled in the art to which it appertains, and we desire it to be understood that changes in the form, proportion, and the minor details of construction may be resorted to without departing from the principle or sacrificing any of the advantages of this invention.

What we claim is—

1. In an apparatus of the class described, the combination of a stand in the form of an open box, a platform arranged within the stand, located at and closing the top thereof and adapted, when unsupported, to fall precipitately to the bottom of the stand, locking devices for rigidly supporting the platform at the top of the stand, alarm mechanism automatically operated by the falling of the platform and adapted to startle a candidate, and means for tripping the platform, substantially as described.

2. An apparatus of the class described, comprising a stand, a platform arranged within the top of the stand and adapted, when unsupported, to fall to the floor, means for rigidly supporting the platform at the top of the stand and for tripping the same by hand, and a flexible covering concealing the platform and projecting beyond the edges thereof, substantially as and for the purpose described.

3. In an apparatus of the class described, the combination of a stand, provided at its top with a platform arranged to fall, when unsupported, to the floor or other supporting-surface, pivoted supporting-bars located at opposite sides of the platform and arranged to project beyond the edges thereof to engage the stand for supporting the platform, a spring-actuated slide connected with the inner ends of the supporting-bars and adapted to swing the same out of engagement with the stand to cause the platform to fall, and means for locking and for tripping the slide, substantially as described.

4. In an apparatus of the class described, the combination of a stand, a platform arranged within the top of the stand and adapted to fall, when unsupported, the pivoted supporting-bars arranged at opposite sides of the platform and adapted to project beyond the same to engage the stand, a spring-actuated slide connected with, and adapted to swing the supporting-bars out of engagement with the stand, a cartridge-receiving chamber located in the path of the slide, whereby the latter is caused to explode a cartridge, and means for setting and tripping the slide, substantially as described.

5. In an apparatus of the class described, the combination of a stand, a platform arranged to fall within the stand, pivoted supporting-bars located at opposite sides of the platform, and adapted to project beyond the same for engaging the stand, a reciprocating spring-actuated slide connected with the inner ends of the supporting-bars and adapted to swing the same out of engagement with the stand to cause the platform to fall, a catch for locking the slide against movement, and a lever arranged to engage the catch for tripping the slides, substantially as described.

6. The combination of a stand, a platform arranged to fall within the stand, means for rigidly supporting and for tripping the platform by hand, a bell, a bell-hammer mechanism for actuating the bell-hammer, and a lever connected with the actuating mechanism and holding the same normally out of operation and arranged to be engaged by the platform in falling, whereby the actuating mechanism is released, substantially as and for the purpose described.

In testimony that we claim the foregoing as our own we have hereto affixed our signatures in the presence of two witnesses.

EDMUND DE MOULIN.
ULYSSES S. DE MOULIN.

Witnesses:
JOSEPH E. WRIGHT,
JOHN MCALISTER.

U. S. DE MOULIN.
COMBINED LIFTING AND SPANKING MACHINE.
APPLICATION FILED SEPT. 2, 1908.

920,837.

Patented May 4, 1909.

UNITED STATES PATENT OFFICE.

ULYSSES S. DE MOULIN, OF GREENVILLE, ILLINOIS.

COMBINED LIFTING AND SPANKING MACHINE.

No. 920,837.   Specification of Letters Patent.   Patented May 4, 1909.

Application filed September 2, 1908. Serial No. 451,418.

To all whom it may concern:

Be it known that I, ULYSSES S. DE MOULIN, a citizen of the United States, residing at Greenville, in the county of Bond and State of Illinois, have invented a new and useful Combined Lifting and Spanking Machine, of which the following is a specification.

This invention relates to initiation devices and more particularly to a combined lifting and spanking machine of the type described and claimed in Patent No. 654,611, bearing date of July 31, 1900.

The object of the invention is to provide a trick device of this character used ostensibly as a weight lifting machine but which, when actuated operates to release a spring actuated electro-generator and a spring actuated paddle, the current of electricity being directed into the person actuating the machine while the paddle at the same time strikes him.

A further object is to provide simple and efficient means operated by the lifting handles for releasing the paddle and generator actuating mechanisms.

A still further object is to provide a paddle having means operated by its impact against the body, for exploding a cartridge or other detonating device carried thereby.

With these and other objects in view the invention consists of certain novel features of construction and combinations of parts which will be hereinafter more fully described and pointed out in the claims.

In the accompanying drawings is shown the preferred form of the invention.

In said drawings: Figure 1 is a perspective view of the complete device. Fig. 2 is a bottom plan view thereof. Fig. 3 is a vertical longitudinal section. Fig. 4 is a detail view of the engaging portions of the pivot frame and paddle stem.

Referring to the figures by characters of reference, 1 designates a box-like platform and mounted within this platform adjacent one end are vertically movable rods 2 provided at their upper ends with handles 3 designed to be gripped by the user. The lower ends of the rods 2 are attached to a cross strip 4 disposed within the platform and having its ends slidably mounted in guide grooves 5. Springs 6 surround the rods 2 above the strip 4 and are designed to hold said strip normally in lowered position. One of the rods 2 is insulated from the cross strip 4 and is electrically connected as by means of a wire 7 with an electro-generator 8 while another electrical connection, such as wire 9, connects the cross strip 4 with the generator 8.

The generator 8, which may be of any desired type, is designed to be driven by a spring motor 10 through a train of gears 11 and one of these gears has a stop pin 12 outstanding from one face thereof. Pivotally mounted on a bracket 13 is a locking lever 14 normally held, by means of a spring 15, inside the circle described by the pin 12 when the gears are rotating. A stop bracket 16 is provided for limiting the movement of this lever in one direction. Another bracket 17 is secured within the platform and has a latch lever 18 pivoted thereon and mounted to swing in a vertical plane whereas the lever 14 is designed to swing in a horizontal plane. One end of the latch lever projects above the cross strip 4 and a spring 19 is connected to said lever and to the bracket 17 for the purpose of holding the latch lever normally in position to automatically engage and lock the lever 14 against the stress of spring 15. When lever 14 is thus locked one end of it projects into the path of pin 12 and the train of gears 11 is thus prevented from operating.

Arranged longitudinally within the platform preferably along the center thereof are guide strips 20 between which is mounted a slide 21. A strap 22 connects these guides and constitutes a keeper designed to be engaged by a spring metal tongue 23 extending from one end of the slide and having a head which automatically engages a strap or keeper 22 when brought into contact therewith. Another strap 24 extends from the other end of slide 21 and is pivotally connected to a bolt or rod 25 mounted within the terminus of an elongated yoke 26. The terminal portions of this yoke extend through a slot 27 in the platform and are pivotally mounted upon brackets 28 secured to the platform. Springs 29 connect the bolt 25 with one end of the platform so as to normally hold the slide 21 removed from the strap or keeper 22 and the yoke 26 normally at a predetermined angle to the platform. This yoke has included in its structure preferably two superposed angular collars 30 provided with inwardly directed lugs 31. Said collars are designed to receive the stem 32 of a paddle 33, said stem having a longitudinal groove 34 for the reception of the lug 31.

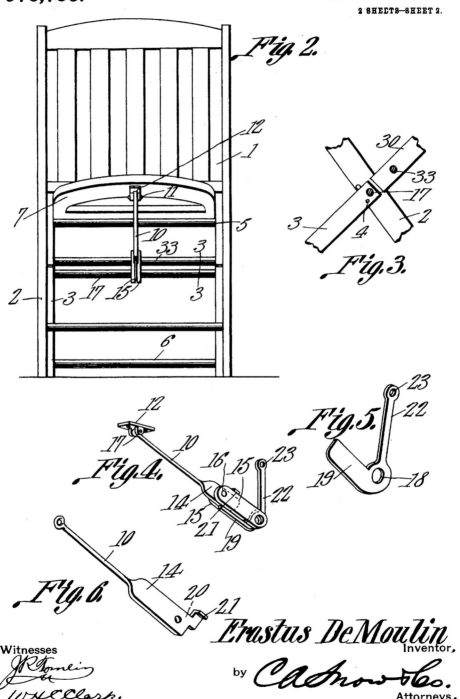

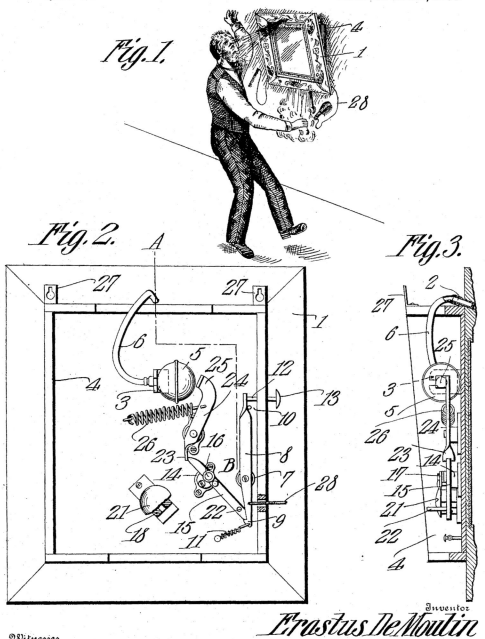

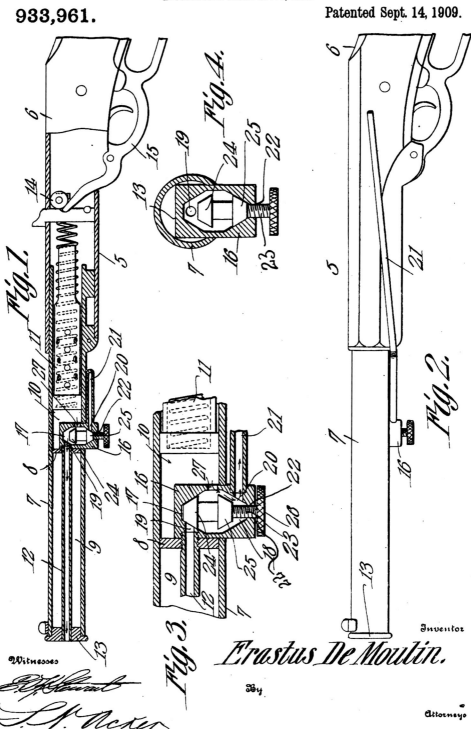

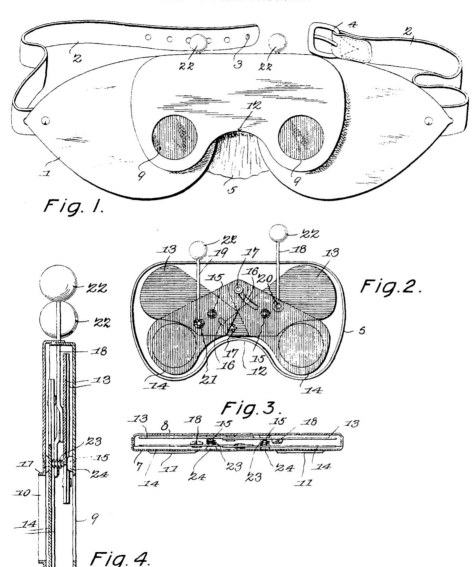

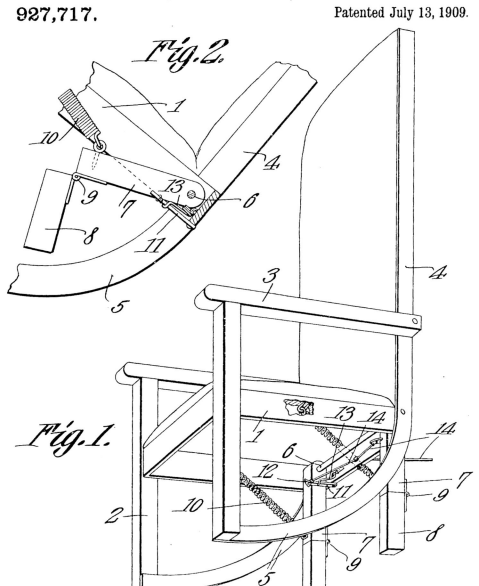

APPENDIX III

FURTHER CEREMONIAL WARES
FROM DEMOULIN BROS.

DeMoulin Bros. & Co., Greenville, Ill.

HOLY VESSELS

Tongs   Snuffer   Hinge   Censer   Spoon   Candlestick   Basin   Bowl

1655R—Bowl, covered with real gold leaf.........$ 8.25
1656R—Tongs, covered with real gold leaf; per pair 10.50
1657R—Snuffers, covered with real gold leaf; per pair 5.90
1658R—Basin, covered with real gold leaf......... 8.00
1659R—Spoons, covered with real gold leaf; per pair 4.15
1660R—Candlesticks, covered with real gold leaf; per pair 7.00
1661R—Censer, covered with real gold leaf........ 9.00
1662R—Hinge, covered with real gold leaf........ 7.90

1663R—Complete set 60.70

1664R—Bowl, covered with gilt bronze ....$ 4.70
1665R—Tongs, covered with gilt bronze; per pair.. 4.10
1666R—Snuffers, covered with gilt bronze; per pair 2.50
1667R—Basin, covered with gilt bronze........... 4.50
1668R—Spoons, covered with gilt bronze; per pair.. 2.80
1669R—Candlesticks, covered with gilt bronze; per pair 4.15
1670R—Censer, covered with gilt bronze 2.70
1671R—Hinge, covered with gilt bronze 4.10

1672R—Complete set 29.55

TABLES OF THE LAW

1673R

1673R—Tables of the Law, large size, seasoned wood, finished to imitate stone; the Ten Commandments finely painted in Hebrew characters ....$ 6.15
1674R—Tables of the Law, same as 1673R, but small size...... 4.00

BOOK OF THE LAW

1675R—Book of the Law, printed on parchment in Hebrew, with roll and slat, tied with ribbon ....$ 4.00
1676R—Book of the Law, same as No. 1675R, enclosed in tube.. 4.15
1677R—Book of the Law, printed on parchment in English in plain type, with roll and slat; tied with ribbon 5.00
1678R—Book of the Law, printed on heavy linen in English in plain type, with roll and slat; tied with ribbon (Indiana regulation) 3.65

MANNA POT

1679R—Manna Pot, of wood, with cover, full bronzed ....$ 1.80
1680R—Manna Pot, spun brass, handsome design, with cover, gilt finish 3.35

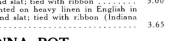
1679R

BUDDED RODS

1681R

1681R—Budded Rod, large size, carved wood, showing buds and green leaves ....$ 3.00
1682R—Budded Rod, small size, carved wood, painted ....$ 1.80

SERPENTINE STAFF

1683R, 1684R

1683R—Serpentine Staff, 48 inches long, handsomely carved and painted ....$ 7.60
1684R—Serpentine Staff, 36 inches long, handsomely carved and painted 6.45

SERPENT ON STAFF

1685R

1685R—Serpent on Staff, 32 inches long, handsomely carved and painted ....$ 3.90
1686R—Serpent on Staff, 32 inches long, painted 2.90

ARCHES AND PILLARS

1690R-1695R

1690R—Arch and Pillars, 9 feet to top of keystone, 5½ feet wide; fluted columns, elaborate capitals, fancy bases with carved emblems; elegant arch with fine lettering and removable keystone; both the arch and pillars covered with real gold leaf; complete, boxed $215.00

1691R—Arch only, same as 1690R.. 58.00

1692R—Arch and Pillars, same as 1690R, but very fine gold bronze instead of gold leaf..................... 135.00

1693R—Arch only, same as 1690R, but very fine gold bronze instead of gold leaf 32.80

1694R—Arch and Pillars, 7½ feet to top of keystone, 4½ feet wide; fluted columns with capitals and fancy bases; neat arch with lettering and removable keystone; both the arch and pillars finely gold bronzed; complete, boxed 102.00

1695R—Arch only, same as 1694R... 27.00

TABERNACLES OR VEILS

Closed

Half Open

Open
1696R-1700R

Our tabernacle folds compactly, occupying a space only 1x5x6½ feet when folded. One man can put it up or fold it almost instantly. The frame is unusually substantial, being joined by strong hinges and all corners braced. The side curtains always remain smooth, making a neat appearance at all times. Both the side and cross curtains are made in proper colors. Dimensions open, 15 feet long, 5 feet wide and 6½ feet high. We make any size to order.

1696R—Tabernacle with cross curtains of fine silk plush...$180.00
1697R—Tabernacle with cross curtains of fine silk finished velvet 128.50
1698R—Tabernacle with cross curtains of fine satin serge 124.35
1699R—Tabernacle with cross curtains of moire (imitation of watered silk) 113.25
1700R—Tabernacle with cross curtains of mercerized cashmere 97.15

COSTUMES

HIGH PRIEST
ROBES

Full lined; collar with open work gold lace and doubled gold bullion fringe; outer sleeves with open work gold lace, doubled gold bullion fringe, 4-inch gold bullion tassels and extra fine gold brocaded satin lining; inner sleeves with two rows of gold lace and lace shirring; skirt with wide white lace, elaborate applique, embroidery and gilt bells; belt and pendant caps of fine gold brocaded satin trimmed with gold lace; pendants of fine satin elaborately silk embroidered and trimmed with gold lace and woven silk-and-gilt pomegranates. Ephod of very fine gold brocaded satin, lined and interlined, trimmed with gold lace and doubled gold bullion fringe.

2041R—Finest quality silk plush and fine guaranteed Skinner's satin $116.50
2042R—Fine guaranteed Skinner's satin 107.00
2043R—Fine silk plush and satin... 103.75
2044R—Fine silk poplin 96.40
2045R—Fine silk finished velvet and silk poplin 94.80
2046R—Fine satin serge 89.75

MITRES

Flexible body; with curtain; body with bands trimmed with gold lace and colored jewels; curtain of very fine gold brocaded satin trimmed with gold lace and gold bullion fringe; plate on front with the words "Holiness to the Lord."

2047R—Finest quality silk plush Skinner's satin $26.65
2048R—Fine satin 25.00
2049R—Fine silk poplin 25.60
2050R—Fine satin serge 25.40

2041R-2050R

ROBES

Full lined; collar and outer sleeves trimmed with open work gold lace and gold bullion fringe; inner sleeves with two rows of gold lace; skirt with wide white lace, open work gold lace; gilt bells and woven silk-and-gilt pomegranates; belt and pendants of fine gold brocaded satin trimmed with gold lace and pomegranates. Ephod of extra fine gold brocaded satin, lined and interlined, trimmed with bands of satin, gold lace, and gold bullion fringe.

2051R—Finest quality silk plush and fine guaranteed Skinner's satin $100.00
2052R—Fine guaranteed Skinner's satin 92.70
2053R—Fine silk plush and satin... 90.40
2054R—Fine silk poplin 84.35
2055R—Fine silk-finished velvet and silk poplin 82.80
2056R—Fine satin serge 78.00

MITRES

Flexible body; with curtain; embroidered design on front of body; trimmed with gold lace and gold bullion fringe; heavily gold plated plate on front with words "Holiness to the Lord."

2057R—Fine guaranteed Skinner's satin $11.00
2058R—Fine satin 9.50
2059R—Fine silk poplin 8.75
2060R—Fine satin serge 8.50

2051R-2060R

ROBES

Full lined; outer sleeves trimmed with open work gold lace and gold bullion fringe; inner sleeves with gold lace; skirt with open work gold lace, gilt bells and woven silk-and gilt pomegranates; belt and pendant of fine gold brocade satin trimmed with gold lace and pomegranates. Ephod of fine gold brocaded satin, lined and interlined, trimmed with bands of satin, gold lace and gold bullion fringe.

2061R—Finest quality silk, plush and guaranteed Skinner's satin .. $63.40
2062R—Fine guaranteed Skinner's satin 59.50
2063R—Fine silk plush and satin.... 57.30
2064R—Fine silk poplin 50.00
2065R—Fine silk-finished velvet and silk poplin 48.55
2066R—Fine satin serge 44.00

MITRES

Flexible body; with curtain; trimmed with gold lace and gold bullion fringe; plate on front with words "Holiness to the Lord."

2067R—Fine guaranteed Skinner's satin $10.80
2068R—Fine satin 9.40
2069R—Fine silk poplin 8.55
2070R—Fine satin serge 8.40

Breast Plates listed on Page 18.

2061R-2070R

HIGH PRIEST—Continued
ROBES

Full lined; white inner sleeves, bands and lower skirt of same material as robe; bands trimmed with gold lace; lower skirt with wide white lace; girdle with tassels.

2072R—Finest quality silk plush and fine guaranteed Skinner's satin $41.00
2073R—Fine guaranteed Skinner's satin 37.35
2074R—Fine silk plush and satin.... 35.25
2075R—Fine silk poplin 28.25
2076R—Fine silk finished velvet and silk poplin 27.10
2077R—Fine satin serge 23.00
2078R—Moire 18.65
2079R—Mercerized sateen 13.45
2080R—Mercerized cashmere 12.90

MITRES

Flexible body; band trimmed with gold lace.

2081R—Finest quality silk plush.... $6.25
2082R—Finest guaranteed Skinner's satin 6.10
2083R—Fine silk plush 6.00
2084R—Fine silk poplin 5.50
2085R—Fine silk finished velvet.... 5.25
2086R—Fine satin serge 5.00
2087R—Moire 4.10
2088R—Mercerized sateen 3.90
2089R—Mercerized cashmere 3.75

2072R-2089R

KING
MANTLES AND CAPES

Mantle, very long and full, elaborately silk embroidered on entire front edges and around bottom. Cape of crushed and dotted silk plush which is a close imitation of ermine fur and far more satisfactory; neat ribbon bow at shoulders; large silk cord and tassels.

2090R—Mantle of fine guaranteed Skinner's satin, cape as described above. Both the mantle and cape lined with fine silk poplin $65.00
2091R—Mantle of fine satin, cape as described above. Both the mantle and cape lined with fine silk poplin 55.60
2092R—Mantle of fine silk poplin, cape as described above. Both the mantle and cape lined with fine imitation of watered silk 41.65
2093R—Mantle of fine satin serge, cape as described above. Both the mantle and cape lined with fine mercerized sateen 33.50

CROWNS

Very elaborate metal frame, gold plated and elaborately set with jewels.

2094R—Fine guaranteed Skinner's satin $17.50
2095R—Fine satin 16.50
2096R—Fine silk poplin 15.85
2097R—Fine satin serge 15.50

2090R-2097R

The Armor Coat, Hose and Sandals illustrated above are listed and illustrated on page 51 where a better idea of the coat trimmings may be obtained. The Mantle, Cape and Crown make a very suitable outfit for King without the coat, hose and sandals, but the appearance is enhanced when the coat, hose and sandals are used.

ROBES

Full lined; front panel silk embroidered; band of crushed and dotted plush which is a close imitation of ermine down edges of front panel and around sleeves and bottom; elaborate embroidered designs at outer edge of ermine bands and on cuffs of inner sleeves; collar of crushed and dotted plush, trimmed with fine fringe.

2098R—Finest quality silk plush and guaranteed Skinner's satin ... $71.00
2099R—Fine guaranteed Skinner's satin 53.85
2100R—Fine silk plush and satin.... 52.25
2101R—Fine satin 48.45
2102R—Fine silk poplin 42.25
2103R—Fine silk-finished velvet and satin poplin 41.10
2104R—Fine satin serge 38.85

CROWNS

Fine gold plated frame with flaring polished points and elaborately set with jewels.

2105R—Fine guaranteed Skinner's satin $7.50
2106R—Fine satin 6.80
2107R—Fine silk poplin 6.50
2108R—Fine satin serge 6.10

2098R-2108R

1 *2* *3*

CHARLES SCHNEIDER obtained his first novelty catalog—A Johnson-Smith pamphlet ordered from a comic book—at the age of ten and never looked back. He is the editor of the influential *CAD: A Handbook for Heels*, has written cartoons for Warner Brothers' *Tom and Jerry Tales*, appeared as the morbid comedian in the film *Ghost World*, and created the murderer's paintings for *Art School Confidential*.

DAVID COPPERFIELD is an Emmy Award-winning American illusionist, his achievements as a stage magician alone are unparalleled in magic history. He holds 11 Guinness World Records and has the largest private collection of magic artifacts on earth. His career earnings as a magician are the highest ever recorded and he performs the largest illusion show ever staged. He performs more magic shows in a year than any other performer and holds the record of the most tickets sold worldwide by a solo entertainer.

WILLIAM D. MOORE is an Associate Professor of History at the University of North Carolina Wilmington and the author of *Masonic Temples* published by the University of Tennessee Press. Although not a Freemason, he previously served as the director of the Livingston Masonic Library and Museum of the Grand Lodge, F. & A.M., of New York. He holds an A.B. from Harvard and a Ph.D. from Boston University.